Governing religious diversity in global comparative perspective

This book presents comparative analyses of different modes of the governance of religious diversity and state-religion connections and relations in twenty-three countries in five world regions: Western Europe, Southern and South-Eastern Europe, Central and Eastern Europe, the MENA region, and South and Southeast Asia

Debates and controversies around the governance of religious diversity have become important features of the social and political landscape in different regions and countries across the world. The historical influences and legacies and the contemporary circumstances provoking these debates vary between contexts, and there have been a range of state and scholarly responses to how, and why, particular understandings and arrangements of state-religion relations should be preferred over others. The analyses of country cases and regions presented in this volume are based on extensive reviews of secondary literature and of legal and policy landscapes and in some cases on interviews.

This book will be a great resource for academics, researchers, and advanced students interested in the sociology of religion, religious studies, politics, multiculturalism and migration studies. The contributions in this volume arise out of the Horizon2020 funded GREASE project. It was originally published as a special issue of *Religion, State & Society*.

Tariq Modood is Professor of Sociology, Politics, and Public Policy and founding Director of the Centre for the Study of Ethnicity and Citizenship at the University of Bristol, UK. He was awarded an MBE for services to social sciences and ethnic relations in 2001, made Fellow of the Academy of Social Sciences in 2004, and elected Fellow of the British Academy in 2017. He has held over 40 grants and consultancies and has over 35 (co-) authored and (co-)edited books and reports and over 200 articles and chapters. His latest book is *Essays on Secularism and Multiculturalism* (2019) and as Special Issues co-editor, with T. Sealy, "Beyond Euro-Americancentric Forms of Racism and Anti-racism (Political Quarterly, 2022). He has a YouTube Channel (*Tariq Modood*) and his website is tariqmodood.com

Thomas Sealy is Lecturer in Ethnicity and Race in the School of Sociology, Politics, and International Studies at the University of Bristol, UK. He researches and has published on multiculturalism, the governance of religious diversity, forms of racism, and Islamophobia and converts to Islam in Britain. His monograph, *Religiosity and Recognition: Multiculturalism and British Converts to Islam*, was published in 2021 and as Special Issues co-editor, with T. Modood, "Beyond Euro-Americancentric Forms of Racism and Anti-racism (Political Quarterly, 2022).

Governing religious diversity in global comparative perspective

Edited by
Tariq Modood and Thomas Sealy

LONDON AND NEW YORK

First published 2024
by Routledge
4 Park Square, Milton Park, Abingdon, Oxon, OX14 4RN

and by Routledge
605 Third Avenue, New York, NY 10158

Routledge is an imprint of the Taylor & Francis Group, an informa business

Preface and Chapter 4 © 2024 Taylor & Francis
Afterword: Normative vs. Actual Secularism(s) © 2024 Haldun Gülalp
Afterword: Some Reflections on State-Religion Relationships and Political
Secularism in the Contemporary World © 2024 Gurpreet Mahajan
Introduction © 2022 Tariq Modood and Thomas Sealy.Originally published as Open
Access.
Chapter 1 © 2022 Thomas Sealy and Tariq Modood. Originally published as Open
Access.
Chapter 2 © 2022 Tina Magazzini, Anna Triandafyllidou and Liliya Yakova. Originally
published as Open Access.
Chapter 3 © 2022 Daniel Vekony, Marat Iliyasov and Egdūnas Račius. Originally
published as Open Access.
Chapter 5 © 2022 Thomas Sealy, Zawawi Ibrahim, Pradana Boy Zulian and Imran
Mohd Rasid. Originally published as Open Access.
Chapter 6 © 2022 Thomas Sealy and Tariq Modood. Originally published as Open
Access.

With the exception of Introduction, Chapters 1–3, 5 and 6, no part of this book may
be reprinted or reproduced or utilised in any form or by any electronic, mechanical,
or other means, now known or hereafter invented, including photocopying and
recording, or in any information storage or retrieval system, without permission in
writing from the publishers. For details on the rights for Introduction, Chapters 1–3,
5 and 6, please see the chapters' Open Access footnotes.

Trademark notice: Product or corporate names may be trademarks or registered
trademarks, and are used only for identification and explanation without intent to
infringe.

British Library Cataloguing in Publication Data
A catalogue record for this book is available from the British Library

ISBN13: 978-1-032-45205-0 (hbk)
ISBN13: 978-1-032-45684-3 (pbk)
ISBN13: 978-1-003-37590-6 (ebk)

DOI: 10.4324/9781003375906

Typeset in Myriad Pro
by codeMantra

Publisher's Note
The publisher accepts responsibility for any inconsistencies that may have arisen
during the conversion of this book from journal articles to book chapters, namely
the inclusion of journal terminology.

Disclaimer
Every effort has been made to contact copyright holders for their permission to
reprint material in this book. The publishers would be grateful to hear from any
copyright holder who is not here acknowledged and will undertake to rectify any
errors or omissions in future editions of this book.

Contents

Citation Information	vii
Notes on Contributors	ix
Preface	xii

1 Developing a framework for a global comparative analysis of the governance of religious diversity   1
Tariq Modood and Thomas Sealy

2 Western Europe and Australia: negotiating freedoms of religion   17
Thomas Sealy and Tariq Modood

3 State-religion relations in Southern and Southeastern Europe: moderate secularism with majoritarian undertones   35
Tina Magazzini, Anna Triandafyllidou and Liliya Yakova

4 Dynamics in state-religion relations in postcommunist Central Eastern Europe and Russia   54
Daniel Vekony, Marat Iliyasov and Egdūnas Račius

5 Negotiating religion-state relations in the MENA region: actors' dynamics, modes, and norms   75
Georges Fahmi and Mehdi Lahlou

6 South and Southeast Asia: deep diversity under strain   91
Thomas Sealy, Zawawi Ibrahim, Pradana Boy Zulian and Imran Mohd Rasid

7 Diversities and dynamics in the governance of religion: inter-regional comparative themes   108
Thomas Sealy and Tariq Modood

Afterwords: Normative vs. Actual Secularism(s)   125
Haldun Gülalp

Some reflections on state-religion relationships and political secularism in
the contemporary world 133
Gurpreet Mahajan

Index 139

Citation Information

The following chapters were originally published in the journal *Religion, State & Society*, volume 50, issue 4 (2022). When citing this material, please use the original page numbering for each article, as follows:

Chapter 1
Developing a framework for a global comparative analysis of the governance of religious diversity
Tariq Modood and Thomas Sealy
Religion, State & Society, volume 50, issue 4 (2022) pp. 362–377

Chapter 2
Western Europe and Australia: negotiating freedoms of religion
Thomas Sealy and Tariq Modood
Religion, State & Society, volume 50, issue 4 (2022) pp. 378–395

Chapter 3
State-religion relations in Southern and Southeastern Europe: moderate secularism with majoritarian undertones
Tina Magazzini, Anna Triandafyllidou and Liliya Yakova
Religion, State & Society, volume 50, issue 4 (2022) pp. 396–414

Chapter 4
Dynamics in state-religion relations in postcommunist Central Eastern Europe and Russia
Daniel Vekony, Marat Iliyasov and Egdūnas Račius
Religion, State & Society, volume 50, issue 4 (2022) pp. 415–435

Chapter 5
Negotiating religion-state relations in the MENA region: actors' dynamics, modes, and norms
Georges Fahmi and Mehdi Lahlou
Religion, State & Society, volume 50, issue 4 (2022) pp. 436–451

Chapter 6
South and Southeast Asia: deep diversity under strain
Thomas Sealy, Zawawi Ibrahim, Pradana Boy Zulian and Imran Mohd Rasid
Religion, State & Society, volume 50, issue 4 (2022) pp. 452–468

Chapter 7

Diversities and dynamics in the governance of religion: inter-regional comparative themes
Thomas Sealy and Tariq Modood
Religion, State & Society, volume 50, issue 4 (2022) pp. 469–485

For any permission-related enquiries please visit:
http://www.tandfonline.com/page/help/permissions

Notes on Contributors

Daniel Nilsson DeHanas is Senior Lecturer in Political Science and Religion at King's College London, UK. His research focuses on political issues involving British Muslims and on the roles of religion in right-wing populism. He is the co-editor of the journal *Religion, State & Society*.

Georges Fahmi is part-time Assistant Professor at the Robert Schuman Centre for Advanced Studies in Florence, Italy, and Associate Fellow at Chatham House, London, UK. He received his PhD in Political Science from the European University Institute in 2013.

Haldun Gülalp taught Sociology at Hamilton College, USA, and Boğaziçi University, Istanbul, and Political Science at the Middle East Technical University, Ankara, Turkey, and Yıldız Technical University, Istanbul. He also held visiting professorships at George Washington University, Northwestern University, and UCLA, and research fellowships at the Woodrow Wilson International Center for Scholars and Oxford University. Since his retirement from teaching in 2015, he has been participating in international collaborative research projects.

Zawawi Ibrahim was affiliated with Malaysia's Strategic Information and Research Development Centre, where he worked as Professor of Anthropology in the Faculty of Arts & Social Sciences and the Institute of Asian Studies at University Brunei Darussalam (UBD). A Malaysian citizen, Zawawi earned his PhD in Social Anthropology from Monash University, Melbourne, Australia. He passed away in 2022.

Marat Iliyasov is a part-time researcher at Vytautas Magnus University, Kaunas, Lithuania. In 2022 he concluded his post-doctoral research at Wisconsin-Madison University, USA, and took up his position at Miami University, Oxford, USA. His academic interest is situated at the crossroad of several strands of international relations, including peace studies, political demography, radicalisation, religious governance, and memory politics. His main research field is the Russian Federation with a particular focus on post-war Chechnya.

Mehdi Lahlou is Professor of Economics at the National Institute of Statistics and Applied Economics (INSEA), Rabat, Morocco, and Associated Professor at University Mohammed V, Rabat, Morocco. He received his PhD in Economics from the University of Paris 1 Panthéon-Sorbonne, France, in 1982.

Tina Magazzini is Senior Researcher in the Department of Mobility and Migration of the Czech Academy of Sciences and a Visiting Fellow at the University of Lisbon.

NOTES ON CONTRIBUTORS

Gurpreet Mahajan was Professor at the Centre for Political Science at Jawaharlal Nehru University, New Delhi, India, till 2021. Her writings cover a range of subjects, from issues related to hermeneutic method and philosophy, to multiculturalism, secularism, and civil society. Her publications include *Explanation and Understanding in the Human Sciences* (1992; 1997; 2011), *Identities and Rights: Aspects of Liberal Democracy in India* (1998), and *India: Political Ideas and the Making of a Democratic Discourse* (2013).

Tariq Modood is Professor of Sociology, Politics, and Public Policy and founding Director of the Centre for the Study of Ethnicity and Citizenship at the University of Bristol, UK. He was awarded an MBE for services to social sciences and ethnic relations in 2001, made Fellow of the Academy of Social Sciences in 2004, and elected Fellow of the British Academy in 2017. He has held over 40 grants and consultancies and has over 35 (co-) authored and (co-)edited books and reports and over 200 articles and chapters. His latest book is *Essays on Secularism and Multiculturalism* (2019) and as Special Issues co-editor, with T. Sealy, "Beyond Euro-Americancentric Forms of Racism and Anti-racism (Political Quarterly, 2022). He has a YouTube Channel (*Tariq Modood*) and his website is tariqmodood.com

Egdūnas Račius is Professor of Middle Eastern and Islamic studies at Vytautas Magnus University, Kaunas, Lithuania. His research interests encompass Eastern European Muslim communities and the governance of religion (particularly Islam) in postcommunist Europe. His most recent monograph is *Islam in Post-Communist Eastern Europe: between Churchification and Securitization* (2020). He serves on the Editorial Boards of the *Journal of Muslims in Europe* and the *Yearbook of Muslims in Europe*.

Imran Mohd Rasid is a graduate student and Research Fellow at the Strategic Information and Research Development Centre, Malaysia. His area of research includes critical theory, Malaysian political history, global political economy, and the phenomenon of transnational and trans-local religious-political movements. His research has been presented in several academic conferences, and some published as book chapters. He has also co-founded an organisation called Imagined Malaysia, a research group that strives to push for greater historical literacy in Malaysia.

Thomas Sealy is Lecturer in Ethnicity and Race in the School of Sociology, Politics, and International Studies at the University of Bristol, UK. He researches and has published on multiculturalism, the governance of religious diversity, forms of racism, and Islamophobia and converts to Islam in Britain. His monograph, *Religiosity and Recognition: Multiculturalism and British Converts to Islam*, was published in 2021 and as Special Issues co-editor, with T. Modood, "Beyond Euro-Americancentric Forms of Racism and Anti-racism" (Political Quarterly, 2022).

Marat Shterin is Professor of the Sociology of Religion at King's College London, UK. He has published widely on the intersections between religion, politics, and law in Russia and Britain. He is the co-editor of the journal *Religion, State & Society*. His latest co-edited volume is *Islam in Russia: Religion, Politics & Society* (2023).

Anna Triandafyllidou holds The Canada Excellence Research Chair in Migration and Integration at Toronto Metropolitan University (formerly Ryerson University), Canada. Prior to this she held Robert Schuman Chair at the Global Governance Programme at a Robert Schuman Centre for Advanced Studies at European University Institute, Italy.

She is the editor of the *Journal of Immigrant & Refugee Studies*. Her recent authored books include *What is Europe* (with R. Gropas, 2nd edition, 2022) and *Rethinking Migration and Return in Southeastern Europe* (with E. Gemi, 2021).

Daniel Vekony is Senior Lecturer at the Corvinus University of Budapest, Hungary, and a part-time researcher at the Vytautas Magnus University, Kaunas, Lithuania. His main research foci are European Muslims and the prospects of multiculturalism as a political theory and a model of cohabitation. Recently he has focused his attention on collective memory narratives about Islam and Muslims in British and Hungarian societies. His other professional interest is the field of relations between Hungary and the Middle East during the Cold War.

Liliya Yakova works on Centre for the Study of Democracy (CSD) Sociological Programme projects related to ethnic minorities, vulnerable groups, radicalisation, and socioeconomic disparity. Her areas of interests include marginalised populations, social justice, communication and policy for social change, peacebuilding, and organisational policy. Before joining CSD, Liliya was Associate Director of Operations for the Purdue Peace Project (USA), a violence prevention initiative in West Africa and Central America.

Pradana Boy Zulian is Lecturer in Islamic Legal Studies at the Faculty of Islamic Studies at the University of Muhammadiyah Malang, Indonesia, where between 2015 and 2018 he led the Centre for the Study of Islam and Philosophy (Pusat Studi Islam dan Filsafat). He trained as an Islamic legal scholar at the University of Muhammadiyah Malang, Indonesia, and received his PhD from the Department of Malay Studies at the National University of Singapore, Singapore. His monograph *Fatwa in Indonesia: An Analysis of Dominant Legal Ideas and Modes of Thought of Fatwa-Making Agencies and Their Implications in the Post-New Order Period* was published in 2018.

Preface

All states must make choices in how they govern religious diversity. In the worst cases, states will actively perpetuate inequalities or oppression through these choices. But even in the best cases, it is inevitable that compromises will be made and successes can only be partial. It is therefore essential that we not only seek to understand how states navigate the challenge of religious diversity, but that we do so in comparative perspective. Then mutual learning across imperfect choices becomes possible.

This book presents findings from a major new project (2018–2022), Radicalisation, Secularism, and the Governance of Religion (GREASE). GREASE compares approaches to the governance of religious diversity in 23 countries across five world regions: the Middle East and North Africa (MENA), South and Southeast Asia, Central and Eastern Europe, Southern and Southeastern Europe, and Western Europe, with Australia added to this final European 'region' as a complementary case.

This book was originally published as a special issue of the journal we edit, *Religion, State & Society*, guest edited by Tariq Modood and Thomas Sealy. Tariq Modood is Professor of Sociology, Politics, and Public Policy at Bristol University and the founding Director of the Centre for the Study of Ethnicity and Citizenship. Thomas Sealy is Lecturer in Ethnicity and Race at Bristol University where he is also an active contributor to the intellectual life of the Ethnicity Centre. They led the Bristol team that was one of ten partners in this EU Horizon 2020-funded global institutional consortium.

We join them in thanking the anonymous reviewers of the original special issue, as well as all of the contributors for their participation in this writing venture and in the wider GREASE project. This book draws upon the GREASE project's unprecedented global scope to the study of religion and diversity. It begins with an introduction that proposes a framework with new conceptual tools for understanding the governance of religious diversity, incorporates a focused contribution on each of the five world regions, and, finally, concludes with a contribution that compares the regions and cases. In a world in which religious freedoms, restrictions, and appropriate levels of state intervention remain hotly contested topics, this book makes many important empirical and normative contributions.

Daniel Nilsson DeHanas
Department of Theology and Religious Studies, King's College London

Marat Shterin
Department of Theology and Religious Studies, King's College London

ə OPEN ACCESS

Developing a framework for a global comparative analysis of the governance of religious diversity

Tariq Modood and Thomas Sealy

ABSTRACT
Between and within different world regions today religious diversity remains a significant challenge and researchers have identified a wide variety of church-state relations as well as of legal, institutional, and political arrangements related to state-religion connections. These variations in type and degree owe something to distinctive political, institutional, theological, and historical inheritances and have led to different normative conceptions of secularism and of state-religion relations and connections. This first contribution begins by mapping the ground of existing conceptions of secularism and state-religion connections. Our discussion first assesses normative approaches that emanate from 'the West' as well as from perspectives outside of 'the West' (such as India), and which might directly challenge the former. It then turns to outline a new framework of five modes of governance of religious diversity, presenting each in relation to a series of constitutive features or norms that characterise it and which distinguish it from other modes. This typology of modes forms the basis of the intra- and inter-regional comparative analyses presented in the regionally focused contributions to this collection. We finally provide an overview of these contributions and their application of the typology.

Introduction

Debates and controversies around the governance of religious diversity have become, and in fact have long been, important features of the social and political landscape in different regions and countries across the world. The contemporary circumstances provoking these debates, and the significant aspects of historical legacies and how these influence and shape present-day conditions vary between contexts, and accordingly there have been a range of state as well as scholarly responses to how, and why, particular understandings and arrangements of state-religion relations should be preferred.

This collection presents a framework for a global comparative analysis of the governance of religious diversity developed as part of the Horizon 2020-funded GREASE project. The analyses presented throughout the contributions to this collection are based on extensive review of secondary literature, of legal and policy landscapes, and

---

This is an Open Access article distributed under the terms of the Creative Commons Attribution-NonCommercial-NoDerivatives License (http://creativecommons.org/licenses/by-nc-nd/4.0/), which permits non-commercial re-use, distribution, and reproduction in any medium, provided the original work is properly cited, and is not altered, transformed, or built upon in any way.

in some cases on interviews, in each country case. Our use of governance here, as will become apparent throughout the contributions to this collection, includes legal and policy measures as well as connections and cooperation between state and civil society actors. The contributions apply this framework to present comparative analyses of different modes of the governance of religious diversity and state-religion connections and relations covering 23 countries in five world regions: Western Europe, Southern and Southeastern Europe, Central and Eastern Europe, the MENA region, South and Southeast Asia and, finally, Australia (which we here analyse with Western Europe, with which it shares many key characteristics). While any form of clustering of this kind will have its drawbacks, and the choice of these regional clusters has a geographical and presentational function, the groupings also have a certain analytical purchase. There is, we suggest, sufficient commonality between the country cases to warrant their grouping, though we will also note that each regional cluster has a notable exception. Following the focused discussions based on regional comparative cases, the final contribution to this collection reflects on these points further as part of an inter-regional comparative analysis.

This first contribution to the collection begins by mapping the ground of existing conceptions of secularism and state-religion connections. Our discussion first assesses normative approaches that emanate from Europe, especially Western Europe, before turning to perspectives from outside of the West, and which might directly challenge them. It then turns to outline a new framework of five modes of governance of religious diversity, presenting each in relation to a series of constitutive features or norms. This typology of modes forms the basis of the intra-regional comparative analyses presented in the regionally focused contributions to the collection. We finally provide an overview of the contributions and their application of the typology.

New accommodationist responses

In Europe, especially Western Europe, decline in religious belief and in the importance of religion in society shows no sign of reversing. Many Europeans are happy to think of their countries and their continent as post-Christian. It is important to note here, though, the variation within Europe. Countries in Eastern and Southern Europe report higher degrees of religiosity and higher levels of importance for religion as a core part of national identity than do Western European countries (Pew Research 2018), while also exhibiting early stages of the secularisation that characterises Western Europe. Alongside this trend, it is clear that many European states are now highly exercised by the challenges posed by post-immigration ethno-religious diversity. Although issues in European regions relate to different religious traditions, questions that have been raised throughout Europe share a common reference to their Muslim minority populations, and often it is the new Muslim settlements of the last 50 years or so that are at the centre of it. For some the pivotal date is 9/11, but 1988–89 better marks its origins. This was the period of *The Satanic Verses Affair* in the UK and *l'affaire du foulard* in France (Modood 2012), which brought Muslims – and in many ways the issue of public religion, oriented around non-Christian religious minorities – to the foreground of public and political, and subsequently scholarly, debate. Occurring between 1989 and 1991 depending on the state, this also marks the beginning of the fall of communism in Europe and of Soviet-bloc state secularisms imposed from above. Since that collapse, in parts of Central and Eastern Europe states and resurgent dominant religions have grappled with both the 'old' religious diversity of historic communities and minorities alongside 'new' minorities from more recent immigration flows.

The rethinking of secularism in Europe, then, is largely due to the fact of newer, and especially non-Christian, religious diversity. In response, some have (re)asserted a strong or muscular secularism, a position prominent, for example, in some political discourse and among some *neo-laïcité* and New Atheist movements, while others have emphasised the Christian history and character of these countries that must be protected.

Liberal theorists have, by contrast, at least in part accepted critiques of secularist pre-eminence and that this pre-eminence is not merely a political ambition but built into the very concepts of liberalism (Rawls 1997; Habermas 2006). More recent liberal accounts of secularism have also sought to rethink liberalism's ideas of neutrality and state-religion separation or connections. 'Open secularism' (Bouchard and Taylor 2008; Maclure and Taylor 2011) makes an important distinction. On the one hand are the *ends of* secularism (its 'essential outcomes', according to Bouchard and Taylor 2008, 21]), referring to the moral equality of persons, and freedom of conscience and religion. On the other hand are the *means of* secularism, referring to the separation of church and state and state neutrality in respect of religious and deep-seated secular convictions. It does so to argue that the latter pair might not be necessary for the realisation of the former pair.

In her important 2017 book, Cécile Laborde has allowed that some state-religion connections (SRCs) are compatible with liberalism. Yet, in arguing against SRCs, Laborde contends that these will inevitably lead to the alienation of minorities. For Laborde this entails two things: that governments express objective attitudes (2017, 135), and that this 'objective social meaning is context-dependent but not individual-dependent; it turns on how a reasonable (and reasonably well-informed) member of a community would understand the actions of public officials who undertake to display material that has religious content' (Laborde 2017, 85). The reference to the reasonable person being reasonably informed suggests that (s)he needs to take into account some empirical data, and presumably it would be reasonable that this should include the view of Muslims (and others) rather than an abstract 'reasonable' person (Modood and Thompson 2022).

Furthermore, Laborde's position presumes that the negative status of minority religious identity is sustained by symbolic establishment and not, for example, by racialisation, cultural 'othering', or muscular forms of liberal secularism that would squeeze religion from the public sphere. If we look for empirical evidence of the alienation of Muslims in Britain as an example, it is the case that they do seem to feel excluded and alienated by certain aspects of British, and indeed European, society (Murad 2020). Yet there is no record of any criticism by a Muslim group against the establishment of the Church of England (on these points see Modood 2019; also Martin 2017). However, many Muslims complain that Britain is too unreligious and anti-religious, too hedonistic, too consumerist, too materialist, and so on (Murad 2020; something they share with many Christians). Muslims protest far more vigorously about secularist bans on modest female clothing than they do about 'establishment' or Christian privileges. When Prime Minister David Cameron, during the 2011 Christmas season, said that it should be asserted that Britain is 'a Christian country' (BBC 2015) – the first time a British prime minister had spoken like that in a long time – it was welcomed by Ibrahim Mogra, then the chairman of the Mosque Committee of the Muslim Council of Britain, and later its assistant secretary general.[1] These matters do not support the mistaken view that Islamophobia is not an issue in Britain, or that Muslims do not feel alienated in Britain, but highlight that religious minorities such as Muslims are more likely to be alienated by the kind of secular state that Laborde argues for, and that their concerns make very little reference to Christianity, let alone the establishment of the Church of England.

So, we should not assume that state recognition of one or some religions is the only potential source of alienation on this matter; strict state-religion separation can also alienate or aggrieve those whose religious identity is especially important, and subjectively and objectively diminish their civic standing. Indeed, that calls for disestablishment come overwhelmingly from secularists rather than from minority faith groups is telling, as is that some Christians can also feel alienated from the secular state.

Notable in these liberal accounts is that, in order to ensure and protect the liberty of sovereign individuals within a state struggling to be neutral, equality is principally conceived to mean equality of individuals. In contrast to these liberal positions, Modood (2019) has argued that a rethinking of liberalism is necessary to ensure equality and recognition not just of individuals but also of ethno-religious groups, and his arguments in relation to moderate secularism emphasise the public good of religion and SRCs (Modood 2017). As a matter of fact, models that argue for church-state separation do not approximate particularly closely to church-state relations among Western European countries beyond France, and a variety of patterns of legal-constitutional and non-legal constitutional regulation and relations can be found. It is forms of connection between state and religions that emphasise the public good of religion, such as institutional connections in areas such as welfare provision and education for instance, that constitute the 'moderate' of this form of secularism in contrast to those which emphasise stricter forms of separation or state interference. Moreover, despite institutional connections between state and religion, one could only dispute that Western European states such as the UK, Germany, Belgium, and Denmark are secular if one had some narrow, abstract model of secularism that one insisted on applying to the varieties of empirical cases.

From this it is clear that we are already talking about multiple secularisms, but this gains extra traction when we look outside of the West, and some thinkers situated in non-western contexts have also entered these Anglophone debates in both commenting on secularism in Europe as well as furthering the debates through considering non-western forms of secularism and SRCs.

Deep diversity: non-European responses

Outside of Europe, in quite different historical and contemporary contexts, states have also faced questions of the governance of religious diversity. In the MENA region, debates between secularists and Islamists over the relationship between religion and state, law and politics again resurfaced with the Arab Spring, and Turkey under Erdoğan has seen a renewed centrality for religion in the political sphere. In South and Southeast Asia also, questions over the secular or religious character of the state and of relations between majority and minority religions have loomed large in several countries since gaining independence from European colonial powers in the mid-twentieth century.

With the re-emergence of debates over secularism in Western Europe, from the 1990s political theorists from outside the West or originating in the South began to make prominent contributions to political thinking and theorising on debates about secularism, many bringing an alternative perspective to western debates and issues. These contributions themselves were provoked by both issues arising in the West as well as in the country or region of the writer. This can be seen in the work of Talal Asad, whose genealogical interest was as much in the colonial secularism of Egypt as with how countries like Britain and France were managing their new Muslim populations (Asad 1993, 2003). Bhargava (1998) was one of the first to spark these normative debates. His intervention was provoked by considerations and debates in India, notably the Shah Bano case in 1985 and the demolition of Babri Masjid in Ayodha in 1992 (marked in India as major blows to its state secularism). But he also addressed the perceived 'crisis' of secularism in the West and highlighted its supposed lack of capacity to accommodate extra-Christian religious diversity (see also Mahajan 2007), and this idea of a crisis of secularism in the West underpins his contributions to Anglophone debates.

The West, Bhargava insists, is better served by looking sideways to India in order to view secularism's future than by looking at its own past (2009, 2014, 2015). It is along these lines that Bhargava seeks to rehabilitate secularism drawing on the Indian experience. Bhargava's (2009) model of secularism is based on his conception of 'principled distance' and is comprised of three characteristics: 1) a disconnection between state and religion at the levels of ends and institutions such that the relationship is guided by shared motives and values (he names the French tripartite liberty, fraternity, and equality), but not the same disconnection at the level of law and policy; 2) a differentiated citizenship; and 3) state interference in religion (where it may actively support or be hostile to different aspects of religion).

In contrast to both those who would seek an alternative to secularism (Madan 1998; Nandy 1998; Bader 2007) as well as those who would universalise a particular model and understanding of secularism, Bhargava seeks a form of *contextual secularism*, both in the sense of varying from place to place as well as in forms of moral reasoning (2009, 106). He notes, for example, that western conceptions of political secularism 'do not appear to have travelled all that well in other societies' (2013, 71). A problem here, however, is that Bhargava argues for a contextual approach, but simultaneously asserts the travelability of the Indian model.

An alternative position is that described by Gurpreet Mahajan, also with reference to the case of India and its 'long history of living with religious differences and the absence of a homogeneous public sphere' (2017, 80). Mahajan argues that a moderate form of secularism (as that in most of Western Europe) is certainly preferable to the US or French models, at least as an 'enabling condition' (Mahajan 2017, 85). Yet for Mahajan, moderate secularism is not sufficient for accommodating and valuing religious and cultural diversity if it does not embrace the idea that the state assist (often by making necessary arrangements for) the collective observance of religious practices for all communities, including the majority.

Subsequently, Mahajan argues that 'while [western secular states] help to secure freedom of belief and conscience for all, their attitude towards *religious practices* is, at best, ambiguous [. . .] they consider them to be like any other lifestyle preference or set of freely chosen beliefs, ignoring that religious observances are closely tied to a person's sense of dignity and respect, a constitutive element of their very self, and hence [experienced as] something more than [merely] an infringement of one's basic freedom [of 'choice']' (Mahajan 2017, 76–77, emphasis added). In India, by contrast, differentiated legal and policy outcomes for different religious groups and their individual members mean that rather than individual freedom liberating the individual *from* the group, 'individuals enjoyed the liberty to live in accordance with the customs and practices of their community. In fact, the state was expected to ensure that facilities necessary for the exercise of this liberty were provided' (Mahajan 2007, 331). This emphasis, therefore, falls much more on group-related rights and freedoms.

These normative analyses of the distinctive nature of the Indian case can be considered not necessarily as exemplary but as illustrative of the issues involved once religious diversity rather than individual freedom sets the challenge for political secularism. Stepan's (2011) pioneering work points to a set of multiple secularisms of alternative arrangements and pictures of secularism owing to different historical and demographic contexts, including legacies of European colonialism. The one which interests us here is the 'Respect All, Positive Cooperation, Principled Distance' model, which he outlines from the contextual cases of Indonesia, Senegal, and India and their responses of 'innovative formulas of accommodation' (Stepan 2011, 140) to the circumstances and challenges of governing newly independent and religiously heterogenous states.

As with moderately secular countries, Stepan's 'Respect All, Positive Cooperation, Principled Distance' model is based on 'mutual autonomy', yet, as with Mahajan, it contrasts with moderate secularism in important ways in that it represents a more pronounced form of religion and religious diversity occupying a more emphasised position in the public sphere. Three features distinguish the model. The first is *respect for minority and majority religions in the public sphere*, through official recognition of multiple religions which the state positively supports and protects in the public sphere, which contrasts with the patterns of majority privilege found in moderately secular Europe. The second feature, *positive cooperation*, denotes not just positive accommodation, but forms of policy cooperation (Stepan 2011, 131). This promotes the multivocality of religions, which in turn provides scope for religious reasons and religious arguments in public debates. This contrasts with the absence of religious language and reasoning in political debate in European contexts; as an example, in relation to the UK we can note that the arguments for 'religious clauses', advocated for and gained as part of the Equality Act 2010 by a range of faith groups, adopted a rights-based discourse rather than religious discourse (Hunt 2012). The third feature is that of *principled distance*, which Stepan borrows from Bhargava, and which posits both support for all religions alongside legitimate state interference to contend with both interreligious and intrareligious domination. A further recent concept that has been analysed in relation to South and Southeast Asia is 'covenantal pluralism' (Stewart et al. 2020), which again reflects the deep diversity of the region. It emphasises, in contrast to above, legal equality along with recognition and respect for cultural difference. Covenantal pluralism, while contextually inspired, nevertheless remains to date normatively abstract and aspirational.

These positions are not without their own problems, however, as recent events in India, Indonesia, and Malaysia show trends of increasing majoritarianism, even state and communal persecution, which is putting religious diversity and freedom of religion in the region under severe strain. What is noteworthy about those trends is not just that they consist of forms of majoritarianism that go beyond the majoritarianism of the contemporary moderate secularism of Western Europe, but also that they are occurring despite the diversity-friendliness and group accommodation of political secularism and constitutional provision in countries such as India. Not only can political frameworks be more idealistic than what happens in practice – communal, religious, caste discrimination, and violence were features even in the heyday of 'secular' India – but secular modes of governance can be rendered inoperable or be radically deformed in the light of social dynamics and forces such as racism, nationalism, and populism (Sikka 2022). Analysis of a mode of secularism therefore must attend to both its normative aspiration as well as to the political practice and social reality, and be alert to changes taking place at each of these levels: the normative, political practice, and societal dynamics.

Throughout this collection we are concerned with normative questions of secularism and state-religion connections. Yet, we are also deeply exercised by contextualism. In this way, covenantal pluralism or the minimalist secularism of Laborde fall short of being able to outline and explain actual empirical cases and, moreover, challenges and shifts within concrete contexts. As well as contextualist, our concern is also comparative, and so we do not (as, for instance, Bhargava does) propose a one model outline that we suggest other contexts should follow. Our approach is rather to highlight what can be said about secularism in a minimalist sense, that is, what our different contexts can be said to share, and then work up to develop a contextual framework of how religious diversity is governed. This allows us to identify key similarities and differences as well as to account for shifts occurring as a result of challenges and debates in different contexts. The following sections outline our approach.

What is political secularism?

From the discussion above, it is clear we are talking of 'multiple secularisms' both by widening our scope outside the West, but also within the West (Taylor 1998; Casanova 2009; Calhoun, Juergensmeyer, and Van Antwerpen 2011; Stepan 2011). Taking this point further, we recognise that multiple secularisms are an aspect of the wider theoretical and sociological understanding; and in this sense are related to 'multiple modernities' (Eisenstadt 2000).

Accordingly, we adopt a minimalist definition of political secularism. This minimalist definition offers two distinct advantages. Others tend to start with freedom of religion or toleration, but they then cannot explain in what ways plainly secularist regimes like the former USSR and China are secularist states. Moreover, too thick a definition of secularism with, for instance, a focus on a strict church-state separation may fail to see states with state-religion connections of various extents and types as 'properly' secular. This is significant not least because 'no country worldwide can be classified as adopting the pure, theorised "separation" model' (Perez and Fox 2018, 2). It is better, then, to start with what all secularisms have in common and then build up towards a normative account. This also allows us to observe the variety of political secularisms – both normatively and across the world – and the ways in which they differ. The minimalist definition of political secularism we work with is:

> The core idea of political secularism is the idea of *political autonomy*, namely that politics or the state has a *raison d'etre* of its own and should not be subordinated to religious authority, religious purposes or religious reasons (Modood 2017, 354).

To this minimal secularism, liberal states have extended political autonomy to *mutual autonomy* (or something more akin to Stepan's 'twin tolerations' [2000]), namely, not just the non-subordination of the political to the religious, but vice-versa too, the non-subordination of the religious to the state. Similarly, such states make equally central the idea that religion is a matter of personal choice or conscience, indeed this becomes a core principle of liberalism. For many theorists and publics, this liberal secularism becomes 'secularism' as such and the platform for all discussion. However, as will be evident from this collection, this is not the universal meaning and practice of secularism and the exercise of political autonomy or the state governance of religion. To begin with, liberal democratic secularism may be appropriate in some political and normative contexts but it is a Eurocentric bias as far as a global study of the governance of religion is concerned. We therefore begin with the above minimalist definition of secularism and develop a framework of different modes of the governance of religious diversity, which we outline in the following section.

Towards a comparative framework

The framework we develop, following the discussion above, differs in important ways from existing typologies. Different approaches for understanding how religious diversity in Europe is managed have highlighted, for example, a distinctly European model (in contrast with the United States) (Madeley 2009; Ferrari 1999, 2012), historical-confessional character (Madeley 2003; Knippenberg 2007; also Minkenberg 2008), immigration and cultural integration (Minkenberg 2008; Koenig 2009), disaggregating different types of establishment (see Bader 2007, 203; Stepan 2011; Minkenberg 2008), and the two-way relations between institutions and actors (Bader 2009). There are also those edited collections that bring together country case studies, such as those that focus on the varying forms of secularism outside the West (for example, Künkler, Madeley, and Shankar 2018; van der Vyver and Witte 1996; Burchardt, Wohlrab-Sahr, and Middell 2015), but without developing a comparative typology. Other studies have focused on religious repression or discrimination, whether more narrowly, such as in non-democracies (Sarkissian 2015), or more widely, and based on large data sets (Fox 2020). Fox's (2008) is a truly global survey, taking in some 175 countries, and looking at government involvement in religion. Focused on debates of secularisation-modernisation and explaining government involvement, this study makes a number of interesting observations and identifies 'patterns', but again its focus is not in developing a typology of governance.

As well as the reasons outlined in the previous section, there are further reasons that also lead us to a separate and new framework. We suggest that there is not a 'European model' (cf Ferrari, Madeley) despite some commonalities (see Sealy and Modood; Magazzini, Triandafyllidou and Yakova; and Vekony, Iliyasov and Račius in this collection). Whilst we are alert to historical legacies, we also seek to avoid being trapped by path dependency (Enyedi 2003); because of notable comparative overlaps we find and that, as Bader puts it, 'history is not destiny' (2007, 875). Whilst we might characterise our approach as 'inductive generalisation', we seek to avoid an over proliferation of modes and patterns (Bader 2007, 876). Our framework also extends the focus beyond Europe or Europe-United States comparisons (cf Madeley, Koenig, Bader, Minkenberg, and Ferrari) to provide a comparative global framework. This set of groupings and country cases we discuss of course has omissions, both 'regional' as well as individual countries. The study is necessarily limited in the number of country cases it could include, but we hope that what we develop will have wider applicability than we are able to cover here (and might indeed be developed further in light of this).

Nevertheless, in developing our typology, our approach is closest to Stepan (2011), although we differ in how we draw our distinctions. Our focus is also distinct: we are not just focused on technical matters of state-church connections (established/not established, levels of separation or the fact of connections), although these are important. Based on the fact of state-religion connections in states regardless of where they would fall under such typologies, our focus is more on the *qualitative character of state-religion connections* and the norms of governance of religion and religious diversity. That is to say, our typology and the analytical strategy it employs focus not just on the fact of state-religion connections and relations, but on the character of these, the levels of control or support, for instance. It is this factor that we argue requires greater emphasis and attention.

In developing a framework to comparatively analyse the aspects and trends we have begun to discuss above, along with our empirical country cases, we identify five 'modes' of the governance of religious diversity. These are designed to capture different modes of governance and they relate to and reflect the minimalist definition of political secularism outlined above in different ways. This will be explored in more detail in the final contribution to this collection; for now we outline our five modes. While these modes identify and delineate distinct general approaches to the governance of religious diversity, approximating ideal types, they are insufficient for comparatively analysing the overlaps and distinctions between and within regions as well as capturing trends, developments, and changes or gaps and shifts between formal arrangements and practices. As such, each mode is broken down into constituent norms that distinguish them. In this way, while a dominant mode could be identified for different cases, it also allows us the flexibility to capture the dynamic character of how religious diversity is governed and how responses to present challenges are being shaped. The five modes and their associated disaggregated norms are presented in Table 1.

While noting no country is a perfect match with any one mode and in some countries more than one mode will be at work, we can make a few important initial observations about these modes. Modes 1 and 2 can be characterised as anti-diversity approaches (or at least not pro-diversity in any public sense). It is worth noting that our mode of secularist statism might only be present as a dominant mode in one country (from the case studies here), this being France (see Sealy and Modood in this collection). But its inclusion reflects also that more countries would have been characterised by it until the past few decades, particularly several in Central and Eastern Europe, and we cannot discount the possibility of its future (re)occurrence and so our framework must be able to capture this particular form.

Mode 3 emphasises a conception of public neutrality (even if restricted in some way). It is not anti- or pro-diversity and might emphasise either way, often depending on how it is modified or qualified by norms from other modes. Modes 3 and 4 are both founded on political liberalism and give primacy to individual liberty and equality, although mode 4, developed from Modood (2017), goes furthest in extending this to groups. This feature of

Table 1. Modes and norms for the governance of religious diversity.

1. Incorporated within Majoritarian Nationalism	• Strong state identification with one religion • May or may not include toleration for other religions • May or may not include personal religious laws • In radical cases the state takes over or controls the institutions and followers of one or more religions (e.g. Diyanet) • The state may come to be controlled by religious parties (e.g. AKP, Muslim Brotherhood)
2. Secularist Statism	• State control of religion • The state excludes religion from the political and the civic, confining religious freedom largely to the private sphere • This mode of secularism may be self-defined as part of the national identity. • May include some support of some religions, but religion mainly seen as belonging to the private sphere
3. Liberal Neutralism	• Moral individualism – freedom of conscience • Anti-assimilation and equal civic standing of all religions • Religions are officially and socially tolerated • Active 'de-othering' but no 'recognition'
4. Moderate Secularism	• Moral individualism – freedom of conscience • Religions may enjoy equal or unequal status but all are officially and socially tolerated • Religion seen as a public good in need of support (e.g. funding of faith schools) • Religion might also be seen as in need of regulation (to match some prevailing values e.g. issues of women bishops/single sex marriage) e.g. social attitudes that undermine tolerance and respect for religion and religious diversity (in interfaith relations and beyond religion) • Mutual autonomy but restricted neutrality, including 'weak' establishment and unequal recognition • Religious and non-religious citizens give each other generally accessible/dialogical reasons in politics
5. Pluralistic ('unity in diversity') Nationalism	• Multiculturalising moderate secularism • Difference-sensitive identity recognition • Institutional accommodation of religious diversity • 'Respect All, Positive Cooperation, Principled Distance' • Religion active and present in public and political life • Policy cooperation – religious reasons in political sphere • Accommodative of differentiated legal status, religious personal laws • Primacy of group autonomy and social support for deep diversity

balancing or alternatively emphasising group rights as well as individual rights becomes an important point of difference for modes 4 and 5.

Modes 4 and 5 can be characterised as pro-diversity approaches, although exactly how this diversity looks and how it might also be limited is modified by features from the other modes. Both give some emphasis to group liberty and differentiated group equality, with neutrality much weaker, although mode 5 goes considerably further in including a range of cases from some group recognition to moral groupism.

We should also note that we do not include a mode to capture theocratic countries, such as Iran, not because we don't recognise the distinction of these types of connections, but because none of our country case studies reflect these kinds of arrangements.

Applying the framework: an outline of the collection

Each mode of governance is unpacked by highlighting a number of constituent norms (some of which may overlap with one or more other modes of governance, as in the case of freedom of conscience). In applying these norms to an analysis of the governance of religious diversity, we make a further important distinction. Firstly, we designate the constituent norms of each mode (those in the right-hand column) as *operative norms*. Following what Parekh calls 'operative public values', this means that they are the norms that provide the 'context and point of orientation' (2000 [2006], 267) for discussions and debate over public religion. Our further distinction here, however, is to identify and distinguish between what we call *dominant operative norms* (DONs) and *qualifying operative norms* (QONs) in each given country context. DONs are those norms that we can see as operating at a more basic and underpinning level, they provide the 'centre of gravity' for the discussions and debates in a particular context, they are more pervasive and do most of the work in terms of how religion is governed. Often these are found in basic constitutional articles, but this is not necessarily or rigidly definitional of DONs. What is significant is that they are operative in how religion is governed. If norms or principles are stated in constitutional documents but are not actually effective in how religion is governed, for instance, they would not constitute DONs.

QONs are equally important and serve to limit, adjust, or modify how DONs function. They are present in a way that is significant for a state's approach to diversity and serve to highlight important differences between country contexts that cannot be explained by reference to a single mode, and without seeing how other norms interact with it. QONs are not as prominent as DONs, but serve to qualify how DONs operate in important ways. Thus, in cases where two country cases might have the same DONs but different QONs, we would see a marked difference in governance. To be clear, the distinction between DONs and QONs is not that between *de jure* and *de facto* norms, or ideal and practice; it is between norms that do most of the work and norms that are also present and operative but not so powerfully, so they moderate the way that the dominant norms work. As such, the norms in the table above are not dominant or qualifying in any essential sense, rather they are contingent, potentially variable, and what norms are dominant or qualifying in any particular case is a matter of analysis of that case. This in turn is an important way in which our typology avoids static interpretations, as the norms, and whether they operate as DONs or QONs, have the potential to change.

Our modes then represent ideal types, each with a collection of norms that serve to constitute each mode and distinguish it from others. As we have seen above, our position is that context matters when it comes to conceiving secularism and its effects, and each of the contributions demonstrates this in relation to our five regions and their country case studies. As contextually derived, these modes can be said to roughly reflect empirical cases. Yet, as ideal types they also do not necessarily reflect all important aspects of any given context. As a result, what is centrally important in our framework, and central to its analytical innovation, is how norms may interact not just within, but also across modes, and how this can track as well as indicate directions of travel and shifts in governance of religious diversity. We are then not simply interested in a static 'model' view of state-religion relations, but in developing a comparative framework that allows us to analyse changes and developments in ways that might lean towards measures and arrangements that are diversity enhancing or equalising upwards, on the one hand, or towards diversity restricting or equalising downwards, on the other hand.

Making this distinction provides two analytical advantages reflected in each of our regional-based contributions to this collection. Firstly, it allows us to identify and specify intra-regional similarity and difference when countries may reflect the same general mode at a regional level, but have significant differences between countries below the regional level. In this way, it allows us to assess how the norms travel in a way which is contextually sensitive (and reflects a method of 'iterative contextualism', Modood and Thompson 2018).

Fahmi and Lahlou, for instance, show how overall, the MENA region represents majoritarian nationalism through the strong control exerted by the state whilst it promulgates religious identity as a core aspect of citizenship. This, moreover, is despite features of legal and institutional pluralism as well as legal frames that insist on the freedom of conscience, but which are not particularly operative. A general exception in the region, however, is Lebanon, which has institutionalised (limited) diversity. Sealy and Modood likewise show how Western European states and Australia share a basic conception of freedom of religion based in freedom of conscience, moral individualism, and toleration. However, important distinctions in the region revolve around the character of state-religion institutional connections, which mark France out as an exceptional case in the region. Looking at Central and Eastern Europe, the contribution by Vekony, Iliyasov and Račius shows that despite a common formal foundation of freedom of religion, in many countries the state identifies with one denomination and only the institutionalised forms of religion (registered religious organisations) are allowed to operate publicly. This is restrictive of diversity and there has been a rise of religious nationalism of an identitarian nature throughout much of the region, and where Lithuania stands out as an exception.

A second analytical advantage of our approach is that it allows us to see how different countries, despite being predominantly captured by one of our five modes, also include norms from other modes that have a significant bearing on the governance of religious diversity in that country. The contribution by Magazzini, Triandafyllidou and Yakova shows that Southern and Southeastern Europe as a whole also rests on moral individualism, freedom of conscience, and toleration for all religions. Yet how these regional points of similarity look and contrast within the region is shaped by the variance and emphasis of other norms that operate in each country, with aspects of moderate secularism and majoritarian nationalism making significant qualifications in different countries.

This, furthermore, allows us to look at how shifts and changes take place in directions that might be diversity enhancing or restricting as one or more norms become more pronounced and salient in contrast to others, again in ways that may not affect the overall mode that a country could be seen to reflect. We are then able to identify the factors that can explain the evolution in the different countries and the current challenges posed to or by how religious diversity is governed. For example, Sealy et al. identify in relation to South and Southeast Asia that while, on the whole, the region may be considered an example that reflects pluralistic nationalism (in line with Stepan's position), the region is also (increasingly) characterised by qualifying norms of strong currents of diversity-limiting ethno-religious nationalism, and which might operate through the legal system and political processes, including policy-making, and be argued to have constitutional grounding. Also in this vein, in relation to Western Europe, Sealy and Modood show that countries that reflect a mode of moderate secularism might also have important operative norms from other modes, and which might be diversity-enhancing norms (such as institutional accommodation) or diversity-restricting norms (such as state control of religion), particularly in contexts marked by responses to threats of (violent) radicalisation.

The separate contributions apply the framework to intra-regional analyses of each of our five regions. The final, concluding contribution then draws some comparative threads from across our regional case studies. Through analysing the norms, institutional arrangements, policies, and practices, these contributions present comparative studies of selected country case studies within each region, which seek to identify both intra-regional differences as well as what can be said about the region as a whole. Each contribution presents an historical overview of state-religion connections and secularism, outlines key contemporary challenges, and analyses developments and shifts in relation to how religion and religious diversity are governed. As a collection, these contributions represent a comparative analysis of the governance of religious diversity with a global scope.

Note

1. See BBC (2011) 'David Cameron Says the UK is a Christian Country'. 16 December. Online at https://www.bbc.co.uk/news/uk-politics-16224394; also WWRN (2014) 'David Cameron Christianity claim backed by religious groups'. 21 April. Online at https://wwrn.org/articles/42235/.

Acknowledgments

We are grateful to two anonymous reviewers and the journal editors for their comments on this contribution; and to all the contributors for their participation in this collection, as well as in the project, GREASE, which is the basis of this collection.

Disclosure statement

No potential conflict of interest was reported by the author(s).

Funding

The GREASE project, on which this contribution is based, has received funding from the European Union's Horizon 2020 research and innovation programme under grant agreement number 770640.

ORCID

Tariq Modood (iD) http://orcid.org/0000-0001-8712-5508
Thomas Sealy (iD) http://orcid.org/0000-0002-3211-6900

References

Asad, T. 1993. *Genealogies of Religion: Discipline and Reasons of Power in Christianity and Islam*. London: The Johns Hopkins University Press.

Asad, T. 2003. *Formations of the Secular: Christianity, Islam, Modernity*. Stanford: Stanford University Press.

Bader, V. 2007. *Secularism or Democracy? Associational Governance of Religious Diversity*. Amsterdam: Amsterdam University Press.

Bader, V. 2009. "The Governance of Religious Diversity: Theory, Research and Practice." In *International Migration and the Governance of Religious Diversity*, edited by P. Bramadat and M. Koenig, 43–72. Montreal: McGill-Queen's University Press.

BBC. 2015. "Most British Muslims 'Oppose Muhammad Cartoons Reprisals'." February 25. Last Accessed 2 June 2015. http://www.bbc.com/news/uk-31293196.

Bhargava, R. 1998. "What is Secularism For?" In *Secularism and Its Critics*, edited by R. Bhargava, 486–542. New Delhi: Oxford University Press.

Bhargava, R. 2009. "Political Secularism: Why It is Needed and What Can Be Learnt from Its Indian Version?" In *Secularism, Religion and Multicultural Citizenship*, edited by G. B. Levey and T. Modood, 82–109. Cambridge: Cambridge University Press.

Bhargava, R. 2013. "Can Secularism Be Rehabilitated?." In *Secular States and Religious Diversity*, edited by B. J. Berman, R. Bhargava, and A. Lalliberté, 69–97. Vancouver: University of British Columbia Press.

Bhargava, R. 2014. "How Secular is European Secularism?" *European Societies* 16 (3): 329–336. doi:10.1080/14616696.2014.916335.

Bhargava, R. 2015. "Beyond Moderate Secularism." In *Secularism, Religion, and Politics: India and Europe*, edited by P. Losonczi and W. Van Herck, 57–64. London: Routledge.

Bouchard, G., and C. Taylor. 2008. *Building the Future: A Time for Reconciliation*. Montreal: Gouvernement du Québec.

Burchardt, M., M. Wohlrab-Sahr, and M. Middell, eds. 2015. *Multiple Secularities Beyond the West: Religion and Modernity in the Global Age*. Berlin: De Gruyter.

Calhoun, C., M. Juergensmeyer, and J. Van Antwerpen, eds. 2011. *Rethinking Secularism*. Oxford: Oxford University Press.

Casanova, J. 2009. "The Secular and Secularisms." *Social Research: An International Quarterly* 76 (4): 1049–1066. doi:10.1353/sor.2009.0064.

Eisenstadt, S. N. 2000. "Multiple Modernities." *Daedalus* 129 (1): 1–29.

Enyedi, Z. 2003. "Conclusion: Emerging Issues in the Study of Church–state Relations." *West European Politics* 26 (1): 218–232. doi:10.1080/01402380412331300277.

Ferrari, S. 1999. "The New Wine and the Old Cask. Tolerance, Religion and the Law Incontemporary Europe." *Ratio Juris* 10 (1): 75–89. doi:10.1111/1467-9337.00043.

Ferrari, S. 2012. "Law and Religion in a Secular World: A European Perspective." *Ecclesiastical Law Journal* 14: 355–370. doi:10.1017/S0956618X1200035X.

Fox, J. 2008. *A World Survey of Religion and the State*. Cambridge: Cambridge University Press.

Fox, J. 2020. *Thou Shalt Have No Other Gods Before Me: Why Governments Discriminate Against Religious Minorities*. Cambridge: Cambridge University Press.

Habermas, J. 2006. "Religion in the Public Sphere." *European Journal of Philosophy* 14 (1): 1–25. doi:10.1111/j.1468-0378.2006.00241.x.

Hunt, S. 2012. "Negotiating Equality in the Equality Act 2010 (United Kingdom): Church-State Relations in a Post-Christian Society." *Journal of Church and State* 55 (4): 690–711. doi:10.1093/jcs/css078.

Knippenberg, H. 2007. "The Political Geography of Religion: Historical State-Church Relations in Europe and Recent Challenges." *GeoJournal* 67 (4): 253–265. doi:10.1007/s10708-007-9068-x.

Koenig, M. 2009. "How Nations-States Respond to Religious Diversity." In *International Migration and the Governance of Religious Diversity*, edited by P. Bramadat and M. Koenig, 293–322. Montreal: McGill-Queen's University Press.

Künkler, M., J. Madeley, and S. Shankar, eds. 2018. *A Secular Age Beyond the West: Religion, Law and the State in Asia, the Middle East and North Africa*. Cambridge: Cambridge University Press.

Laborde, C. 2017. *Liberalism's Religion*. London: Harvard University Press.

Maclure, J., and C. Taylor. 2011. *Secularism and Freedom of Conscience*. London: Harvard University Press.

Madan, T. N. 1998. "Secularism in Its Place." In *Secularism and Its Critics*, edited by R. Bhargava, 297–320. New Delhi: Oxford University Press.

Madeley, J. 2003. "A Framework for the Comparative Analysis of Church–state Relations in Europe." *West European Politics* 26 (1): 23–50. doi:10.1080/01402380412331300187.

Madeley, J. 2009. "Unequally Yoked: The Antinomies of Church–state Separation in Europe and the USA." *European Political Science* 8 (3): 273–288. doi:10.1057/eps.2009.16.

Mahajan, G. 2007. "Multiculturalism in the Age of Terror: Confronting the Challenges." *Political Studies Review* 5: 317–336. doi:10.1111/j.1478-9299.2007.00133.x.

Mahajan, G., A. Triandafyllidou and T. Modood. 2017. "Living with Religious Diversity: The Limits of the Secular Paradigm." In *The Problem of Religious Diversity: European Challenges, Asian Approaches*, edited by A. Triandafyllidou and T. Modood, 75–92. Edinburgh: Edinburgh University Press.

Martin, N. 2017. "Are British Muslims Alienated from Mainstream Politics by Islamophobia and British Foreign Policy?" *Ethnicities* 17 (3): 350–370. doi:10.1177/1468796816656674.

Minkenberg, M. 2008. "Religious Legacies and the Politics of Multiculturalism: A Comparative Analysis of Integration Policies in Western Democracies." In *Immigration, Integration, and Security: America and Europe in Comparative Perspective*, edited by A. C. d'Appollonia and S. Reich, 44–66. Pittsburgh: University of Pittsburgh Press.

Modood, T. 2012. "Is There a Crisis of Secularism in Western Europe?" *Sociology of Religion* 72 (2): 130–149. doi:10.1093/socrel/srs028.

Modood, T. 2017. "Multiculturalism and Moderate Secularism." In *The Problem of Religious Diversity European Challenges, Asian Approaches*, edited by A. Triandafyllidou and T. Modood, 52–74. Edinburgh: Edinburgh University Press.

Modood, T. 2019. *Essays on Secularism and Multiculturalism*. London: Rowman-Littlefield and European Consortium of Political Science.

Modood, T., and S. Thompson. 2018. "Revisiting Contextualism in Political Theory: Putting Principles into Context." *Res Publica* 24 (3): 339–357. doi:10.1007/s11158-017-9358-1.

Modood, T., and S. Thompson. 2022. "Othering, Alienation and Establishment." *Political Studies* 70 (3): 780–796. doi:10.1177/0032321720986698.

Murad, A. H. 2020. *Travelling Home: Essays on Islam in Europe*. Cambridge: The Quilliam Press.

Nandy, A. 1998. "The Politics of Secularism and the Recovery of Religious Toleration." In *Secularism and Its Critics*, edited by R. Bhargava, 321–344. New Delhi: Oxford University Press.

Parekh, B. 20002006. *Rethinking Multiculturalism: Cultural Diversity and Political Theory*. Basingstoke: Macmillan.

Perez, N., and J. Fox. 2018. "Normative Theorizing and Political Data: Toward a Data-Sensitive Understanding of the Separation Between Religion and State in Political Theory." *Critical Review of International Social and Political Philosophy* 4: 485–509.

Pew Research. 2018. "Eastern and Western Europeans Differ on Importance of Religion, Views of Minorities, and Key Social Issues." Accessed 28 December 2018. https://www.pewforum.org/2018/10/29/eastern-and-western-europeans-differ-on-importance-of-religion-views-of-minorities-and-key-social-issues/.

Rawls, J. 1997. "The Idea of Public Reason Revisited." *The University of Chicago Law Review* 64 (3): 765–807. doi:10.2307/1600311.

Sarkissian, A. 2015. *The Varieties of Religious Repression: Why Governments Restrict Religion.* Oxford: Oxford University Press.

Sikka, S. 2022. "Indian Islamophobia as Racism." *The Political Quarterly* 93 (3). doi:10.1111/1467-923X.13152.

Stepan, A. 2000. "Religion, Democracy, and the 'Twin Tolerations'." *Journal of Democracy* 11 (4): 37–67. doi:10.1353/jod.2000.0088.

Stepan, A. 2011. "The Multiple Secularisms of Modern Democratic and Non-Democratic Regimes." In *Rethinking Secularism,* edited by C. Calhoun, M. Juergensmeyer, and J. Van Antwerpen, 114–144. Oxford: Oxford University Press.

Stewart, W. C., C. Seiple, and D. R. Hoover. 2020. "Global Covenant of Peaceable Neighborhood: Introducing the Philosophy of Covenantal Pluralism." *The Review of Faith & International Affairs* 18 (4): 1–17. doi:10.1080/15570274.2020.1835029.

Taylor, C. 1998. "Modes of Secularism." In *Secularism and Its Critics,* edited by R. Bhargava, 31–53. New Delhi: Oxford University Press.

van der Vyver, J. D., and J. Witte, eds. 1996. *Religious Human Rights in Global Perspective: Legal Perspectives.* London: Martinus Nijhoff Publishers.

ô OPEN ACCESS

Western Europe and Australia: negotiating freedoms of religion

Thomas Sealy ⓘ and Tariq Modood ⓘ

ABSTRACT
Newly established religious minorities in Western European countries and Australia have sparked fresh questions about the public place of religion. The current situation in the region reflects a certain agonism over the place of public religion and its relation to liberal secular order. This has especially been the case for the region's Muslims in a context marked by fears of radicalisation and extremism. This contribution considers these responses in relation to Belgium, France, Germany, and the UK; and Australia. The contribution explores the norm of freedom of religion that forms the region's core similarity but also the ground on which divergences in norms of state-religion connections can be found. It identifies key norms that operate in the region in order to draw out similarities as well as important differences between the countries. Exploring how the governance of religious diversity comes to reflect diversity-enhancing or diversity-limiting features, it assesses the ways and extent to which the region can be characterised under 'moderate secularism'.

Introduction

Western Europe, it has been said, has been undergoing a significant challenge, or even crisis, of secularism and multiculturalism in its struggles to include religious minorities that have arrived since the mid-twentieth century (Bhargava 1998, 2009, 2016, 2017; Mahajan 2007; Roy 2007). While this may be something of an overstatement (Modood 2012), the meaning and parameters of secularism have become the focus of renewed attention provoked by contemporary extra-Christian religious diversity.

Some of the key political and public debates have revolved around the presence and accommodation of religious signs and symbols, issues of free speech, particularly those prompted by books (the Rushdie Affair), cartoons (the Danish cartoon affair; Charlie Hebdo) and their reproduction or use, and debates over the place and content of Islamic (Sharia) law in relation to civil law. In this vein, it is the prominence of and focus on Muslims and Islam that has been at the forefront of debates and controversies, and which have been seen to do most to challenge the region's liberal secular states (see for example, Joppke 2015; Modood 2019).

This is an Open Access article distributed under the terms of the Creative Commons Attribution License (http://creativecommons.org/licenses/by/4.0/), which permits unrestricted use, distribution, and reproduction in any medium, provided the original work is properly cited.

This contribution considers what can be said about Western Europe as a region when it comes to the governance of religious diversity; is there something we can call a Western European approach? To do so we apply a new framework for the comparative analysis of the governance of religious diversity (see Modood and Sealy, this collection) to the cases of the UK, France, Germany, and Belgium (see Figure 1). We also include Australia in this group given its historical outgrowth from the UK. The analysis presented is based on extensive research of secondary literature, and legal and policy measures. We look at similarities and differences between these countries, and how these relate to issues of secularism and freedom of religion. The contribution begins with an historical overview before going on to assess two simultaneous trends: on the one hand, a more accommodationist, multicultural response; on the other hand, a more secularist, 'muscular' liberalism, more intolerant of visible and audible religion in the public sphere. We therefore further ask: what mode(s) and norms of governance of religious diversity operate in the region? How do these modes bear on the responses of our country cases to issues and controversies of accommodating religious diversity? And, conversely, how do these issues and controversies bear on the mode(s) of governance? We also address the idea of freedom of religion in the region, how this has come to differ between our country cases, and how this forms a particularly significant fault line between them.

Historical overview to contemporary relevance

The Westphalian settlement (1648), in retrospect, set in motion a trajectory that would pass through ideas of religious tolerance, state neutrality, and privatised religion. Along with developments resulting from the growth of modern capitalism and the early modern

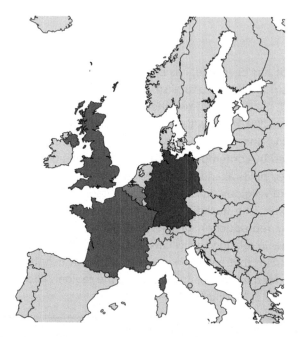

Figure 1. Western European countries covered in this contribution: Belgium, France, Germany, and the UK.

scientific revolution, religion came to be gradually and increasingly circumscribed from politics through the nineteenth century; notable incidents including the German *Kulturkampf* (1872–1878) (Großbölting 2017; Hatfield 1981; Henkel 2006), Belgian 'school wars' (1879–1884) (Dobbelaere and Voyé 1990), and secularisation laws under the Third Republic (1875–1905) in France culminating in the law of 1905 on church-state separation (Gunn 2004). In England also, various functions such as education and welfare began to be taken over by the state and direct financial ties between state and established Church of England were cut (such as tithes and grants). Australia was initially occupied as a penal colony by the British before it became a colonial settler society, and a long shadow of systematic dispossession, displacement, and denial of the continent's indigenous Aboriginal and Torres Strait Islander peoples hangs over its historical development. Prior to federalisation (1901), relations were marked by Protestant-Catholic sectarianism.

Nevertheless, state-religion connections across the region persisted, albeit in revised forms recontoured by a norm of political secularism in which political authority was separated from religious authority and the latter made subordinate to the former. Reformed arrangements and connections began to settle as the twentieth century progressed. In Germany, principles from the earlier Weimar Constitution (1919) were enshrined in the new (1949) German Basic Law (*Grundgesetz*), adopting the principle of separation between church and state as well as protecting religious freedoms, retaining subsidies and privileges for the Protestant and Catholic churches, and codifying cooperation between church and state, especially on matters of education and welfare, through the status of 'corporation under public law' (*Körperschaft des öffentlichen Rechts*). The number of groups granted public corporation status has grown since, although as the granting of this status is devolved to each *Land* (federated state), and conditions of size and permanency are important determining factors, there is variation in this process. To take a few examples, in Bavaria/Berlin: Methodists (1922/1973), Jews (1947/1951), Greek Orthodox (1975/1976), Baptists (1982/1974), Romanian Orthodox (2006/[no date given]), and Jehovah's Witnesses (2009/2006) have, amongst others, all been granted public corporation status (Hofhansel 2013); in Bavaria, humanist organisations were also granted this status in 1947 and 2012; and in Hesse a Bahá'í and a Muslim group are also recognised (Körs 2017).[1] The takeover of social functions by the state in the UK continued but some ties, such as reserved seats in the House of Lords, were preserved and the Church of England also gained greater autonomy in its own affairs (as they became). State-religion connections with the diversity of minority religions have also been extended. In Belgium, the system of pillarisation brought about as a result of the school wars, which had separated Catholic, Liberal, and Socialist social institutions and organisations, loosened but strong connections between state and religion remain, notably in education and the role the Catholic Church plays in public life (Franken 2016a, 2016b), and further religious groups gained official state recognition. Since the 1970s, and the repeal of its 'White Australia' policy, Australia has cultivated a multiculturalism that builds on earlier state support and accommodation of religious groups (Levey 2017). In France, historical connections persisted in the form of recognised representative organisations for Catholics, Protestants, and Jews, and funding for faith (principally Catholic) schools and places of worship.

The historical legacy has meant that religions in the region continue to play important public roles, and that the state-religion connections facilitate, support, encourage, and also colour many of those roles. Accommodations and exemptions for certain aspects of dress, funeral practices, religious buildings, ritual slaughter, and educational provision, for instance, have been claimed, debated, sometimes made, and sometimes refused or revoked.

Since the late 1980s, the region has seen a re-emergence of public religion. So-called New Religious Movements (NRMs) have been extremely controversial (going back to the 1960s), perhaps especially in France and Germany, and subject to state control (see Richardson 2004). There have also been more recent high-profile legal cases involving Christians, particularly related to sexuality, such as the gay cake row in Northern Ireland (*Lee v Ashers Baking Company Ltd and others*), which went to the European Court of Human Rights (ECtHR), and Christian hotel owners in England who refused to allow a gay couple a double room in England (*Bull vs Hall*) (for discussion on both cases, see Velasco Ibarra 2020). The issue of public religion in Western Europe has, nevertheless, largely focused on religious minorities, and especially Muslims.

There are two sets of arguments we are interested in here. One sees the current state-religion connections extant across Western Europe as a problem for the inclusion of minority religions; even arguing that the modes of secularism in the region are 'irretrievably flawed' (Bhargava 2014, 2017) in their ability to accommodate religious minorities, in part because of the region's Christian inheritance. Laborde (2013, 2017) has made a related argument in so far as she sees church-state connections, particularly those with a dominant church, as necessarily alienating for minorities.

We argue that these positions are mistaken. These state-religion connections can help the accommodation and inclusion of minority religions, and in fact religious minorities do not seem to protest the position of, for example, the established Church of England, instead appreciating these arrangements as a recognition by the state of the public and national significance of religion (Modood and Thompson 2021; also see Modood 1997; Perez, Fox and McClure 2017; Fetzer and Soper 2005). Moreover, recent research on populism strongly indicates that recognised religions can dilute or neutralise far-right backlashes against religious minorities (Cremer 2021). We seek to show that state-religion connections recognise the public good of religion and that this can be positively accommodative of minority religions, notwithstanding certain constraints.

The other type of argument we are concerned with characterises the understanding and mode of secularism in the region. Some have seen French *laïcité* as representing 'mainstream western secularism' (Bhargava 2009) or as a European and not just a French value (Willaime 2009). Others see French *laïcité* as neutral towards religion (Joppke 2007; cf Jansen 2013). It is important to note that this is not a consensus view (see for example Kuru 2008; Modood and Sealy in this collection). One key contrast is that between the 'moderate' secularism of most of Western Europe and Australia, and the 'radical' secularism of France (Modood 2010; Levey 2017). It is this latter characterisation that we elaborate on, where our modes of moderate secularism and secularist statism develop from Modood's earlier distinction.

We can first note what is held in common across our country cases and so forms the norms of the region,[2] and we can state this quite briefly and uncontroversially. Underpinned by a political secularism (see above), Western European and Australian norms rest on a foundation of freedom of religion based in freedom of conscience and moral individualism, and these rights are found enshrined in constitutions or primary legislation.

Yet there are two religious freedoms here: freedom of conscience and freedom of practice. Both are guaranteed in each country and while one's private religious convictions are not really at issue, the latter becomes the key point of normative divergence between our country cases. We seek to show how and why, despite this common baseline of political secularism and freedom of religion, the modes and their constitutive norms vary within our region. What orients our study is not structures of governance *per se*, although these are extremely important, but the norms that underpin them and how they operate (see Modood and Sealy in this collection). That is, it is not the fact of state-religion connections or even necessarily – and certainly not only – their form, but rather the extent, character, and quality of these connections and relations that we are concerned with foremost (cf Modood 2010).

Our analysis is organised into two main sections. The first splits our cases into two groups to elaborate on the modes and norms that characterise and differentiate them (represented in Table 1) in relation to diversity-enhancing norms. The second turns to more diversity-restricting norms and focuses especially on recent trends and challenges to religious diversity that have emerged in relation to countries' Muslim populations. In both cases, it identifies which norms are operative, and distinguishes between *dominant operative norms* (DONs), which are those norms most dominant in how religion is governed in a particular case, and *qualifying operative norms* (QONs), which are equally important and serve to limit, adjust, or modify how DONs function (for further discussion of this distinction see Modood and Sealy, this collection).

Accommodation of religious diversity

Moderate secularism: religion as a public good

Four of our countries represent a mode of moderate secularism: the UK, Belgium, Germany, and to a lesser extent Australia, yet all have state-religion connections of different sorts. The UK is the only case here with a formally established church. The Church of England remains (weakly) established and certain privileges, such as reserved seats for bishops in the upper chamber of parliament, remain. The German Basic Law, by contrast, establishes a formal separation between church and state (Article 137 (1)), whilst in Belgium it is not a formal constitutional separation. An immediate point to make,

Table 1. Modes and norms for the governance of religious diversity.

Secularist Statism	• State control of religion • The state excludes religion from the political and the civic, confining religious freedom largely to the private sphere • May include some support of some religions, but religion mainly seen as belonging to the private sphere
Moderate Secularism	• Moral individualism – freedom of conscience • Religions may enjoy equal or unequal status but all are officially and socially tolerated • Religion seen as a public good in need of support (funding of faith schools) • Religion might also be seen as in need of regulation (to match some prevailing values e.g. issues of women bishops/single sex marriage) e.g. social attitudes that undermine tolerance and respect for religion and religious diversity (in interfaith relations and beyond religion) • Mutual autonomy but restricted neutrality, including 'weak' establishment and unequal recognition • Generally accessible/dialogical reasons

therefore, is that these countries being examples of moderate secularism is not based on a point of sameness of constitutional recognition between church and state. Rather, it is the political secularism of the state along with the normative provision of positive connections, allowing for variety in the exact form of these connections, that forms the common ground between them.

Despite these differences in 'establishment', state-religion connections are constitutionally guaranteed in both Belgium and Germany, and in both countries religions can gain formal recognition status; in Germany, for example, through gaining public corporation status. In the UK, which lacks a formal written constitution, the position of religion is secured through other legislation. In England, the 'advancement of religion' is recognised as a charitable purpose under the Charities Act 2011, for instance, and it is from gaining charitable status that financial benefits in terms of tax relief are open to religious bodies. Cooperation between state and religion is secured in areas such as education and social welfare, chaplains in public institutions such as schools, hospitals, prisons and the armed forces, as well as a number of other areas.

When it comes to newer religious minorities more specifically, routes to formal recognition have also been available under these legal provisions and their terms, and a number of religions, as well as humanist groups, are recognised. Also, institutional connections have been expanded through, for instance, the German Islam Conferences (*Deutsche Islam Konferenz*) or 'democratic constellation' of Muslim organisations (Modood 2013 [2007]) in the UK. As well as these formal mechanisms, measures that are pragmatic or ad hoc have also filled gaps.

Through this kind of cooperation, the norms in these states go beyond a privatised view of religion in society as merely a matter of individual conscience. Religion is seen as a public good, providing significant public services, and is supported, in no small part as a result of the historical importance of churches in these areas. Two main areas in which religion is seen as a public good are education and welfare service provision. In terms of welfare service provision, it is perhaps not too much of an exaggeration to say that state welfare would be severely disabled, if not collapse, without the roles of and partnerships with churches and faith-based organisations (see for example Dinham 2015, 109; 2009 on the UK; and on Germany, Barker 2000; Lewicki 2014; Franken 2016b, 2017; and on Belgium, Franken 2015, 2016b; Adam and Torrekens 2015).

Religions also play a central role in education, where they operate in the public school system with government funding as well as run private schools, and might take the form of involvement in setting or providing the curriculum for religious education, worship, or running what are loosely referred to as faith schools (Bribosia et al. 2011; Franken 2017; Brems 2020; Long and Danechi 2019). These, moreover, have generally increased in the last couple of decades even if Christian-based schools predominate. Here the characteristic of pragmatic accommodation is evident in some German *Länder* (federated states), where, for instance, religious groups without public corporation status have informal arrangements to teach religious education, including Muslim and Buddhist groups (Körs 2017, 2019).

As well as these types of connections, a large degree of mutual autonomy is assured. There are, for instance, some exemptions from equalities legislation (particularly on gender and sexuality) as applied to the labour market for some positions where doctrinal specifications are in conflict. State control of and interference in religion are also limited, such as in matters of doctrine. In Belgium, for example, the Constitution prohibits the state from 'interven[ing] either in the appointment or in the installation of ministers of any religion whatsoever' (Article 21), and in the UK, government interference in Church of England affairs has receded gradually, and since 2007 the prime minister no longer plays an active role in Church appointments.

Through these kinds of norms and connections between state and religion, we can also see some features of a different mode of governance playing a qualifying role, that of pluralistic nationalism (see Modood and Sealy in this collection), and this is perhaps strongest in the UK; namely, through aspects of difference-sensitive recognition, institutional accommodation, and areas of policy cooperation. Yet, moderate secularism differs from pluralistic nationalism in the depth and extent of these features, and the basic principles of moral individualism and political secularism mentioned above as the common regional norms are fundamental to why these are qualifying rather than dominant norms. In this way, despite the positive public presence and role of religion, this is very much within parameters contoured by political secularism.

Turning to Australia, overall, the way in which the Australian Constitution treats religious freedom has for many decades operated on the principle that religious beliefs and practices are voluntary and private matters for its citizens, with weaker positive protection and connections for religious rights and freedoms in comparison to similar countries (Meyerson 2009, 529) such as our three European cases of moderate secularism (the UK, Belgium, and Germany). Constitutionally, this forms a key point of difference here, and has elsewhere been characterised as liberal separationism (Chavura, Gascoigne, and Tregenza 2019).

Nevertheless, as we saw above, accommodation of religious groups was foundational to Australian multiculturalism. Although connections and provisions are not part of the Constitution, Australia maintains a list of Registered Religious Institutions through the Australian Tax Office, which may be eligible for a range of tax benefits and concessions. The most significant recent developments at national level to trends within state-religion connections in Australia have arisen as a result of the 2018 Religious Freedoms Review (see Grossman et al. 2021). In its response the Australian government has stated that freedom of religion is not subordinate to other freedoms and 'accepts [...] that there is an opportunity to further protect, and better promote and balance, the right to freedom of religion under Australian law and in the public sphere' (Australian Government 2018, 4). The debate over this legislation both points to a strong current of moderate secularism (perhaps even with some weaker elements of pluralistic nationalism), but which can be hotly contested on more liberal neutralist grounds. Emerging from the Review, a new Religious Discrimination Act has stalled; having passed the lower house, at the time of writing it is yet to pass through the Senate and come into law owing to tensions with sex and sexuality discrimination rights.[3]

At State and Territory levels, we find a more pronounced moderate secularism. Australia's federated system has left States and Territories free to legislate on various religious matters and the status of religions is unevenly distributed as a result (for further discussion see Grossman et al. 2021). There are a range of Commonwealth agency-based funding programmes for religious and cultural groups and some Australian States and Territories specifically make funds available to minority ethno-religious groups, including expansion of the provision for Special Religious Instruction in government schools to reflect more recent religious diversity in some states although not others. This can be uneven between States and Territories, however; and new legislation in Victoria is set to restrict religious organisations and schools' ability to discriminate on the basis of sexuality, gender, and marital status in staff recruitment,[4] something which may bring it into tension with the Religious Discrimination Act should that pass into law.

Secularist statism: religion privatised

France forms somewhat of an exception from the moderate secularism of the region (cf Willaime 2009; Jansen 2011), and more closely reflects a mode of secularist statism.[5] France is, for instance, the only EU state to explicitly define itself as secular in its constitution. This variance is grounded in a form of civic nationhood antithetical to recognising group difference and a form of republican egalitarian individualism which the granting of group rights is seen to undermine. Religious difference is therefore restricted to the private sphere more fully than is the case in the UK, Germany, and Belgium, and state control is much more prominent.

It is important to appreciate that the precise meaning and parameters of *laïcité* have always been disputed. One strand was historically clerical and monarchist, but today is characterised by being more pluralistic and open (Baubérot 2010; Jansen 2013). Yet it is the other, more combative, version of *laïcité*, which came to connote a particular anti-clerical attitude and policies (Gunn 2004), that has become increasingly prominent, and which for some has come to represent a distortion of the 1905 law (Baubérot 2014). This approach emphasises freedom *from* rather than *of* religion, with the state's role one of protecting citizens in this regard. This is also reflected in the 'cultural layers of laicism' (Jansen 2013, 198) or 'narrative secularism' (Ferrari 2009), with a hardening of a cultural discourse of *laïcité* underlain by presuppositions of assimilationism and the disappearance of public religion. We might say, then, that France is distinct in having stronger ties between nation and secularism, where public identity and how the state relates to citizens is more strongly secularist in identity terms. This is not just a feature of the French state but regarded as central to the country; for some it is what it means to live in France and to be French.

This does not preclude some connections and support and there is a degree to which religions are supported through institutional connections with the state. Legal institutional status has been granted to representative bodies for Catholics, Protestants, and Jews, and a representative body for Muslims was created. This comes with tax exemptions and assistance in access to public spaces and building places of worship. There are state-paid chaplains who operate in public schools, prisons, hospitals, and the military. There are also faith-based private schools and hospitals that receive government funding, providing they meet appropriate criteria.

Nevertheless, there is a normative difference between these types of state-religion connections under our modes of moderate secularism (discussed above) and secularist statism. Key to understanding this difference is not the fact of state-religion connections, but that these connections are based in operating principles qualitatively different enough to warrant their distinction. Moderate secularism is significantly oriented around religion seen as a public good and state-religion connections that support a public role for religion. Secularist statism, by contrast, seeks to restrict religion to the private sphere to a greater degree, religion is seen as a problem, and state-religion connections are characterised by greater state interference and control. In France, public religion is more restricted and tightly controlled by the state, with autonomy more one-way than elsewhere in the region. In France, obtaining the status of 'religion' rather than just 'association' is difficult and requires the State Council to undertake 'a substantive review' of its purposes and practices (Gunn 2009, 978). Moreover, the state maintains a high degree of interference, in majority as well as minority religions. Before the pope appoints new bishops, for example, the minister of the interior checks that the values of the nominees are not incompatible with those of the Republic (Troper 2016, 327). It is also heavily involved in making decisions about employees and the curriculum in the religious schools it funds. Moreover, debates around public funding for a Grand Mosque in Marseille have revolved around it acting as a cultural rather than religious centre, and offering classes open to all (Maussen and Talbi 2017). Churches built before 1905 are state owned and largely state maintained (in a quirk of the arrangement under which the state pays significant subsidies towards the maintenance of the religious buildings it previously appropriated and now allows the religions to use), and religious bodies cannot operate in public schools.

An objection might be raised here with reference to the region of Alsace-Moselle, which gives public recognition to four faiths (Catholicism, Calvinism, Lutheranism, and Judaism). These receive greater financial support than prevails in the rest of France and are taught in state schools for one hour a week. This represents, however, an historical exception that does not disprove the rule. This exception is a result of the region having been part of Germany at the time of the 1905 law, and it was agreed when the region became part of France after the First World War that the 1905 law would not apply (see Troper 2016).

France's exceptionalism here serves to highlight both the common basis in freedom of religion and moral individualism in the region, but also how this can be understood and put into practice quite differently. This is a result of how a different set of norms, from a mode of secularist statism, characterises the governance of religion and religious diversity in the country, and what it can mean in political and policy terms for the relationship between state and religion (see also Champion and Ghouri 2021).

The discussion in this section has mainly oriented around elaborating the public good aspect of moderate secularism contrasted with the secularist statism of France. This sought to establish that, beyond the basic norms of freedom of religion and moral individualism, the character and qualities of structures of governance and their rationales diverged. The following section now goes on to a similar assessment, yet this time oriented around religion seen as a public danger or harm.

The limits and lines in the sand of freedom of religion

If in the previous section we have argued that, despite a shared basis, there is a normative difference between the two modes of moderate secularism and secularist statism on the grounds of how religions are positively, or not, included in the public sphere, a further way of articulating France's non-exceptionalism has been in relation to diversity-restricting measures, particularly those involving the regions' Muslim populations (for example, Jansen 2011). While the aspect of control is a feature of France's approach in a more general sense, the kinds of norms and policies that this emphasis gives rise to can also be seen reflected in countries more characterised by moderate secularism. This section turns to explore this issue in relation to our five country cases and modes of governance. It argues that despite some similarities, France's exceptionalism remains. Two significant aspects of governance relevant here are increased regulation and interference through institutionalisation and increasing restrictions on the public visibility and presence of religious signs and symbols. These two are taken in turn in the rest of this section.

Institutionalisation and regulation

Just as institutionalisation can be the way in which minority religions gain a foothold in a country's political environment and the structures of governance, so too it can be the form through which greater government interference, regulation or control, and restrictions or conditions on diversity occur. This much we have already begun to see in the previous section.

In terms of more diversity-restricting measures, we can begin by noting how in relation to our countries of moderate secularism, despite the positive forms of accommodation discussed above, in practice newer religious minorities have often struggled to fully enjoy statuses of recognition, and where they do, they might be incomplete.

Pre-existing arrangements between state and church have often proven unwieldy when applied to non-Christian religious traditions, especially in relation to their Muslim populations, which have struggled to institutionalise Islam through national representative bodies seen as legitimate by both the state and the communities they were supposed to represent. In part this is to do with the diversity of Muslims (ethnically, nationally, and doctrinally) along with the lack of a centralised authority in Islam comparable to those found in Protestantism or Catholicism. In this sense the demands from the state in terms of the infrastructure of governance can be their own barriers, and might even be aggravated by transnational influences (see, for example, Çitak 2010).

But perhaps more importantly for our concerns is that as well as religion seen as a public good, religion can also be seen as posing a public danger or harm. In this sense, institutional arrangements and conditions might be conducted and formed in such ways as to regulate or control religion. In a context marked by concerns over aligned social and political values, especially those around gender and sexuality, as well as by security concerns and state responses to (violent) radicalisation, Islam and Muslims have come under greater scrutiny, suspicion and, as a result, have had more conditions imposed upon their accommodation and presence in Western European polities. States have had larger roles and exercised more interference in appointing members in Muslim representative organisations,[6] and as a result Muslim organisations and mosques have had erratic and politically contingent relationships with governments.

In contexts marked by fears over Islamist extremism, mosques have also come under greater scrutiny and surveillance than other religious places of worship, and foreign influence has become a particular concern. For instance, in a recent move the Belgian government terminated Saudi Arabia's lease on the Grand Mosque of Brussels over concerns it was promoting radicalism,[7] and in Flanders, in order to be recognised, mosques must have written documents stating and proving their commitment to their use of Dutch as their *lingua operandi* (with the exception of the *khutba* or sermon), their respect for the Constitution and basic rights and liberties, and their not being involved in terrorist activities (Adam and Torrekens 2015).

One might then reason that the situations between our modes of secularist statism and moderate secularism look somewhat similar. Nevertheless, we maintain that there is a normative qualitative difference operating here. We should first note that the notion of religion (or a particular religion as the case may be) as a public danger/harm is compatible with moderate secularism, and so this fact alone does not determine the choice of mode. Importantly, in our countries of moderate secularism, what we see is the regulative aspects becoming enhanced but without actually calling into question the public good function of religion or state-religion connections on this basis. Rather the tension between the two becomes prominent. In France, by contrast, the exertion of state control becomes emphasised such that it becomes increasingly extended and intolerant, crowding out more moderate forces.

We can see this in recent moves by the French state. Following the 2020 terrorist incidents, the beheading of Samuel Paty in Paris and murder of three people in a church in Nice, French President Emmanuel Macron asked Muslim leaders to accept a 'charter of republican values' (although this is not without precedent, see Cesari 2002), and a new anti-separatism bill, passed in August 2021, has been extremely controversial for expanding state powers, restricting religious freedoms, and implicitly targeting Muslims. A number of mosques and Muslim organisations, some engaged in anti-racism work, have been shut down, and greater controls have been placed on religious and cultural organisations in the name of combatting 'political' and 'separatist' Islam. The French state has also announced the creation of an inter-ministerial committee on *laïcité* to ensure 'the respect and promotion of *laïcité* by all public institutions'.[8] These measures all serve to highlight France's secularist statist DONs against those that appear more accommodative and closer to those of moderate secularism, again suggesting France's exceptionalism in this regard in Western Europe.

Signs and symbols

A further area relevant here is in relation to religious signs and symbols, especially the *hijab*, *niqab*, and *burqa*. France's well-known headscarf affairs, beginning in 1989, were both provoked by and aimed at Muslim women's clothing. Ostentatious religious signs and symbols were banned in public schools in 2004, and this was followed by the banning of full-face coverings in public in 2011 (see Bowen 2009; Jansen 2011, 2013). Moreover, the French ban in schools, although provoked by the desire to regulate Muslims, applied in general (it would be illegal for it to do so otherwise). It therefore had more indiscriminate effects for people of other faiths and wider effects for the public visibility of religious diversity as such; Sikh students wearing turbans, Jewish students wearing yarmulkes, and Christians wearing 'big' crosses were also expelled under the 2004 law (see for example Howard 2012).

In relation to our other country cases, we should begin by noting that the UK and Australia have not brought in such bans, and in the UK bans of this kind have never really garnered serious political attention. Bans have appeared in Germany and Belgium, but with qualitative differences in extent, how these have occurred, and the principles underlying them reflecting the distinction between moderate secularism and secularist statism.

While Belgium has introduced a criminal ban on face-covering in the public sphere, a general ban on headscarves has not been brought in (unlike in French public schools). Headscarf bans have appeared but in more ad hoc and inconsistent ways (Brems 2020; Adam and Torrekens 2015) and there can be considerable pressure and discrimination. Public schools run by the Flemish community have prohibited the wearing of religious signs for both teachers and pupils, teachers of religious education classes excepted. For Flemish private schools, as for both public and private schools in Francophone Belgium, the decision is left to the discretion of the individual school authorities. Bans have also been introduced for employees of the French Community Parliament when in contact with the public, as also in some local municipalities, although a general public sector ban has not been brought in. A recent Constitutional Court ruling stipulated that it is not unconstitutional for universities to bring in bans, although this is a decision for each institution. Many universities have stated that they will not be introducing a ban on headscarves, and some existing bans in Wallonia have in fact been revoked following the ruling.[9]

In Germany, there are two important points to note. The first is that a blanket ban on religious symbols (focused on a case where the headscarf was the issue) was ruled unconstitutional by the Federal Constitutional Court, stipulating individual *Länder* would need to introduce separate legislation to institute such bans, and bans have appeared unevenly as a result. The subsequent variation follows political lines of the *Länder* governments, with those on the left favouring general bans of religious symbols, and those on the right selectively targeting the Islamic headscarf, distinguishing it from Christian symbols on the basis of the former's supposed political content and the latter being more cultural and historical (Joppke 2007; see also Jones and Braun 2017). Bans and their rationales then are variable and ad hoc rather than being centralised points of normative principle.

A further important feature of the bans in Germany is that the legal debate, prompted by the case of teacher Fereshta Ludin, revolved around freedom of religion on the one hand, and an understanding of neutrality in schools where a teacher is seen as a *Beamter* (public servant), on the other (Schiffauer 2006). The bans and the initial case itself were focused on teachers and their roles as neutral public servants. A recent law has also been passed to regulate the appearance of civil servants over concerns about their neutrality, prompted by far-right tattoos and including ideological symbols in general, such as political and religious signs.[10] This draws a sharp contrast with France, where there was something much stronger going on. The French state was, on its own understanding, protecting the positive liberty and autonomy of the girls (Tourkochoriti 2012, 825–826). Schools, according to this vision, are a place of 'emancipation' and *mise á distance* where community identities and ties are left at the door (Kuru 2009, 125; Jansen 2013; Joppke 2007; Bowen 2009). Nevertheless, it has been argued that the ban has had a negative effect on socioeconomic integration in the long run, affecting the educational attainment and labour market trajectories of French Muslim women (Abdelgadir and Fouka 2020).

On the one hand then, France exhibits some connections that appear similar to those of moderate secularism, while on the other hand, countries of moderate secularism have also adopted some measures that appear similar to those of France. It is for these reasons that for some the difference, and France's exceptionalism, can seem overwrought.

Nevertheless, there are important differences here in the extent and quality of the connections and of the restrictions that bear on our modes and norms.

Conclusion

The current situation in the region reflects a certain agonism over the place of public religion and its relation to liberal secular order in general. The presence of Muslims in particular has stretched the existing arrangements and forced, in some instances, renewed thinking and attention to how accommodation and inclusion might be achieved, or in other instances, a contraction in pro-diversity arrangements and policies.

Western Europe's regional foundations can properly be said to be freedom of conscience based in moral individualism and toleration; these are the dominant operative norms. However, the region is also characterised by qualifying norms of state-religion institutional connections. Whether or not, however, this results in recognition of religion as a public good or the emphasis is rather religion as a public danger remains politically contingent and often applied in unsystematic ways. Religion can be positively encouraged and may lead to further pro-diversity qualifying norms and policies such as difference-sensitive recognition and institutional accommodations. Yet, religion and its connections to the state might also be an aspect of its management by the state. This can be seen in France's general approach with its secularist statist rendering of *laïcité*, where state control and privatisation are dominant norms. It is also particularly evident in relation to Muslims throughout the region through aspects such as security measures, restrictions on public visibility, or institutional conditions, although these are better seen as qualifying norms in countries of moderate secularism.

The basic underlying principles and the steering provided by the state produce different outcomes for public religion and diversity. Across the discussions above, in terms of freedom of religion as practice or manifestation, we find significant variance between our modes and the reasoning of the norms, resulting in different outcomes both institutionally as well as in terms of public visibility. One notable contrast is that in countries characterised by moderate secularism, aspects of interference and regulation are not only less severe than those under secularist statism, but are also less systematic and less likely to impact religious diversity and religion as a public good *as such*. The structures of governance of religious diversity in the region, although underpinned by common norms of political secularism and freedom of religion based in freedom of conscience and moral individualism, vary in significant ways when it comes to public religion, religion's role as a public good and state-religion connections, and freedom to practise or manifest religion in the public sphere.

Although we maintain the distinction of France's exceptionalism in the region, this contrast is not to say that these trends in countries characterised by moderate secularism are not concerning, and they certainly point to some of the limits of recognition under moderate secularism. Rather it is to suggest that they do not constitute a change of mode sufficient such that all these country cases can be considered indistinguishable from each other in their basic norms of governance. This itself is also not to suggest that such a situation could not occur, that countries currently characterised by moderate secularism couldn't move to an alternative mode, for instance. Rather, it is to point to the much wider shifts that would be necessary for this to be the case. Here, alternative configurations in some other European countries (see Magazzini, Triandafyllidou and Yakova, and Vekony, Iliyasov and Račius in this collection), which also have DONs of moderate secularism but these are qualified in different ways, might make interesting comparisons.

A question that therefore lingers over the issue of the governance of religious diversity in Western Europe, and is relevant for Australia also, is whether and when, and in relation to whom, such governance will come to reflect to a greater degree a more multicultural accommodationist approach or lean more heavily on 'muscular' forms of liberal neutralism or even secularist statism. This shows that moderate secularism itself should perhaps be thought of as a project, ongoing and never quite fully settled or achieved, but whose parameters are to some extent under constant negotiation.

Notes

1. Lists of recognised groups by region can be found on: https://www.personenstandsrecht.de/Webs/PERS/DE/informationen/religionsgemeinschaften/religionsgemeinschaften-node.html.
2. Our use of region indicates our five country cases rather than Australia and Western Europe *in toto*, although we suggest some general relevance of the arguments we present.
3. For reporting of the Bill, see, for example, Josh Butler (2022), 'What's happened to the religious discrimination bill – and where to next?' *The Guardian*, 10 February. Online at https://www.theguardian.com/australia-news/2022/feb/10/whats-happened-to-the-religious-discrimination-bill-and-where-to-next; Jake Evans (2022), 'Government shelves religious freedom bill indefinitely, leaving election promise hanging in uncertainty'. *ABC News*, 9 February. Online at https://www.abc.net.au/news/2022-02-10/government-consults-religious-groups-discrimination-bill/100818568.
4. See Royce Millar and Ben Schneiders (2021), 'Religious schools in Victoria to lose the right to sack LGBTQ staff'. *The Age*, 16 September. Online at https://www.theage.com.au/national/victoria/religious-schools-in-victoria-to-lose-the-right-to-sack-lgbtq-staff-20210915-p58rx5.html.
5. We might note that on different indices, France scores lower on freedom of religion and higher in state interference than its European neighbours and Australia. See, for instance, the World Bank's index (2018 figures) and Pew's government restrictions index.
6. For example, on France see Kastoryano (2004, 2006); Bowen (2009); Cesari (2002); on Belgium, Çitak (2010); Franken (2016b); on Germany see Körs (2017, 2019); Lewicki (2014); on the UK see Modood (2010, 2013[2007]).
7. See (no name) (2018), 'Muslims and politicians react to Belgium's decision to take back Grand Mosque'. *Euro-Islam*, March 29. Online at http://www.euro-islam.info/2018/03/29/muslims-politicians-react-belgiums-decision-take-back-grand-mosque/.
8. See https://www.gouvernement.fr/partage/12316-creation-du-comite-interministeriel-de-la-laicite.
9. See Maïthé Chini (2021), 'Belgian universities stress that they will not ban headscarves'. *The Brussels Times*, 16 June. Online at https://www.brusselstimes.com/117067/belgian-universities-stress-that-they-will-not-ban-headscarves-in-class; (no name) (2021), 'Lifting of hijab ban in southern Belgium offers hope for Muslim women'. *TRT World*, 18 January. Online at https://www.trtworld.com/magazine/lifting-of-hijab-ban-in-southern-belgium-offers-hope-for-muslim-women-43365.
10. See https://www.beamtenbesoldung.org/. Full face veils are banned in some regions for pupils, although there is no general ban of this type in public spaces.

Acknowledgments

We are indebted to our GREASE partners Michele Grossman, Vivian Gerrand, Vanessa Barolsky, of Deakin University, for the discussion of Australia, and to Geoff Brahm Levey who read and commented on an earlier draft. We are grateful to two anonymous reviewers and the journal editors for their comments on this contribution.

Disclosure statement

No potential conflict of interest was reported by the author(s).

Funding

The GREASE project, on which this contribution is based, has received funding from the European Union's Horizon 2020 research and innovation programme under grant agreement number 770640.

ORCID

Thomas Sealy http://orcid.org/0000-0002-3211-6900
Tariq Modood http://orcid.org/0000-0001-8712-5508

References

Abdelgadir, A., and V. Fouka. 2020. "Political Secularism and Muslim Integration in the West: Assessing the Effects of the French Headscarf Ban." *The American Political Science Review* 114 (3): 707–723. doi:10.1017/S0003055420000106.
Adam, I., and C. Torrekens. 2015. "Different Regional Approaches to Immigration Related Cultural Diversity: Interpreting the Belgian Cultural Diversity Policy Paradox." *Régionalisme Et Fédéralisme* 15.
Australian Government. 2018. "Australian Government Response to the Religious Freedom Review." 13 December: https://www.pm.gov.au/media/government-response-religious-freedom-review.
Barker, C. R. 2000. "Church and State Relationships in German 'Public Benefit' Law." *The International Journal of Not-For-Profit Law* 3 (2). Available at http://www.icnl.org/research/journal/vol3iss2/art_1.htm. Accessed 28 June 2019.

Baubérot, J. 2010. "The Evolution of Secularism in France: Between Two Civil Religions." In *Comparative Secularisms in a Global Age*, edited by L. E. Cady and E. S. Hurd, 57–68. New York: Palgrave.

Baubérot, J. 2014. *La laïcité Falsifiée*. Paris: La Découverte.

Bhargava, R., Ed. 1998. *What is Secularism For?*. New Delhi: Oxford University Press.

Bhargava, R. 2009. "Political Secularism: Why It is Needed and What Can Be Learnt from Its Indian Version?" In *Secularism, Religion and Multicultural Citizenship*, edited by G. B. Levey and T. Modood, 82–109. Cambridge: Cambridge University Press.

Bhargava, R. 2014. "How Secular is European Secularism?" *European Societies* 16 (3): 329–336. doi:10.1080/14616696.2014.916335.

Bhargava, R. 2016. "Is European Secularism Secular Enough?" In *Religion, Secularism, and Constitutional Democracy*, edited by J. L. Cohen and C. Laborde, 157–181. Chichester: Columbia University Press.

Bhargava, R. 2017. "Beyond Moderate Secularism." In *Secularism, Religion, and Politics: India and Europe*, edited by P. Losonczi and W. Van Herck, 57–64. London: Routledge.

Bowen, J. R. 2009. *Can Islam Be French? Pluralism and Pragmatism in a Secularist State*. Oxford: Princeton University Press.

Brems, E. 2020. "Discrimination Against Muslims in Belgium." In *State, Religion and Muslims: Between Discrimination and Protection at the Legislative, Executive and Judicial Levels*, edited by M. Saral and Ş. O. Bahçecik, 65–108. Leiden: Brill.

Bribosia, E., A. Rea, J. Ringelheim, and I. Rorive. 2011. "Reasonable Accommodation of Religious Diversity in Europe and in Belgium: Law and Practice." In *The Others in Europe: Legal and Social Categorization In Context*, edited by A. Rea, S. Bonjour, and D. Jacobs, 91–116. Brussels: PUB.

Cesari, J. 2002. "Islam in France: The Shaping of a Religious Minority." In *Muslims in the West, from Sojourners to Citizens*, edited by Y. Haddad-Yazbek, 36–51. Oxford: Oxford University Press.

Champion, A., and A. Ghouri. 2021. "Secularism, Islam and Legal Pluralism in Europe: A Case Study on the Use of Headscarf in the UK and France." In *Abraham and the Secular: Fracture and Composition*, edited by S. Raudino and U. A. Barton, 221–235. Cham: Palgrave Macmillan.

Chavura, S., J. Gascoigne, and I. Tregenza. 2019. *Reason, Religion and the Australian Polity: A Secular State?*. London and New York: Routledge.

Çitak, Z. 2010. "Religion, Ethnicity and Transnationalism: Turkish Islam in Belgium." *Journal of Church and State* 53 (2): 222–242. doi:10.1093/jcs/csq105.

Cremer, T. 2021. "Nations Under God: How Church–state Relations Shape Christian Responses to Right-Wing Populism in Germany and the United States." *Religions* 12 (4): 254. doi:10.3390/rel12040254.

Dinham, A. 2009. *Faiths, Public Policy and Civil Society: Problems, Policies, Controversies*. Basingstoke: Palgrave Macmillan.

Dinham, A. 2015. "Religious Literacy and Welfare." In *Religious Literacy in Policy and Practice*, edited by A. Dinham and M. Francis, 101–112. Bristol: Policy Press.

Dobbelaere, K., and L. Voyé. 1990. "From Pillar to Postmodernity: The Changing Situation of Religion in Belgium." *Sociological Analysis* 51 (S): S1–S13. doi:10.2307/3711670.

Ferrari, A. 2009. "De la Politique à la Technique: Laïcité Narrative et Laïcité du Droit. Pour une Comparaison France/Italie." In *Le Droit Ecclésiastique En Europe Et À Ses Marges (XVIIIe-Xxe Siècles): Actes du Colloque du Centre Droit Et Sociétés Religieuses*, edited by B. Basdevant-Gaudemet, F. Jankowiak and J-P. Delannoy, 333–344. Leuven: Peeters.

Fetzer, J. S., and J. Christopher Soper. 2005. *Muslims and the State in Britain, France, and Germany*. Cambridge: Cambridge University Press.

Franken, L. 2015. "State Support for Religion in Belgium: A Critical Evaluation." *Journal of Church and State* 59 (1): 59–80.

Franken, L. 2016a. "The Freedom of Religion and the Freedom of Education in Twenty-First-Century Belgium: A Critical Approach." *British Journal of Religious Education* 38 (3): 308–324. doi:10.1080/01416200.2015.1113934.

Franken, L. 2016b. *Liberal Neutrality and State Support for Religion*. Cham: Springer.

Franken, L. 2017. "Islamic Education in Belgium: Past, Present, and Future." *Religious Education* 112 (5): 491–503. doi:10.1080/00344087.2017.1303300.

Großbölting, T. 2017. *Losing Heaven: Religion in Germany Since 1945*, Ed. A. Skinner. Oxford: Berghahn.

Grossman, M., V. Gerrand, and A. Halafoff. 2021. "Australia: Diversity, Neutrality, and Exceptionalism." In *Routledge Handbook on the Governance of Religious Diversity*, edited by A. Triandafyllidou and T. Magazzini, 296–308. London: Routledge.

Gunn, T. J. 2004. "Under God but Not the Scarf: The Founding Myths of Religious Freedom in the United States and Laïcité in France." *Journal of Church and State* 46 (1): 7–24. doi:10.1093/jcs/46.1.7.

Gunn, T. J. 2009. "Religion and Law in France: Secularism. Separation, and State Intervention." *Drake Law Review* 57: 949–984.

Hatfield, D. W. 1981. "'Kulturkampf: The Relationship of Church and State and the Failure of German Political Reform." *Journal of Church and State* 23 (3): 465–484. doi:10.1093/jcs/23.3.465.

Henkel, R. 2006. "State–church Relationships in Germany: Past and Present." *GeoJournal* 67: 307–316. doi:10.1007/s10708-007-9063-2.

Hofhansel, C. 2013. "Recognition Regimes for Religious Minorities in Europe: Institutional Change and Reproduction." *Journal of Church and State* 57 (1): 90–118. doi:10.1093/jcs/cst030.

Howard, E. 2012. *Law and the Wearing of Religious Symbols: European Bans on the Wearing of Religious Symbols in Education*. Abingdon: Routledge.

Jansen, Y. 2011. "Secularism and Religious (In-)Security: Reinterpreting the French Headscarf Debates." *Krisis* 2: 2–19.

Jansen, Y. 2013. *Secularism, Assimilation and the Crisis of Multiculturalism: French Modernist Legacies*. Amsterdam: Amsterdam University Press.

Jones, N., and K. Braun. 2017. "Secularism and State Neutrality: The Headscarf in French and German Public Schools." *Australian Journal of Human Rights* 23 (1): 61–89. doi:10.1080/1323238X.2017.1314441.

Joppke, C. 2007. "State Neutrality and Islamic Headscarf Laws in France and Germany." *Theory & Society* 36 (4): 313–342. doi:10.1007/s11186-007-9036-y.

Joppke, C. 2015. *The Secular State Under Siege: Religion and Politics in Europe and America*. Cambridge: Polity Press.

Kastoryano, R. 2004. "Religion and Incorporation: Islam in France and Germany." *The International Migration Review* 38(3): 1234–1255.

Kastoryano, R. 2006. "French Secularism and Islam: France's Headscarf Affair"." In *Multiculturalism, Muslims and Citizenship: A European Approach*, edited by T. Modood, A. Triandafyllidou, and R. Zapata-Barrero, 57–69. Abingdon: Routledge.

Körs, A. 2017. "The Plurality of Peter Berger's 'Two Pluralisms' in Germany." *Society* 54 (5): 445–453.

Körs, A. 2019. "Contract Governance of Religious Diversity in a German City-State and Its Ambivalences." *Religion, State & Society* 47 (4–5): 456–473. doi:10.1080/09637494.2019.1682445.

Kuru, A. T. 2008. "Secularism, State Policies, and Muslims in Europe: Analyzing French Exceptionalism." *Comparative Politics* 41 (1): 1–19.

Kuru, A. T. 2009. *Secularism and State Policies Toward. Religion: The United States France, and Turkey*. Cambridge, Cambridge University Press.

Laborde, C. 2013. "Political Liberalism and Religion: On Separation and Establishment." *The Journal of Political Philosophy* 21 (1): 67–86. doi:10.1111/j.1467-9760.2011.00404.x.

Laborde, C. 2017. *Liberalism's Religion*. London: Harvard University Press.

Levey, G. B. 2017. "Secularism as Proto-Multiculturalism: The Case of Australia." In *The Problem of Religious Diversity European Challenges, Asian Approaches*, edited by A. Triandafyllidou and T. Modood, 228–249. Edinburgh: Edinburgh University Press.

Lewicki, A. 2014. *Social Justice Through Citizenship? The Politics of Muslim Integration in Germany and Great Britain*. Basingstoke: Palgrave Macmillan.

Long, R., and S. Danechi. 2019. "Faith Schools in England: FAQs." House of Commons Library, Briefing Paper No.06972, 20 December 2019. Available at https://researchbriefings.files.parliament.uk/documents/SN06972/SN06972.pdf. Accessed 31 May 2022.

Mahajan, G. 2007. "Multiculturalism in the Age of Terror: Confronting the Challenges." *Political Studies Review* 5: 317–336.

Maussen, M., and M. Talbi. 2017. "Islam in Europe and European Islam." In *'De-Radicalisation': Scientific Insights for Policy*, edited by L. Colaert, 137–156. Brussels: Flemish Peace Institute.

Meyerson, D. 2009. "The Protection of Religious Rights Under Australian Law." *BYU Law Review* 3: 529–553.

Modood, T., Ed. 1997. *Church, State and Religious Minorities*. London: Policy Studies Institute.

Modood, T. 2010. "Moderate Secularism, Religion as Identity and Respect for Religion." *The Political Quarterly* 81 (1): 4–14. doi:10.1111/j.1467-923X.2010.02075.x.

Modood, T. 2012. "Is There a Crisis of Secularism in Western Europe?" *Sociology of Religion* 72 (2): 130–149.

Modood, T. 2013 [2007]. *Multiculturalism: A Civic Idea*. 2nd. Cambridge: Polity.

Modood, T. 2019. *Essays on Secularism and Multiculturalism*. London: Rowman-Littlefield and European Consortium of Political Science.

Modood, T., and S. Thompson. 2021. "Othering, Alienation and Establishment." *Political Studies*. doi:10.1177/0032321720986698.

Perez, N., J. Fox, and J. M. McClure. 2017. "Unequal State Support of Religion: On Resentment, Equality, and the Separation of Religion and State." *Politics, Religion & Ideology* 18 (4): 431–448.

Richardson, J. T., Ed. 2004. *Regulating Religion: Case Studies from Around the Globe*. New York: Springer.

Roy, O. 2007. *Secularism Confronts Islam*. Chichester: Columbia University Press.

Schiffauer, W. 2006. "Enemies Within the Gates: The Debate About the Citizenship of Muslims in Germany." In *Multiculturalism, Muslims and Citizenship: A European Approach*, edited by T. Modood, A. Triandafyllidou, and R. Zapata-Barrero, 94–116. Abingdon: Routledge.

Tourkochoriti, I. 2012. "The Burka Ban: Divergent Approaches to Freedom of Religion in France and in the U.S.A." *William & Mary Bill of Rights Journal* 20 (79): 791–852.

Troper, M. 2016. "Republicanism and Freedom of Religion in France." In *Religion, Secularism, and Constitutional Democracy*, edited by J. L. Cohen and C. Laborde, 316–337. Chichester: Columbia University Press.

Velasco Ibarra, E. 2020. "Lee v Ashers Baking Company Ltd and Others: The Inapplicability of Discrimination Law to an Illusory Conflict of Rights." *The Modern Law Review* 83 (1): 190–201.

Willaime, J.-P. 2009. "European Integration, Laïcité and Religion." *Religion, State & Society* 37 (1–2): 23–35.

ⓐ OPEN ACCESS

State-religion relations in Southern and Southeastern Europe: moderate secularism with majoritarian undertones

Tina Magazzini ⓘ, Anna Triandafyllidou ⓘ and Liliya Yakova ⓘ

ABSTRACT
This contribution studies comparatively three Southern European countries (Italy, Spain, and Greece) and three Southeastern European countries (Albania, Bosnia and Herzegovina, and Bulgaria). Looking beyond historical path-dependencies, we investigate recent developments in terms of state-religion relations. Starting with a thick description of the historical legacies and post-1989 developments, we focus on issues of the last decade, such as the rise of populism and nationalism, the path to EU accession for Bosnia and Albania, the economic and Eurozone crisis of the 2010s, and the refugee emergency of 2015. Our aim is to assess how these have shaped state-religion relations and to categorise the six countries within the typology proposed in the introductory contribution to this collection. Our findings suggest that moderate secularism and liberal neutralism prevail in all six countries. There are, however, important variations in terms of the relevance of majoritarian nationalism in some of them, as the state defines the prevailing religion and has strong historical and institutional ties with that religion. The contribution elaborates on these specificities and concludes with some questions on the importance of the notion of dominant vs qualifying norms and on the role of current challenges in shaping further state-religion relations.

Introduction

Southern Europe, or Mediterranean Europe, is a region that has often been studied in 'clusters', separating the majority-Catholic South West from the Orthodox-majority South East (Madeley 2003; Knippenberg 2007; Sealy et al. 2021). While a sense of historicity is important to grasp the diversity in political, socioeconomic, religious, and cultural patterns, this study shows that, if we focus on the preponderant conceptual characterisation of state-religion relations, the region is made up by more commonalities than differences.

The reason for looking at the six countries highlighted in Figure 1, while acknowledging the significant differences between them, is threefold. A departing consideration is that, as argued by Bracewell and Drace-Francis (1999), we find it important to avoid

---

This is an Open Access article distributed under the terms of the Creative Commons Attribution License (http://creativecommons.org/licenses/by/4.0/), which permits unrestricted use, distribution, and reproduction in any medium, provided the original work is properly cited.

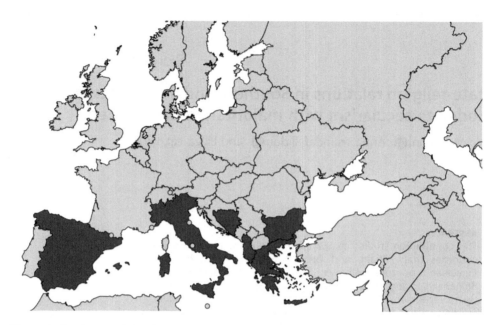

Figure 1. Southern and Southeastern countries covered in this contribution: Albania, Bosnia and Herzegovina, Bulgaria, Greece, Italy, and Spain.

portraying South East Europe as a residual category analysed as a mere reflection or 'defiant mirror' held up to the countries of the North West.

Secondly, we purposefully selected these six countries because while they are seldom taken together, they can be seen as complementary according to the method of difference, as they span the entire spectrum of typologies of relations between the nation and religion (Triandafyllidou and Magazzini 2021, 312). All exhibit different structural conditions, which allows us to infer on the importance of key variables in shaping their governance of religion, namely: Greece has strong ties with a single religion (Orthodox Christianity); Italy and Spain have weak ties with a single religion (Catholicism); Bosnia and Herzegovina has strong plural ties (with Islam, Orthodox Christianity, and Catholicism); and Albania weak plural ties (with Islam, Orthodox Christianity, and to a lesser degree with Catholicism). Rather than studying these countries in pairs along geopolitical dimensions (as southern vs former communist; EU vs non-EU members) or religious ones (Catholic vs Orthodox vs mixed), we explore their complexity and overlapping linkages.

A third and final consideration is a practical one, which has to do with data availability stemming from a research project that focused on these countries and produced original findings between 2018 and 2022,[1] and upon which this contribution is based. Regarding data used and methodology employed, this contribution builds on extensive research of secondary literature, legal and policy measures, and applies the categories and modes outlined in Modood and Sealy, this collection, to the cases of Albania, Bosnia and Herzegovina (BiH), Bulgaria, Greece, Italy, and Spain, looking at both similarities and differences between these countries, and how these relate to issues of secularism and freedom of religion.

During the last twenty years, wide sociopolitical developments have taken place in Southeastern Europe: BiH and Albania are still negotiating a timeline for their incorporation into the EU and grappling with socioeconomic and political fragility, while Bulgaria joined the EU in 2007, which has created a more stable socioeconomic and political context, including for issues of minority rights and state-religion relations. Meanwhile, these three countries and Greece share historical, cultural, and geopolitical commonalities that can be attributed to their geographical position and their Ottoman past: late nation formation, underlying ethno-religious diversity (which in Greece was largely assimilated into a dominant concept of the homogenous Greek nation), territorial sensitivities that exist to this day, and the importance of Turkey as an important kin-state and geopolitical actor in the southeastern neighbourhood (Gülalp 2017; Triandafyllidou et al. 2019).

However, fissures exist also within 'Southern Europe', where Greece, Italy, and Spain have been members of the EU for a long time. These three countries are characterised by some common socioeconomic characteristics, which became more salient during the 2010s as the Eurozone crisis unfolded – but they also differ significantly (Triandafyllidou 2001, 2007). While the 1990s and 2000s emphasised the challenges of reconnecting the central-eastern with the western part of Europe, the 2010s brought back the North-South division. This commonality of 'fate' was further reinforced by the 2015 (still partly ongoing) refugee emergency, where the geographical position of these countries became an important common denominator.

Unlike Albania, Bulgaria, and BiH that remain predominantly countries of origin or transit of migration flows, Greece, Italy, and Spain have experienced significant labour-related migration that has altered their socio-demographic composition. These developments have raised important new challenges for state-religion relations in Southeastern Europe.

This contribution starts with a brief comparative overview of the historical legacies that characterise each country in the pre-1989 period, identifying the main religious groups in their population. We then describe the events that ensued in the post-1989 period with special attention to recent developments in the field of state-religion relations and governance of religious diversity. We follow on by discussing the models that we can identify in the region and the ways in which the main legal frameworks governing state-religion relations (dominant operative norms) and the practical qualifications of the former (qualifying operative norms) play out.

Nation-states and religions in Southern and Southeastern Europe before 1989: a complex picture

Roman Catholicism and Eastern Orthodoxy, resulting from the Great Schism of 1054 that split Christianity into two churches, remain to date the two largest religions practised in the Southern European region, which, however, also hosts significant Muslim populations that constitute majorities in contemporary Albania and BiH. By contrast, Muslim minorities were virtually absent in Spain and Italy between the seventeenth and nineteenth centuries, having been expelled, killed, or forcefully converted, and began to constitute a significant minority as a result of immigration from the 1970s onwards.

The historical past of Albania, BiH, Bulgaria, and Greece is marked by the Ottoman Empire and its gradual dismemberment leading to nation-state formation in Southeastern Europe. An independent Greek state was established in 1821 through a national war of independence against the Ottoman Empire, and an independent national Bulgarian state was established in 1878. Albania became independent from Ottoman rule in 1912 while BiH passed from Ottoman to Austro-Hungarian rule in 1878.

Orthodox Christianity played an important role in both Bulgarian and Greek cultural identity. Under the Ottoman Empire, both Bulgarian and Greek Orthodox Christians maintained the right to religious self-governance – as per the millet system – but Bulgarians were subordinated to the Greek Patriarchate. Following the establishment of the Bulgarian national state in 1878, state-religion relations were shaped by subsequent constitutions: while the first (1879) and the most recent (1991) Bulgarian Constitution establish Orthodox Christianity as the dominant religion over the others, the two socialist Constitutions (of 1947 and 1971) relied on the complete separation of church and state.

Similarly to Bulgaria (except in communist times), Greek national identity has been closely intertwined with Orthodox Christianity. What has been labelled the 'historical anxiety' of the Greek state, fuelled by geopolitical tensions in the Balkans, found expression in a dominant national discourse of ethno-cultural and religious homogeneity that left little room for minorities, particularly Muslims (Baltsiotis 2011, 18). This discourse remained dominant until the 1990s when the quest of the Turkish Muslim minority for further recognition and the arrival of large immigrant populations opened up debate on the accommodation of minority religions.

The cases of BiH and Albania, although sharing the Ottoman legacy with Greece and Bulgaria, differ significantly. BiH represents a unique multi-religious polity, quintessentially 'Balkan' in the sense of diverse but also fragmented (Todorova 1994). From the twelfth century onwards, different historical periods have been dominated by different religious groups. With the Ottoman conquest in the fifteenth and sixteenth centuries, Islam advanced and gained in prominence in BiH with respect to other religions and compared to other Balkan provinces. Towards the end of the seventeenth century, the number of Christians had diminished significantly, whilst the strife between certain groups of Orthodox Christians and Catholics continued. The Muslim population also decreased in the nineteenth century as a result of uprisings leading to the Treaty of Berlin in 1878, and during this period Serbs and Croats started claiming that Muslims from BiH were of Croatian (Catholic) and Serbian (Orthodox) origin. Such claims intensified with the Austro-Hungarian regime (1878–1919), during which Christians were informally privileged.[2]

Albania's historical path was different as the mainly Muslim population remained loyal to the Ottoman Empire until the twentieth century. The Albanian independence movement was largely guided by the Albanian diaspora in neighbouring countries, which led to a strengthening of the Catholic and Orthodox movements (Zhelyazkova 2000, 2001). When Albania became independent from the Ottoman Empire in 1922,[3] religious diversity emerged as a potential problem. The notion of a civil religion emerged therefore as a way to downplay the divisive role of religion for the sake of national unity: the relationship between the state and the religious constituencies was about the presence of a 'supra-religious national consciousness', ultimately guided by the state (Elbasani and Puto 2017, 56).

The 1922 Albanian Constitution set the stage for radical political secularism in the country, incorporating the idea that the state should not have an official religion (Elbasani and Puto 2017; Yakova and Kuneva 2021). With religion viewed as a divisive threat, under the short rule of King Ahmet Zogy (1924–1928) the ideals of unity, a-religiosity, and European modernity gained ground, leading to strict control of religious group activities by the state.

Despite their common historical legacy, it is clear that Albania, BiH, Bulgaria, and Greece have followed different paths in terms of state-religion relations. We can identify some commonalities in the dominant role of religion in shaping national identity and the reluctance to accommodate minorities in Greece and Bulgaria, although Bulgaria's communist interlude has shaped these dynamics in different ways. However, BiH and Albania have sought to address religious diversity differently. Albania has done so through preferring a civic concept of the nation and the state, while BiH – as a member of the former socialist federation of Yugoslavia – relied on the subordination of religious and national dimensions to a broader Yugoslav identity, which eventually proved unsuccessful.

Spain and Italy, with the Catholic Church playing an important part in state formation, present a different historical background. Spain, one of Europe's oldest countries, was largely born out of religious struggles between Islam and Catholicism, with the latter being established as the state religion under the rule of Catholic monarchs during the fifteenth and sixteenth centuries, which were marked by the persecution and expulsion of non-Catholics (Jews, Muslims, 'Moriscos', Roma) and the establishment of the Spanish Inquisition. Spanish Constitutions (1812, 1837, 1845, 1876) all asserted Roman Catholicism as the only official legal religion in Spain, a position confirmed by a Concordat signed in 1851 by the Spanish government and the Holy See. In 1931 the short-lived Spanish Republic renounced the Concordat in its secular Constitution, which was the first measure implementing a strict separation between religious and government affairs in Spain. The Civil War (1936–1939) that ensued became strongly entrenched along religious lines, with the Catholic Church supporting the uprising of Francisco Franco in 1936, and ended with a four-decade-long dictatorship, which re-established Catholicism as the state religion (Urrutia Asua 2016; Magazzini 2021b).

Similarly to Spain, the Catholic Church in Italy has always been, beyond a religious institution, a political one. One of the most powerful entities in the peninsula, the Papal States controlled most of what is now considered central Italy for about a millennium and played a crucial role in the formation of the Italian state. Even though most of its territories were lost to the Kingdom of Sardinia in 1861 (when King Vittorio Emanuele II of Sardinia was proclaimed King of Italy),[4] it was not until 1870 that Italian troops conquered Rome, putting an end to the temporal power of the pope. Following the First World War and the rise to power of Mussolini's fascist dictatorship, Italy signed the Lateran Treaty with the Holy See in 1929, which created the Vatican City State and restored many of the prerogatives of the Catholic Church (Kertzer 2015). This agreement preceded by two decades the one reached between the Holy See and Franco's Spain, with both countries displaying similar features of fascist dictatorships adopting National Catholicism as part of their ideological identity.

During the twentieth century, following the end of the First World War, church-state relations in Southern and Southeastern Europe were marked overall by a stronger state role, which can be seen as a logical consequence of relatively young nation-states consolidating (with the exception of the Iberian peninsula). During the Second World War, the former Kingdom of Yugoslavia and BiH turned into a theatre of embittered conflicts and infighting driven by radical ideologies. In 1941 the Bosniak Young Muslims movement was founded, a kind of pan-Islamism resulting 'from a politicisation of Islam following contact with fascist and communist ideologies' (Bougarel 2017, 66). The state's grip over religion intensified during the communist period, during which Socialist Yugoslavia (1945–1990) promoted a policy of subordination of religious institutions, which came to be viewed as ideological enemies of the new regime (Ballinger and Ghodsee 2011). The period was marked by attempts on behalf of the federal state to address ethno-religious divisions by engineering loyalty to an a-religious nation of Yugoslavs.

Bulgarian society was subjected to a process of forced secularisation, with the Orthodox Church losing its autonomy and public presence (Mancheva 2019, 2021). The Albanian state took the ideas of a-religiosity and national unity to an extreme, officially endorsing atheism in its 1976 Constitution and repressing all forms of religious expression (Zhelyazkova 2000; Yakova 2019; Karataş 2020). Consequently, the state cut off financial support to religious institutions and repurposed most religious buildings, and religious convictions become grounds for persecution and arrest.

Meanwhile, Spain, Italy, and Greece – albeit for different periods of time – all experienced far-right dictatorships centred on the pillars of anti-communism and national ideologies that presented the countries as the outposts of Christian values and civilisation against the threat of anarchism and atheism. Christianity, whether Orthodox or Catholic, played a strong political role in identifying the 'national' community. In Spain, under Franco's dictatorship (1939–1975) 'National Catholicism' represented one of the main tenets of the government's ideology. This meant not only that the Catholic Church's privileges were restored (as well as the monarchy's) and that Catholicism was re-established as the only state religion, but also that the role of the Church in both private and public life reached its peak, sanctioned by the 1953 Concordat (Muñoz Mendoza 2012). It was not until the transition to democracy and the 1978 Constitution that a gradual separation between the Catholic Church and the Spanish state was agreed upon, with Catholicism still holding a privileged position (Griera, Martínez-Ariño, and Clot-Garrell 2021, 5–6).

Similarly, in Greece, long after the end of the junta's rule in 1974 and the establishment of the Third Hellenic Republic, the view of Greece as an Orthodox Christian nation has remained, and the presence of Islam is still largely perceived as a rival cultural element that could threaten the homogeneity of the Greek 'ethnos' (Skoulariki 2010, 302).

In Italy, the form of government (from monarchy to republic) and the overall regulatory framework changed with the democratic 1948 Constitution in the aftermath of the Second World War, which incorporated freedom of religion and the separation of state and church in its fundamental values. However, the framework to regulate relations with the Catholic Church remained that of 1929, and it was only in 1984 that the Lateran Pacts were revised to remove the statement positing Catholicism as Italy's state religion.

Regardless of institutional arrangements, the twentieth century has seen Southern Europe's societies secularise, with a steady decrease in church attendance and religious weddings (Evans and Baronavski 2018). In Southeastern Europe secularisation was imposed by the communist regimes and had strong impact in suppressing religion. However, the importance of religious identity re-emerged in Yugoslavia following Tito's death in 1980, when religious institutions experienced a revival interweaving with ethno-religious identities, and tensions rose in the federation. Nationalist agendas and narratives fostered deep rifts between Serbs, Croats, and Bosniaks, who had co-existed peacefully until then (Kiper and Sosis 2020). After 1989 such religious and ethnic re-awakenings followed suit across the region.

Renegotiating state-religion relations in the post-1989 context

The different experiences of Southern and Southeastern European countries became apparent in the early 1990s as communist regimes imploded after the fall of the Berlin wall, precipitating radical transformations in Southeastern Europe.

The Yugoslav federation broke up with a bloody civil war between its republics, informed by both ethnic and religious divisions. It became apparent that the forced secularisation imposed during communist times had not been successful: in BiH's 1991 census only 6% of its population identified as Yugoslavs while over 90% identified with one of the three major ethno-religious groups (Bosniaks 43.5%, Serbs 31.2%, Croats 17.4%) (Alibašić and Begović 2017, 21). Conflicting ideologies and ethno-religious tensions from the 1940s resurfaced during the 1990s, when a war fought over ethno-religious lines and symbols (1992–1995) left the country divided and in need of reconceptualising state-religion relations and the relationship among its communities. The Dayton Accords established a federal system that presented many shortcomings particularly regarding the implementation of federal decisions at the local level. An attempt was made by the Party of Democratic Action (*Stranka demokratske akcije*) in the 1990s to infuse pan-Islamism into the nascent Muslim nationalism, thus substituting communism with Islam as a political ideology (Bougarel 2017). This, however, failed and brought disenchantment with both politics and religion. Even after the death of the main divisive leaders, the cleavages created during the war remain and the religious institutions revived after the fall of communism continue to be involved, often controversially, in political and public life. As a result, BiH is probably the most 'extreme' case in which ethnic and religious identities are still fused: Muslims commonly identify as Bosniaks, Orthodox Christians as Serbs, and Catholics as Croats. In order to manage such diversity, present-day BiH promotes a model of separation of state and religion including the principles of religious freedom and equality of all religious communities, with an explicit prohibition on religious communities spreading hatred towards other religious communities. However, given the context of the country's divided society the implementation of the principle of equality of religious communities is not always easy nor straightforward.

In Albania, by contrast, the first postcommunist provisional Constitution (1991) declared the country a secular state (Dyrmishi 2016), allowing for freedom of religion. Members of religious communities (mostly Muslims) who had suffered greatly under communism actively supported the New Democratic Party (*Partia Demokrate e Re*) and mobilised in politics. The loose control on religious institutions from the state around this time made it possible for some foreign religious groups from Muslim-majority countries in the Middle East to establish a presence in Albania. By 1998 there were reports that various Islamic organisations from abroad had established political links in Albania to launch terrorist cells in the country (Yakova and Bogdanova 2022; Hayrapetyan 2017). This period coincided with the installation of a Socialist Party (*Partia Socialiste e Shqipërisë*) government, which implemented more stringent security measures, prosecuted suspected terrorists, closed Islamic charities, and expelled from the country those considered to present a threat (Elbasani and Puto 2017).

It was in this context that the current Albanian Constitution (1998) took shape to set up broader provisions for the governance of religious diversity in the country. Apart from declaring state neutrality and no official religion, the Constitution established religious freedom and collaboration between the state and religious institutions for a 'common good', reflecting the notion of a 'civic religion' that characterised the short-lived period of independence before communism. Albania's *laïcité* moved away from total separation between church and state, and secured close state supervision of religion by maintaining close state-religion cooperation. The Muslim community, through the Albanian Muslim Community (*Komuniteti Mysliman i Shqipërisë*), plays an important role in supporting such state supervision. As the only Muslim authority granted permission to negotiate with state institutions, it is seen as acting as intermediary between the state and Muslims and as a safeguard against radical versions of Islam (Elbasani and Puto 2017). However, the state also has close ties with the Bektashis, Catholics, Orthodox Christians, and evangelical Christians. This approach can also be observed in a 2018 official appeal to EU institutions by the leaders of the five major religious communities in support of Albania's EU accession (Agenzia D'Informazione 2018). In 2012 Albania introduced the Law on Non-Discrimination, which also protects freedom of religion and belief (OHCHR 2017).

In Bulgaria the strong policies of promoting atheism came to an end with the fall of the regime in 1989, and the new Bulgarian Constitution (1991) was drafted stating explicitly that – while religious institutions are separated from the state – freedom of religious expression is a fundamental right. The Constitution also stipulates that the state should assist the different denominations in the country to promote interreligious tolerance.[5] According to the Constitution, denominations have equal rights and standing, however the majority Orthodox denomination is identified as a 'traditional' one, which puts it in a favourable position, while minority denominations must register at the Sofia city court to operate in the country. Even though the Orthodox Christian majority (approximately 76%) is privileged in its relations to the state, Bulgaria's various minorities[6] are represented in the Council of Religious Communities and are protected by Bulgaria's institutional framework. The legal protections enshrined in the Constitution are comprehensive, but their practical application is still not always effective, and minority individuals and organisations still try to find everyday solutions for their problems (Grekova, Kyurkchieva, and Kosseva 2013). Overall, having undertaken such institutional reforms in the 1990s, the governance of religious diversity in Bulgaria was not much affected by the EU accession in 2007.

Meanwhile, the early 1990s were the years in which both the Italian and Spanish states reached formal agreements with representatives of minority religions. Spain signed agreements with the Islamic Commission of Spain (*Comisión Islámica de España*), the Federation of Israelite Communities of Spain (*Federación de Comunidades Israelitas de España*) and the Federation of Evangelical Religious Entities of Spain (*Federación de Entidades Religiosas Evangélicas de España*) in 1992, while Italy acknowledged Waldensians, Seventh-Day Adventists, Judaism, evangelical Christians, and Lutherans. The number of religious minorities recognised by the Italian state continued to widen in the 2000s (to include Greek Orthodox Christians, Mormons, Buddhists, and Hindus), but still left out religions perceived to be at odds with Italian law, importantly Islam (which represents the largest minority religion in the country) and Sikhism (Pace 2018; Magazzini 2021a).

In the same decades Greece struggled to improve the socioeconomic and political integration of its native Muslim Turkish minority (Antoniou 2005) while also accommodating a significant influx of migrants from neighbouring former communist countries and from South Asia. Despite contestation, important concessions were made to religious minorities including a law (4301/2014) that defines the procedures through which religious minority groups can be recognised as 'religious legal entities' under civil law (Anagnostou 2019) and which automatically recognises most of the existing minority religions and religious institutions (Law 4301/2014 as amended by Law 4972/2022). These developments are a net improvement in the direction of moderate secularism, compared to the previous situation where the Ministry of National Education and Religious Affairs would give a permit upon considering several issues including the status of a religious minority as known religion and the actual 'need' for establishing a church or place of worship (Triandafyllidou and Gropas 2009, 963). Resistance and hostility towards Islam remain, however, with Athens being the last capital in Europe to have a formal mosque inaugurated in 2020 (Al Jazeera 2020).

Recent asylum-seeking arrivals have exacerbated Islamophobic discourses (Kedikli and Akça 2018). While such narratives are by no means exclusive to Greece, here these trends – along with a severe economic crisis during the first part of the 2010s – have fuelled the rise of the far right and related racist, anti-Semitic, and Islamophobic movements. In Bulgaria too, particularly since the refugee flows of 2015–2016, there has been a rise in far-right discourse against migrants, but also against other minorities (such as LGBTQ+) (Stoynova and Dzhekova 2019; Wesolowsky 2021). Such discourses were also supported by the Bulgarian Orthodox Church, especially around the 2015–2016 refugee emergency (Leustean 2021).

The rise of far-right, anti-immigrant, and Islamophobic discourses identified in Greece and Bulgaria are in evidence in Italy too, where the economic crisis of the 2010s also favoured the rise of extreme right-wing parties such as la Lega (League) and Fratelli d'Italia (Brothers of Italy), which exploit a general frustration with the lack of social mobility by portraying Muslim immigrants as threatening national values and culture (Kaya 2020; Kaya and Tecmen 2021). However, in both Italy and Greece grassroots solidarity movements have also formed and consolidated in recent years with the aim of promoting migrant rights as well as fighting hate discourse. Pope Francis, the current head of the Catholic Church, has been outspoken in highlighting the plight of refugees and migrants, as well as promoting interfaith dialogue, and religious minorities (such as the Waldensians) have also been active in promoting inclusion initiatives towards newcomers (Bauböck and Mourão Permoser forthcoming).

Spain here diverges from the other two countries of Southern Europe: while the legacy of four decades of 'National Catholicism' is still reflected in the Catholic Church's privileged position, and society was also harshly hit by the economic crisis of the 2010s, immigration concerns have so far not led to the same degree of anti-immigrant rhetoric in mainstream political parties. This does not, however, translate into a virtuous governance of religion model, since the strong guarantees of freedom of religion enshrined in the legal system often do not translate into practice (Ruiz Vieytez 2012), and support for the far-right party Vox has been steadily growing since 2016 (Barrio, Alonso Sáenz de Oger, and Field 2021; Zanotti and Turnbull-Dugarte 2022).

Table 1. Modes and norms for the governance of religious diversity.

Incorporated within Majoritarian Nationalism	• Strong state identification with one religion • May or may not include toleration for other religions • May or may not include personal religious laws • In radical cases the state takes over or controls the institutions and followers of one or more religions (e.g. Diyanet) • The state may come to be controlled by religious parties (e.g. AKP, Muslim Brotherhood)
Secularist Statism	• State control of religion • The state excludes religion from the political and the civic, confining religious freedom largely to the private sphere • This mode of secularism may be self-defined as part of the national identity • May include some support of some religions, but religion mainly seen as belonging to the private sphere
Liberal Neutralism	• Moral individualism – freedom of conscience • Anti-assimilation and equal civic standing of all religions • Religions are officially and socially tolerated • Active 'de-othering' but no 'recognition'
Moderate Secularism	• Moral individualism – freedom of conscience • Religions may enjoy equal or unequal status but all are officially and socially tolerated • Religion seen as a public good in need of support (e.g. funding of faith schools) • Religion might also be seen as in need of regulation (to match some prevailing values e.g. issues of women bishops/single sex marriage) e.g. social attitudes that undermine tolerance and respect for religion and religious diversity (in interfaith relations and beyond religion) • Mutual autonomy but restricted neutrality, including 'weak' establishment and unequal recognition • Religious and non-religious citizens give each other generally accessible/dialogical reasons in politics

Modelling state-religion relations in Southern and Southeastern Europe

Our aim in this section is to identify the main models of state-religion relations (see Table 1) that capture the six case studies described above by referring to the framework established in Modood and Sealy, this collection, and applying the distinction between a 'dominant operative norm' (DON), a dominant feature of state-religion relations in a country, and a 'qualifying operative norm' (QON), a provision that limits, adjusts, or modifies the operative norm in a way that tempers (or exacerbates) the state's approach to religious diversity.

On the whole, and despite their diverse historical trajectories, the countries analysed have moderate secularism as their predominant mode of governance. As can be seen in Table 2, which offers an overview of how each country can be classified in relation to its dominant operative and qualifying operative norms, all case studies have strong protections for freedom of religion (which are codified in their constitutions). While the

Table 2. Modelling state-religion relations in Southern and Southeastern Europe.

	Majoritarian nationalism	Secularist statism	Liberal Neutralism	Moderate secularism
Albania		QON		DON
BiH	QON			DON
Bulgaria	QON	QON		DON
Greece	DON			QON
Italy	QON			DON
Spain	QON			DON

QON = Qualifying Operative Norms; DON = Dominant Operative Norms.

dominant features of state-religion relations are largely shared across the different cases, the countries differ with regard to their qualifying norms (QONs), with Albania and Bulgaria displaying some characteristics of secular statism while Greece, Spain, Italy, and BiH show noticeable traits of majoritarian nationalism. Liberal neutralism (a mode that applies to other cases analysed in this collection) is not present in any of the six cases, neither as DON nor as QON.

Constitutional principles, realities on the ground, and the role of qualifying norms

Overall, the Southern and Southeastern European modes of governance of religion analysed here are all rooted in the concept of freedom of religion based in freedom of conscience and moral individualism. This is the dominant operative norm (as defined by Modood and Sealy in this collection), which favours the toleration of different religions and supports the modes of moderate secularism, in which religion is seen as in need of some form of support and regulation.

The freedom of religion element, which is characterised by the promotion of moral individualism and freedom of conscience, with the state officially tolerating all religions, can be found in Article 3 of the Italian Constitution,[7] which enshrines protection from discrimination on the basis of religion (among other characteristics). This principle is further articulated in Articles 19 and 20 of the Constitution, which state that 'Anyone is entitled to freely profess their religious belief in any form, individually or with others' and that 'No special limitation or tax burden may be imposed on the establishment, legal capacity, or activities of any organisation on the ground of its religious nature or its religious or confessional aims'. Additionally, Article 8 posits that 'All religious denominations are equally free before the law'.

In Bosnia and Herzegovina, the Constitution[8] also establishes freedom of religion and prohibits any discrimination on the grounds of religion, while additional legislation stipulates the equal rights of all religious communities and establishes BiH as a multi-confessional country.

In Albania, the recognition of individual freedom of religion serves as a stepping stone for religious community freedom, since all religious communities are regarded by the state as juridical persons. The Albanian Constitution[9] speaks of the rights of minorities and justifies them through the prism of the person's inherent right to dignity, making it explicit that religious communities have the freedom to practise/express their beliefs and their religious belonging.

In the current Spanish framework, religious rights and freedoms are enshrined in the Constitution[10] under the section 'Fundamental rights and public liberties'. Article 16 explicitly guarantees freedom of ideology, religion, and worship for individuals and communities, and that 'no one may be compelled to make statements regarding his religion, beliefs, or ideologies' which represents the cornerstone of an approach based on freedom of conscience and toleration for all religions, therefore placing Spain in the freedom of religion mode.

While moderate secularism is the dominant norm in governing state-religion relations in the region, a closer look at the institutional framework and at additional norms enshrined in law and implemented in practice reveals a more nuanced picture that reflects the specific historical experiences of each country.

In both Spain and Italy, the historical relations between the state and the Catholic Church are reflected in their constitutional and legal frameworks. In Spain, the same Article 16 of the Spanish Constitution which speaks of freedom of religion adds that there shall be no state religion but that 'The public authorities shall take the religious beliefs of Spanish society into account and shall consequently maintain appropriate cooperation with the Catholic Church and the other confessions'. This specification acknowledges that the state's neutrality is limited: public authorities are mandated to cooperate with the Catholic Church, which is therefore given a special level of recognition.

These norms enshrined in Article 16 of the Spanish Constitution are elaborated further in the 1980 Organic Law on Religious Freedom (no.177), which emphasises moral individualism and freedom of conscience. According to this Religious Liberty Law, the only restrictions that the state can impose with regard to the right to religious freedom have to do with public security and with the principle of doing no harm to others. Overall, one can therefore place Spain within the mode that is centred on freedom of religion and moderate secularism, while affording a different degree of support to different religions, with Catholicism benefitting from historical ties to the state.

The same can be said of Italy, where the Constitution references a legal agreement between the Italian state and the Holy See that ensures mutual autonomy between the state and the majority religion. While the Italian Constitution speaks of mutual neutrality, in defining such neutrality between the state and the Catholic Church it refers back to the Lateran Pacts, which were sanctioned in 1929 by Mussolini's dictatorship. Amendments to these Pacts were made in 1985, causing Roman Catholicism to lose its previous status as the official religion of the Italian state. By asserting the political autonomy of the state relative to religion, even though the term secular is never employed ('The State and the Catholic Church are independent and sovereign, each within its own sphere'), the Constitution presents a case of moderate secularism, but one in which the majority religion benefits from unequal support afforded by the state, therefore outlining majoritarian nationalism as a qualifying norm.

Greece offers a case that is close to Italy and Spain in many regards, but includes a stronger focus on the majoritarian religion, including in its Constitution. The Greek Constitution provides for the freedom of religious conscience as inviolable, and for enjoyment of civil rights and liberties independently of religious beliefs (Article 3), and requires all MPs to take a religious or secular oath (in accordance with their beliefs) before entering office (Article 59). However, at Article 3 it also recognises Orthodox Christianity as the 'prevailing religion', thus combining freedom of religion with a strong push for majoritarian nationalism as a qualifying operative norm. The privileged position of the Orthodox Church of Greece (Ορθόδοξη Εκκλησία της Ελλάδας) as a national institution has been embedded in the legal order, where relevant legal acts and policies on religious matters take into consideration the interests of the Church (Tsitselikis 2012, 9) and until recently gave the Church the possibility of providing a consultative opinion on the establishment of other 'known religions'[11] (Hatziprokopiou and Evergeti 2014). It is no coincidence that in a 2018 Pew Research Center study, three-quarters of Greek respondents considered being Orthodox Christian important to being truly Greek, while nearly nine out of ten claimed Greek culture to be superior to others (2018, 6). The Orthodox

Church of Greece enjoys the status of a legal entity in public law, and the majoritarian religion is seen by the state as a public good, complemented by relatively weak institutional accommodation of religious diversity (Gemi 2021).

Overall, Greece, Italy, and Spain exhibit significant similarities in the historical relationship between the state and the church that is reflected in both their constitutional principles and in their institutional frameworks for religious governance. Albania and Bulgaria, meanwhile, exhibit stronger frameworks of separation of church and state emanating from their fully secularist experience under communism. The Bulgarian Constitution[12] promotes moral individualism as well as official neutrality of the state towards religious denominations. While religion still retains a strong influence as an important component of the cultural identity of many Bulgarians, Bulgarian society is highly secularised. The Orthodox Christian Synod and the Chief Muftiate remain weak in the context of the communist legacy and postcommunist political rivalries.

Similarly, the present-day relationship between the Albanian state and religion is characterised by respect for mutual autonomy conforming to the principles of moderate secularism, but it includes the presence of some government control of religion, as well as of limited support for religion and cooperation with some religious organisations for common goals (as per the 1998 Constitution and the institutional-regulatory framework that it established). According to Elbasani and Puto (2017), the relationship between the Albanian state and organised religion was shaped by historical, sociopolitical, socio-demographic, economic, and cultural factors, resulting in a balanced two-way autonomy approach which adapts the French *laicité* mode of separation between church and state to the necessities and goals of Albania, privileging the approach that we characterise as secularist statism.

BiH presents a peculiar case. Its legal framework of state-religion relations, as well as its qualifying norm of favouring one religion over others, coincide perfectly with those of Italy and Spain. They are however the product of very different polities and recent history(ies). Following the war fought over ethno-religious lines and symbols, BiH society had to reconceptualise the relationship between the state and its different religious communities. It also had to face the challenge of governing religious diversity based on the principle of equality and freedom from state interference in religious matters. Present day BiH promotes a mode of separation of state from any one religion and includes the principles of religious freedom and equality of all religious communities. Since only limited toleration exists between religious communities, religious communities are prohibited from spreading hatred against other religious communities in order to protect the multi-confessional character of the state. Despite such laws, ethno-religious tensions – sometimes spilling over into political conflict – characterise this country.

In the context of BiH's religious pluralism and divided society, the implementation of the principles of equality of religious communities has thus been challenging. Since each territorial entity is responsible for its own relationship with the religious communities it hosts, such a relationship has often proven highly favourable to the dominant religious group in each territory, particularly in accessing state-level government representation. This has created situations in which some minority religious groups have not been accommodated or respected in ways equal to the respective majority religious group. One example is Republika Srpska, which has been influenced by the geopolitical aspirations of Serbia through the predominant Serbian Orthodox Church. In this example, the set-up of the BiH system, which has provided substantial powers to local entities, has resulted in the granting of *de facto* privilege to the Serbian Orthodox Christian majority, in the form of funding, construction permits for religious sites, and the distinct status of the Church (Center for the Study of Democracy 2020; Bayrakli and Hafez 2019). Thus, while BiH may adhere to the principles of moderate secularism and freedom of religion, within each of its constitutive entities state-religion relations conform with a majoritarian nationalism mode.

Concluding remarks

Looking at Southern and Southeastern Europe as a whole, despite its numerous internal diversities ranging from historical trajectories to legal systems, the region shares a strong primary legislation rooted in freedom of religion. All countries examined include moral individualism, freedom of conscience, and toleration for all religions in their constitutions and/or primary legislation.

Most countries have built their core legislation on norms of freedom of religion to develop modes of moderate secularism as their way of managing state-religion relations and religious diversity. In practice, this means including provisions to guarantee relative mutual autonomy between state and religion, while offering some support and regulation to religious institutions on behalf of the state.

Moderate secularism constitutes the region's overarching, dominant operative norms in law if not always in fact. In most of Southern Europe, when it comes to strong state-religion connections, religion has played a fundamental role in defining the 'imagined ethnos', thus leading to the emergence of significant qualifying norms that shape the actual sociopolitical reality. This means that, in many instances, national and religious identities are intertwined, and that the attachment to Orthodox Christianity as the core element of nation-state identity in Greece, for instance, or to Catholicism in Spain and Italy, makes it difficult to separate ethnicity from religiosity. Indeed, Greek national identity has been historically constructed in opposition to the religious 'Other' in general, and to the Muslim other in particular. Such historical and political contingencies have forged a genuine mode of religious governance whereby Orthodox Christianity has an especially prominent place in the public sphere under the rubric of the 'prevailing religion', which places it in the majoritarian nationalism mode, showing strong ties with a single religion. While such prevalence of the majoritarian religion is not a preponderant conceptual characterisation in the rest of the region, it is however present as a qualifying norm in the cases of Italy, Spain (both of which have weak ties with a single religion), and BiH (where territorial governance is organised in such a way as to allow each region to favour the local religious majority).

Even if not as strong as in France, a degree of secularist statism can be found in Albania and Bulgaria, as a legacy of forced secularisation under communism, but combined with a respect for mutual autonomy and religious freedom driven at least partly by the desire to access the European Union.

On the whole, while the significant presence of majoritarian nationalism as either a dominant or qualifying norm in the region is a worrying sign for religious diversity management, as long as the legal foundations centred around religious freedom are not completely disregarded in practice, one can hope that ethno-religious conflicts such as those of recent history in the Balkans will not return. Our analysis also shows that historical path dependencies lose their importance as current socioeconomic and political concerns may significantly shape the legal and institutional framework of state-religion relations and the ways in which religious diversity is governed. Thus, the importance of majoritarian nationalism qualifying norms in the case of Italy, Spain, and Greece may also arise as a reaction to an increased immigrant presence and a shifting composition of the population in favour of plurality. By contrast, in Albania and Bulgaria secular communist legacies may find renewed strength in the context of their European integration pathways. Last but not least, in BiH persisting divisions and tensions seem to trump both dominant and qualifying norms, failing to lead to a viable state-religion modality that would allow for greater national unity.

Notes

1. The analysis presented in this contribution is based on country reports elaborated for the Horizon Project GREASE: Radicalisation, Secularism and the Governance of Religion: European and Asian Perspectives (http://grease.eui.eu).
2. Both Catholic and the Orthodox communities benefited from favourable political conditions and significant state subsidies under the Austro-Hungarian Empire, while the Muslim community became marginalised (Tzvetkova and Todorova 2021).
3. While the signatories of the Albanian Declaration of Independence were mostly Sunni Muslims, Bektashi Sufis, Catholics, and Orthodox Christians also contributed to independence (Schwartz 2012).
4. The Kingdom of Sardinia had recognised equal civil and political rights for Jews and Waldensians already in 1848, and favoured a moderate secularism, despite many of its political leaders being Catholics in their private lives (Magazzini 2021a). While maintaining Catholicism as Italy's official religion, the 1848 Constitution adopted a regime of separation between church and state, which was condemned by then Pope Pius IX, who excommunicated the king and the leaders of the Italian government and ordered 'good Catholics' not to recognise its legitimacy (Ercolessi 2009).
5. The Department of Denominations is in charge of easing the dialogue between the state and the denominations. This has also created an informal body, the Council of Religious Communities, composed of representatives from all denominations, and helps foster dialogue between the different denominations and the state.
6. Muslims represent the largest minority at about 10% of the population, but they comprise a diverse range of ethnic communities, from Turks to Roma.
7. Italian Constitution (1948). Official English version available online at: https://www.senato.it/documenti/repository/istituzione/costituzione_inglese.pdf.
8. Bosnia and Herzegovina Constitution of 1995 with Amendments through 2009 (2009). Official English version available at: https://www.constituteproject.org/constitution/Bosnia_Herzegovina_2009.pdf?lang=en.
9. Albania's Constitution of 1998 with Amendments through 2016 (2016). Official English version available at: https://constituteproject.org/constitution/Albania_2016.pdf?lang=en.
10. Spanish Constitution (1978). Official English version available online at: https://www.lamoncloa.gob.es/documents/constitucion_inglescorregido.pdf.
11. The term 'known religion' is referred to in Article 13, paragraph 2 of the Greek Constitution. The full text of the Constitution is available here in Greek: https://www.hellenicparliament.gr/Vouli-ton-Ellinon/To-Politevma/Syntagma/ and in other languages: https://www.hellenicparliament.gr/en/Vouli-ton-Ellinon/To-Politevma/Syntagma. According to the Council of State and the Supreme Court, this term denotes any religion that is public, with no secret rituals or

dogmas, which do not constitute an unlawful union, or a fictitious association or organisation with illegal aims, and its purpose must not negatively affect public order or morals.
12. Constitution of the Republic of Bulgaria (2015). Official English version available online at: https://www.parliament.bg/en/const.

Disclosure statement

No potential conflict of interest was reported by the author(s).

Funding

The research that informs this contribution has received funding from the European Union's Horizon 2020 research and innovation programme under grant agreement number 770640.

ORCID

Tina Magazzini http://orcid.org/0000-0001-8534-0175
Anna Triandafyllidou http://orcid.org/0000-0001-6760-0033
Liliya Yakova http://orcid.org/0000-0003-1927-5525

References

Agenzia D'Informazione. 2018. *"Albania in the EU: Religions Come Together to Support Adhesion to the 'Common European Home'."* https://agensir.it/europa/balcani/2018/04/23/albania-in-the-eu-religions-come-together-to-support-adhesion-to-the-common-european-home/.

Alibašić, A., and N. Begović. 2017. "Reframing the Relations Between State and Religion in Post– War Bosnia: Learning to Be Free!" *Journal of Balkan and Near Eastern Studies* 19 (1): 19–34.

Al Jazeera. 2020. "Athens Finally Gets a Mosque." November 3. https://www.aljazeera.com/news/2020/11/3/athens-first-mosque-opens-doors-to-muslim-worshipers.

Anagnostou, D. 2019. "Implementation and Impact of Strasbourg Court Rulings: The Case of Religious Minorities and Their Convention Freedoms." In *The European Court of Human Rights and the Freedom of Religion and Belief: The 25 Years Since Kokkinakis.* Studies in Religion, Secular Beliefs and Human Rights. 13 vols., edited by J. Temperman, T. J. Gunn, and M. Evans, 388–418. Nijhoff: Brill.

Antoniou, D. 2005. "Western Thracian Muslims in Athens. From Economic Migration to Religious Organisation." *Balkanologie Revue d'études pluridisciplinaires* IX: 1–2. doi:10.4000/balkanologie. 579.

Ballinger, P., and K. Ghodsee. 2011. "Socialist Secularism: Religion, Modernity, and Muslim Women's Emancipation in Bulgaria and Yugoslavia, 1945–1991." *Aspasia* 5 (1): 6–27.

Baltsiotis, L. 2011. "The Muslim Chams of Northwestern Greece." *European Journal of Turkish Studies* 12: 1–31.

Barrio, A., S. Alonso Sáenz de Oger, and B. Field. 2021. "VOX Spain: The Organisational Challenges of a New Radical Right Party." *Politics and Governance* 9 (4): 240–251.

Bauböck, R., and J. Mourão Permoser. forthcoming. "Multiple Levels of Sanctuary in Europe." *Journal of Ethnic and Migration Studies* Special Issue on Multiple Levels of Sanctuary in Europe.

Bayrakli, E., and F. Hafez. 2019. *European Islamophobia Report.* SETA Foundation for Political, Economic and Social Research. http://www.islamophobiaeurope.com/wp-content/uploads/2019/09/EIR_2018.pdf.

Bougarel, X. 2017. *Islam and Nationhood in Bosnia and Herzegovina Surviving Empires*, edited by C. Mobley. London and New York: Bloomsbury Academic.

Bracewell, W., and A. Drace-Francis. 1999. "South-Eastern Europe: History, Concepts, Boundaries." *Balkanologie Revue D'études Pluridiciplinaries* 3 (2): 1–16.

Center for the Study of Democracy. 2020. "Bosnia and Herzegovina." *GREASE Radicalisation and Resilience Case Studies.* http://grease.eui.eu/wp-content/uploads/sites/8/2021/01/WP4-Report_BiH.pdf.

Dyrmishi, A. 2016. *Radicalisation and Religious Governance in Albania.* Sofia: The Center for the Study of Democracy and Governance.

Elbasani, A., and A. Puto. 2017. "Albanian-Style laïcité: A Model for a Multi-Religious European Home?" *Journal of Balkan and Near Eastern Studies* 19 (1): 53–69.

Ercolessi, G. 2009. "Italy: The Contemporary Condition of Italian Laicità." In *Secularism, Women and the State: The Mediterranean World in the 21st Century*, edited by B. A. Kosmin and A. Keysar, 9–28. Hartford, CT: Institute for the Study of Secularism in Society and Culture.

Evans, J., and C. Baronavski. 2018. "How Do European Countries Differ in Religious Commitment?" *Pew Research Centre.* https://www.pewresearch.org/fact-tank/2018/12/05/how-do-european-countries-differ-in-religious-commitment/.

Gemi, E., A. Triandafyllidou and T. Magazzini. 2021. "Greece: The 'Prevailing Religion' and the Governance of Diversity." In *Routledge Handbook on the Governance of Religious Diversity*, edited by A. Triandafyllidou and T. Magazzini, 88–98. New York and London: Routledge.

Grekova, M., I. Kyurkchieva, and M. Kosseva. 2013. "Accommodation of Religious Diversity at the Workplace Through the Prism of State-Religion Relations: The Bulgarian Case." *International Journal of Discrimination and the Law* 13 (2–3): 169–193.

Griera, M., J. Martínez-Ariño, and J. Clot-Garrell. 2021. "Banal Catholicism, Morality Policies and the Politics of Belonging in Spain." *Religions* 12 (5): 293.

Gülalp, H. 2017. "Secularism as a Double-Edged Sword? State Regulation of Religion in Turkey." In *The Problem of Religious Diversity: European Challenges, Asian Approaches*, edited by A. Triandafyllidou and T. Modood, 273–296. Edinburgh: University of Edinburgh Press.

Hatziprokopiou, P., and V. Evergeti. 2014. "Negotiating Muslim Identity and Diversity in Greek Urban Spaces." *Social & Cultural Geography* 15 (6): 603–626.

Hayrapetyan, L. 2017. "Youth Radicalization by Extremisms in the Balkans and Western Europe." *Journal of Humanities, Culture and Social Sciences* 1: 9–14.

Karataş, I. 2020. "State-Sponsored Atheism: The Case of Albania During the Enver Hoxha Era." *Occasional Papers on Religion in Eastern Europe* 40 (6): 93–109.

Kaya, A. 2020. "Right-Wing Populism and Islamophobism in Europe and Their Impact on Turkey–EU Relations." *Turkish Studies* 21 (1): 1–28.

Kaya, A., and A. Tecmen. 2021. "Europe versus Islam?: Right-Wing Populist Discourse and the Construction of a Civilizational Identity." In *A Quarter Century of the "Clash of Civilizations"*, edited by J. Haynes, 49–64. London: Routledge.

Kedikli, U., and M. Akça. 2018. "Rising Islamophobic Discourses in Europe and Fight Against Islamophobia on the Basis of International Organizations." *Mediterranean Journal of Social Sciences* 9 (1): 9–23.

Kertzer, D. I. 2015. *The Pope and Mussolini: The Secret History of Pius XI and the Rise of Fascism in Europe*. Oxford: Oxford University Press.

Kiper, J., and R. Sosis. 2020. "The Systemics of Violent Religious Nationalism: A Case Study of the Yugoslav Wars." *Journal for the Study of Religion, Nature and Culture* 14 (1): 45–70.

Knippenberg, H. 2007. "The Political Geography of Religion: Historical State-Church Relations in Europe and Recent Challenges." *GeoJournal* 67 (4): 253–265.

Leustean, L. N. 2021. "Orthodox Conservatism and the Refugee Crisis in Bulgaria and Moldova." *Communist and Post-Communist Studies* 54 (1–2): 83–101.

Madeley, J. 2003. "A Framework for the Comparative Analysis of Church–state Relations in Europe." *West European Politics* 26 (1): 23–50.

Magazzini, T. 2021a. "The Italian Case. 'Baptised Laicità' and a Changing Demographic." In *Routledge Handbook on the Governance of Religious Diversity*, edited by A. Triandafyllidou and T. Magazzini, 59–73. London and New York: Routledge.

Magazzini, T. 2021b. "Spain. All Religions are Equal, but Some are More Equal Than Others." In *Routledge Handbook on the Governance of Religious Diversity*, edited by A. Triandafyllidou and T. Magazzini, 74–87. London and New York: Routledge.

Mancheva, M. 2019. "Bulgaria." *GREASE Country Reports*. http://grease.eui.eu/wp-content/uploads/sites/8/2019/11/Bulgaria-Profile.pdf

Mancheva, M. 2021. "Bulgaria: Strong Cultural Legacies, Weak Institutions, and Political Instrumentalization of Religion." In *Routledge Handbook on the Governance of Religious Diversity*, edited by A. Triandafyllidou and T. Magazzini, 149–161. London and New York: Routledge.

Muñoz Mendoza, J. 2012. *La construcción política de la identidad española: ¿del nacionalcatolicismo al patriotismo democrático?*. Madrid: Centro de Investigaciones Sociológicas.

OHCHR. 2017. *Preliminary Findings of Country Visit to Albania by Ahmed Shaheed, Special Rapporteur on Freedom of Religion or Belief*. Tirana: Press Statement. https://www.ohchr.org/en/NewsEvents/Pages/DisplayNews.aspx?NewsID=21627&LangID=E.

Pace, E., C. Monnot and J. Stolz. 2018. "Religious Congregations in Italy: Mapping the New Pluralism." In *Congregations in Europe*, edited by C. Monnot and J. Stolz, 139–156. Berlin: Springer.

Pew Research Center. 2018. *Eastern and Western Europeans Differ on Importance of Religion, Views of Minorities, and Key Social Issues*. https://www.pewresearch.org/religion/2018/10/29/eastern-and-western-europeans-differ-on-importance-of-religion-views-of-minorities-and-key-social-issues/.

Ruiz Vieytez, E. J. 2012. *Las Prácticas de Armonización Como Instrumento de Gestión Pública de La Diversidad Religiosa*. Madrid: Observatorio del Pluralismo Religioso en España.

Schwartz, S. 2012. "How Albania's Religious Mix Offers an Example for the Rest of the World." *Huffpost*. 12 November. https://www.huffpost.com/entry/how-albanias-religious-mix-offers-an-example-for-the-rest-of-the-world_b_2199921.

Sealy, T., T. Magazzini, T. Modood, and A. Triandafyllidou. 2021. "Managing Religious Diversity in Europe." In *Oxford Handbook of Religion and Europe*, edited by G. Davie and L. N. Leustean, 568–584. Oxford: Oxford University Press.

Skoulariki, A. 2010. "Old and New Mosques in Greece: A New Debate Haunted by History." In *Mosques in Europe: Why a Solution Has Become a Problem*, edited by S. Allievi, 300–318. London: NEF Network of European Foundations Alliance Publishing Trust.

Stoynova, N., and R. Dzhekova. 2019. "Vigilantism Against Ethnic Minorities and Migrants in Bulgaria." In *Vigilantism Against Migrants and Minorities*, edited by T. Bjørgo and M. Mareš, 164–182. London and New York: Routledge.

Todorova, M. 1994. "The Balkans: From Discovery to Invention." *Slavic Review* 53 (2): 453–482.

Triandafyllidou, A. 2001. *Immigrants and National Identity in Europe*. London: Routledge.

Triandafyllidou, A. 2007. "Mediterranean Migrations: Problems and Prospects for Greece and Italy in the Twenty-First Century." *Mediterranean Politics* 12 (1): 77–84. doi:10.1080/13629390601136855.

Triandafyllidou, A., H. Gülalp, M. Iliyasov, G. Mahajan, and E. Račius. 2019. "Nation and Religion – Reflections on Europe, the MENA Region and South Asia." *GREASE Concept Papers*. http://grease. eui.eu/publications/concept-papers/.

Triandafyllidou, A., and R. Gropas. 2009. "Constructing Difference: The Mosque Debates in Greece." *Journal of Ethnic and Migration Studies* 35 (6): 957–975. doi:10.1080/13691830902957734.

Triandafyllidou, A. and T. Magazzini, eds. 2021. *Routledge Handbook on the Governance of Religious Diversity*. London and New York: Routledge.

Tsitselikis, K. 2012. *Old and New Islam in Greece from Historical Minorities to Immigrant Newcomers*. Leiden: Brill/Nijhoff.

Tzvetkova, G., and R. Todorova. 2021. "Bosnia and Herzegovina: Persisting Ethno-Religious Divide." In *Routledge Handbook on the Governance of Religious Diversity*, edited by A. Triandafyllidou and T. Magazzini, 176–189. London and New York: Routledge.

Urrutia Asua, G. 2016. *Minorías Religiosas Y Derechos Humanos. Reconocimiento Social Y Gestión Pública Del Pluralismo Religioso En El País Vasco*. Madrid: Ediciones Akal.

Wesolowsky, T. 2021. "The Worrying Regression of LGBT Rights in Eastern Europe." *Radio Free Europe Radio Liberty*. https://www.rferl.org/a/lgbt-rights-eastern-europe-backsliding/31622890.html.

Yakova, L. 2019. "Albania." *GREASE Country Reports*. http://grease.eui.eu/wp-content/uploads/sites/8/2019/11/Alb%D0%B0nia-Report.pdf.

Yakova, L., and V. Bogdanova. 2022. "Preventing Religiously Motivated Radicalisation: Lessons from Southeastern Europe." *Policy Brief, EUI Issue 2022/12, April 2022*. www.grease.eui.eu.

Yakova, L., and L. Kuneva. 2021. "Albania: Legacy of Shared Culture and History for Religious Tolerance." In *Routledge Handbook on the Governance of Religious Diversity*, edited by A. Triandafyllidou and T. Magazzini, 162–175. London and New York: Routledge.

Zanotti, L., and S. J. Turnbull-Dugarte. 2022. "Surviving but Not Thriving: VOX and Spain in Times of COVID-19." *Government and Opposition* 1–20. First View. doi:10.1017/gov.2022.7.

Zhelyazkova, A. 2000. *Albanian Identities*. International Centre for Minority Studies and Intercultural Relations (IMIR). http://pdc.ceu.hu/archive/00003852/01/Albanian_Identities.pdf.

Zhelyazkova, A., ed. 2001. *Osobeniat Sluchai" Bosna*. Sofia: IMIR.

𝟄 OPEN ACCESS

Dynamics in state-religion relations in postcommunist Central Eastern Europe and Russia

Daniel Vekony ⓘ, Marat Iliyasov ⓘ and Egdūnas Račius ⓘ

ABSTRACT
The contribution aims to provide an exposition of the recent dynamics in state-religion relations in Central Eastern Europe (specifically in Hungary, Lithuania, and Slovakia) and Russia through the prism of the typology of modes of governance of religious diversity. Additionally, the present research complements this framework by taking into account the unique characteristics of Central and Eastern Europe and Russia. Though the countries of the region of Central Eastern Europe and Russia share much common history and recent experiences, the case studies analysed in this contribution reveal that state-religion relations and modes of governance of religious diversity nonetheless differ across countries. From a liberal secular perspective, adopted by the current authors, the dynamics of state-religion relations in this region look problematic. Of particular concern are state-Islam relations, which in some of the countries covered, namely Slovakia and Hungary, are already at a very low point, with Muslims (particularly of immigrant background) being increasingly securitised by the media, public, and the national political elites.

Introduction

The region of Central Eastern Europe[1] and Russia is known to have undergone profound transformations in state-religion relations in the past hundred years – from formerly amicable in the pre-World War era through exceptionally hostile during the communist intermezzo to somewhat ambivalent in the postcommunist era. The Central Eastern European states covered in this contribution, namely Lithuania, Slovakia, and Hungary, are all member states of the EU, and therefore have to abide – not least in their regimes of governance of religion – by EU values, principles, and standards. Russia, however, though before 16 March 2022 it too had been subject to the jurisdiction of the European Court of Human Rights, has always had its own interpretation of the principles and norms enshrined in the European Convention on Human Rights and therefore has had strained relations with the Council of Europe. In the past two decades Russian domestic politics, not least those pertaining to state-religion relations, have been criticised by the EU and its individual member states, most notably by those located in Central Eastern Europe. Therefore, while the Baltic States and the Višegrad States may be seen as two sub-

---

This is an Open Access article distributed under the terms of the Creative Commons Attribution-NonCommercial-NoDerivatives License (http://creativecommons.org/licenses/by-nc-nd/4.0/), which permits non-commercial re-use, distribution, and reproduction in any medium, provided the original work is properly cited, and is not altered, transformed, or built upon in any way.

regions of Central Eastern Europe and comparable among themselves, Russia stands out as a very different region of its own.

All of the region's countries, though formally secular, have Christian heritage that forms part of their national identities. Even though religion plays an ever-decreasing role in people's everyday lives, the majority of the region's population nominally belongs to one of the main traditional Christian churches, namely Roman Catholic (in Lithuania, Hungary, and Slovakia) or Russian Orthodox (in Russia). Membership of other religions is marginal compared to the different denominations of Christianity, although, in Russia, inhabitants of Muslim cultural background constitute over 6.5%, and possibly up to 12%, of the population (Levada-Center 2013; Malashenko 2011).

State-religion relations in the region vary vastly. While some of the countries recognise a number of religious denominations as 'traditional' to the land, others limit themselves to a single denomination or do not confer such status on anyone. This formal (non)recognition, as is shown further below, often has far-reaching consequences, and not only for the individual faith communities but, and more importantly, in terms of preferences, hierarchies, and inequalities in the general constellation of state-religion relations.

On the social level, though the majority of the population in the region still identify with a (traditional) faith community – chiefly one of the Christian denominations – in practice, as the research findings reveal, a large proportion of this religious identification is intrinsically linked to nationalism (Pew Research Center 2017). However, in recent years decreases in traditional religious observance in some of these countries are being compensated by the appearance and increase of new religious communities (some of the 'New Religious Movements' type, others of historic religions less present in particular countries, including Islam).

Also, lately, Christian primordialist ideology that questions the idea of secular multiculturalism and cohabitation of religions and the very basis of current state-religion relations has also been on the rise. Moreover, in some cases, as is shown in this contribution, this issue has been taken up by political parties which incorporate it in their programmes. In some of the countries of the region, this has already resulted in an overhaul of legislation related to the governance of religion, taking it away from the hitherto burgeoning liberal secularism of the states. Thus, the meaning and parameters of secularism in the region of Central Eastern Europe and Russia in the postcommunist era may not be seen as carved in stone but rather as an object of renewed attention by multiple state and non-state actors and, consequently, subject to change.

This contribution aims at providing an exposition of the recent dynamics in state-religion relations in Central Eastern Europe (on the examples of Hungary, Lithuania, and Slovakia) and Russia (see Figure 1) through the prism of the typology of modes of governance of religious diversity (see the introductory contribution in this collection). Additionally, the present research complements this framework by taking into account the unique characteristics of Central and Eastern Europe and Russia. The authors of this contribution contend that to understand the specificities of the region, we need to look at religion-state relations from an angle that takes into consideration the different historical experiences of the countries of the former communist bloc.

The research for this contribution has been two-fold – it primarily includes qualitative content analysis of relevant national key legal documents and the qualitative analysis of practical policy measures by national governments. We focused on primary legal sources

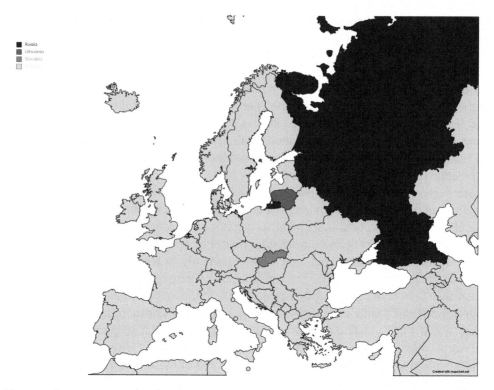

Figure 1. Countries covered in this contribution: Hungary, Lithuania, Slovakia, and Russia.

for the former and secondary sources for the latter part of the research process. The primary sources for the qualitative content analysis were chosen using the purposive sampling method. Except for a short historic overview at the beginning of the contribution, the timeframe applied in the research covers the years from the fall of the Berlin wall until the present day, with special attention given to the years between 2000 and 2021.

We agree with Habermas (2006, 15) that we not only live in a time of postsecular societies, but that this requires an 'epistemic adjustment' in order to accommodate both supporters of secular values and those supporting religious ones in a liberal democratic environment. Provided both secular and religious citizens go through 'complementary learning processes' (Habermas 2006, 16), it is possible to reach an agreement on the limits of secularism. However, this idea of the postsecular only deals with the renegotiation of the limits of secularism in liberal democratic societies. When Habermas (2008, 17) claims that '(t)he controversial term "post-secular society" can only be applied to the affluent societies of Europe or countries such as Canada, Australia and New Zealand, where people's religious ties have steadily or rather quite dramatically lapsed in the post-World War II period', it is unclear whether postcommunist Central Eastern European countries may be considered part of this group.

We support the idea that countries in this region have also entered a postsecular era. Drawing on Eisenstadt's (2000) idea of multiple modernities, we agree with Berger (2014, 78) that in countries with varying historic and political backgrounds, the boundaries between religious groups and the state are drawn differently in a postsecular framework.

This entails, however, that even if postsecular societies show characteristics that Habermas (2008, 20) touched upon, the liberal democratic background Habermas was presupposing may not necessarily be among them. As a result, we agree with Parmaksız (2018) that there is a lack of consensus over the meaning of postsecular.

Further drawing on Parmaksız (2018, 108), his term 'religionormativity' may help us better understand developments concerning the postsecular in Central Eastern European state-church relations: 'A religionormative system organises its social, cultural and/or political spheres around structures of understanding and thinking, as well as practical orientations, which make religiosity privileged' (Parmaksız 2018, 108). This idea is closely related to a negative and positive sense of secularisation (Parmaksız 2018, 108–109). According to the negative sense, secularisation is the weakening of the role of religion in different domains and institutions in society, thus it also entails the weakening of the religionormative political domain. This approach leaves little space for religion in the public sphere. However, according to Parmaksız (2018, 109), secularisation can also be approached in the positive sense,

> as the establishment of a new normative order that cultivates its own sensibilities, practices, values, particular view on life and the human condition. This new seculanormative order creates its own exclusion and control mechanisms over what constitutes legitimate knowledge and thereby privileges certain cognitive structures, ideological and symbolic commitments, along with the practices, habits and reflexes that are attached to these commitments.

This positive postsecularity enables the state to step over the 'classic' normative frameworks of separation and supposed state neutrality and build up its own normative structures based on historical and cultural traditions. Based on distinct cultural and historical heritage, states may emphasise the duty to treat certain religions or religious communities preferentially. This, however, may also entitle the state to keep certain religious communities at arm's length or even to marginalise (and securitise) some of them. In this sense, it becomes justified for the state to grant different levels of recognition to various religious groups.

Churches with privileged status may receive extra government funding to perform certain public goods, such as education, caring for the elderly, or running hospitals. As Roy pointed out, these are the roles the secular states took over from the churches in Europe during the historical period of secularisation (Roy 2019, 16–18). In this sense, what we can observe currently in some Central Eastern European states, most notably Hungary, is a dynamic of de-secularisation initiated by the state, based on certain value sets. Governments may de-secularise certain domains that used to be secular, such as education, granting access to certain privileged churches, such as the traditional Christian churches in the region.

Historical overview of state-religion connections in the region: from established churches to state secularism

Historically, most of the region of Central Eastern Europe and Russia was ruled by two regional empires – the Austro-Hungarian and the Russian. The first was demographically predominantly Catholic, hence, the hegemonic position of the Roman Catholic Church (RCC) in countries that used to be part of that empire. The latter was Russian Orthodox with the Russian Orthodox Church (ROC) as the supreme religious organisation closely intertwined with the state. The region hosted not only other Christian communities but also non-Christians, first of all Jewish but also Muslims. Russia also had many other religious minorities, most of which were incorporated and subjugated as a consequence of the imperial policy of the Russian Empire. Besides the diverse communities of Muslims and Jews, there were Catholics, Protestants, Old Believers, Buddhists, etc. In brief, the societies and their states in the region have a historic tradition of dealing with different religious communities.

However, the level of tolerance towards certain religions and their followers changed over the centuries. For a long time in the Habsburg Empire, the RCC enjoyed a privileged position and members of other religious minorities (like Protestants and Orthodox Christians) were treated as second-class, and – more importantly – as disloyal, citizens (Crews 2003). Under the Romanov monarchy that ruled from the seventeenth to the twentieth century, and during the rule of Ivan IV ('the Terrible', who reigned from 1547 to 1575), non-Orthodox Christians and others were pressured to convert to Orthodox Christianity, at times violently (Geraci and Khodarkovsky 2001, 6). The breakthrough in tolerance towards religious minorities came in the eighteenth century, when 'Edicts of Tolerance' were promulgated in both empires (Crews 2003). As a result, state-founded Islamic religious institutions were created in the Russian Empire by the end of the eighteenth century, and became an instrument in the governance of religion. In the Austro-Hungarian Empire, the Jewish community received formal recognition in 1895 (Raj 1996), followed by formal recognition of Islam and its religious establishment in 1912 (Chudžíková 2011, 41).

The legitimation of Islamic religious institutions was a particularly sensitive topic in both empires. In what is now Russia, Islam *de facto* became one of the country's major religions from the second half of the sixteenth century, when the Moscow Principality started expanding into the territories of the former Golden Horde. The conquests of Kazan and Astrakhan khanates significantly increased its Muslim population. Initially, the state was utterly antagonistic towards its Muslim subjects who, for two centuries, would constantly suffer from state-endorsed Christianisation at the hands of the ROC. With Christianisation policies bringing unsatisfactory results, and inspired by the Enlightenment, Empress Catherine the Great came up with the idea of creating muftiates – the spiritual administrations for governing the Muslim population in the late eighteenth century (Crews 2009, 34; Furman 1989).

In the Austro-Hungarian Empire, recognition of Islam was also problematic because of the proximity of the Muslim Ottoman Empire and the legacy of hostilities and occupations of Austro-Hungarian territories by the Ottomans. A full legal recognition of Islam came only after Bosnia and Hercegovina, with its significant number of Muslims, was occupied in 1878 and annexed by the Austro-Hungarian Empire in 1908 (Sulok 2010). The end of the First World War opened up opportunities for new sovereign nation-states in Central Eastern Europe. Initially they all adopted democratic political systems that enshrined tolerance towards minority religious traditions, albeit where the dominant Christian churches (chiefly, the RCC) retained special status and relations to the state. Though the region of Central Eastern Europe had not experienced the secularising wave seen in Western Europe, in the interwar period secularist ideas finally found their way into the region's societies. Although policies for the governance of religion varied geographically and chronologically across the

Soviet Union, on the whole the Soviet authorities opted for an extreme form of state secularism and turned to suppression of all religious communities and their organisations (Furman 1989). In the early 1920s the authorities experimented with a degree of recognition and even support for some religious minorities (Coleman 2005, 154–197), coupled with repressive measures against the Russian Orthodox Church in particular. Pragmatic wartime and post-war leniency was followed by Nikita Khrushchev's campaign (1958–1964) to eradicate religion as an outdated relic (Konecny 1995; Smolkin 2018, 21–84).

The brief interwar period was followed by the communist era in the entire region, which was marked by the communist regimes' atheistic stance and an extreme form of state secularism (with the exclusively secularist statism mode of governance of religion). This had debilitating and detrimental consequences for all religious groups in the region (Ramet 1989, 2002; Dragadze 2003; Froese 2008; Dunn 2019). The central narrative tried to frame religious beliefs as an anachronism that would disappear with economic and social progress (Ramet 1989; Dunn 2019). All religious communities in the then socialist-communist bloc were closely controlled by the government and only the major denominations (such as traditional Christian, Jewish, and Muslim) managed to continue religious life. But even they, particularly Catholics and Jews, bore the brunt of the atheistic communist policies and actions, which included anti-Zionist, anti-Papal, and wider anti-ecumenical and anti-cosmopolitan campaigns. Christian churches adapted to the political reality and sometimes (particularly Orthodox churches) even went into tactical collaboration with the communist regimes (Ramet 2002; Dragadze 2003; Froese 2008). In some of the countries of the region, however, the Catholic Church took upon itself the role of the preserver and protector of the Catholic identity of the citizens, and some of the clergy, clandestine monks and nuns participated in peaceful resistance to the national communist regimes, for which they often paid with their freedom (Ramet 2002; Dragadze 2003; Froese 2008). Nonetheless, several decades of state secularism resulted in a dramatic decline in religiosity among local populations, and by the end of the communist era a tangible part of the local population had turned away from religion, effectively becoming post-religious (agnostic, if not atheist).

Looking back to these past centuries, the Habsburg and the Russian empires both had very clear religious identities. In each case, this strong religious identity led to the preferential treatment of certain religious groups over others. This also created an asymmetric relationship between the preferred church and the state, where the state became the 'guardian' of the Catholic and the Orthodox churches respectively. Thus, the secularisation process in these empires meant the decreasing control of the state over religious issues paired with an increasing pluralisation, but equal treatment was never on the table. This relationship became extremely asymmetric during the communist era. However, even during this period, state treatment of religions differed, ranging from total marginalisation (of minority religious groups such as Jehovah's Witnesses, or Muslims in Hungary) to strict state control (of traditional churches).

Capturing the intra-regional differences in modes of governance of religious diversity

Following the collapse of the communist regimes in 1989–91 the religious rights of the region's citizens were not only formally reconfirmed, particularly through newly adopted constitutions and laws on religion, but also widely implemented. In Russia, however, the policy of conferring of religious rights and freedoms was limited chiefly to the historical religious collectivities, while the newcomer religious groups, though often formally entitled to them, in practice did not receive the expected religious rights and freedoms. In any case, state-recognised religious communities throughout the region were once again allowed to publicly engage in religious rituals and new religious communities started forming and seeking to register their organisations. The new national constitutions adopted under western liberal influence declared the states to be neutral towards religious organisations. This was a very short-lived liberal neutralism mode of governance of religious diversity, as the RCC and the ROC quickly made use of their, if not always formally conferred then certainly assumed by them, privileged status; the former through the Concordats with the Vatican, the latter through growth of its significance in the sociopolitical life of the country. In Central Europe, the signing of the Concordats created precedents for other traditional religious organisations to apply for similar treatment. The re-establishment of privileged status by the historically dominant churches may be judged as the first step away from liberal neutralism in these countries, towards moderate secularism and, eventually – in the case of Hungary and Slovakia – towards majoritarian nationalism.

Several other faith communities historically found on the territories of the Central Eastern European countries and Russia (like Jewish, Muslim, and some Protestant communities) were incorporated into the institutions that liaise between the state and religion, raising them above the others (non-traditional, registered, and unregistered) but still keeping them below the 'established' Christian denominations. The very distinction of what is officially or informally considered by the states as 'traditional' religious communities from others raises the question of equality between the former and the latter. In practice, the so-called 'traditional' religious communities and their representative organisations are treated preferentially by the state (in the form of financial assistance and wide-ranging social rights) (Račius 2020).

The initially liberal regimes of governance of religion paved the way to a proliferation of groups claiming to be, and registered as, faith communities. And, although in some countries there was concern about the appearance and establishment of ('dangerous') religious cults and sects, most of the groups wishing to register as religious did manage to institutionalise themselves. At the juncture of the millennia, the countries of Central Eastern Europe and Russia hosted a great variety of religious groups in otherwise highly secularised societies. In Hungary alone, for instance, there were more than 300 organisations registered as churches (the official name for registered religious organisations of any faith including those that do not have 'churches' in the Christian sense of the word) by 2010, a huge number compared to the small population of the country (Antalóczy 2013).

Lately, however, some of the countries in the region appear to be turning even further away from liberal secularism and the liberal neutralism mode of governance of religious diversity (Table 1) cherished in the immediate aftermath of the fall of the Iron Curtain. Beginning in the first decade of the twenty-first century, many governments in the region gradually introduced tougher regulations on the registration and operation of religious organisations. One reason for this may have been the securitised environment around certain religious, chiefly Muslim, collectivities after 9/11 (in Russia's case even before) and the terror attacks in European cities in the first decade of the millennium.

Table 1. Modes and norms for the governance of religious diversity.

Majoritarian Nationalism	• Strong state identification with one religion • May or may not include toleration for other religions • May or may not include personal religious laws • In radical cases the state takes over or controls the institutions and followers of one or more religions
Secularist Statism	• State control of religion • The state excludes religion from the political and the civic, confining religious freedom largely to the private sphere • This mode of secularism may be self-defined as part of the national identity • May include some support of some religions, but religion mainly seen as belonging to the private sphere
Liberal Neutralism	• Moral individualism – freedom of conscience • Anti-assimilation and equal civic standing of all religions • Religions are officially and socially tolerated • Active 'de-othering' but no 'recognition'
Moderate Secularism	• Moral individualism – freedom of conscience • Religions may enjoy equal or unequal status but all are officially and socially tolerated • Religion seen as a public good in need of support • Religion might also be seen as in need of regulation • Mutual autonomy but restricted neutrality, including 'weak' establishment and unequal recognition • Religious and non-religious citizens give each other generally accessible/dialogical reasons in politics

Table 2. Modelling state-religion relations in Central Eastern Europe and Russia.

	Liberal neutralism	Moderate secularism	Secularist statism	Majoritarian nationalism
Russia			DON	QON
Hungary		DON		QON
Slovakia		DON		QON
Lithuania	DON	QON		

QON = Qualifying Operative Norms; DON = Dominant Operative Norms.

There are relevant examples of moderate secularism, which could be considered as a dominant operative norm (DON) in a number of countries under research (Table 2). This includes the preferential treatment of certain religions and religious organisations over others, and the unequal status and differential recognition of religions in these countries. In addition, we are of the opinion that majoritarian nationalism is a qualifying operative norm (QON) that is also relevant in the region. Here, we would like to mention the strong identification with Christianity in Russia and Hungary but also in Slovakia, which is also codified in these countries. The increasing role of Christian religious institutions in public life is also worth mentioning here. Finally, the fact that some religious organisations are not recognised or face outright persecution is also remarkable. Looking at the dynamics of state-church relations, in the gradual shift in state-church relations we see a movement away from moderate secularism towards majoritarian nationalism in a number of countries.

Hungary

The current character of state-religion relations in Hungary was established after the coming to power of the current FIDESZ party-dominated government in 2010. Even though religion plays a steadily decreasing role in people's lives, as far the modes and norms of governance are concerned, the current government's policy returns some aspects of religion and religious organisations from the private to the public sphere.

Hungary adopted a new constitution in 2011, which, besides mentioning the appreciation of various religious traditions of the country, emphasises the role of Christianity as a force to preserve the Hungarian nation in its Preamble (Hungarian Parliament 2011). This is a major change from the previous constitution (1989–2011), which did not mention the role of Christianity or God in the text at all (Alkotmany.hu 2011). In this sense, the new constitution could be considered a step away from the secular neutrality of the state, since there is a special, symbolic place for Christianity in the text. Hungary's revised law on religions drastically cut the number of recognised religious organisations – initially to just 14, later to be raised to 27 (Antalóczy 2013) and eventually to 32 (Hungarian Parliament 2011). Due to domestic and international criticism (U.S. Department of State 2017) for curtailing freedom of religion, the Hungarian law on religions has been amended a number of times. The removal of recognition from a number of churches indicated the government's willingness to grant the privileged 'church' status to only a handful of organisations. Among the initial 14 religious organisations recognised there were no Muslim organisations. However, after the amendment of the law, two Muslim organisations also gained recognition.

Although the new constitution still defines the Hungarian state as separate from religious communities (Article VI) (Hungarian Parliament 2011) and freedom of religion is also guaranteed in the text, it also allows the government to cooperate with religious organisations for certain public interests or goals. In practice, this means that the state may decide to sign so-called Comprehensive Cooperation Agreements with certain religious organisations. As a result, these organisations are allowed to take over certain responsibilities from the state in providing public goods (education, social care, etc.) and receive financial assistance in return. This set-up not only erodes the idea of secular neutrality, but essentially de-secularises certain religious communities and the providing of certain public goods. Churches with such Comprehensive Agreements may receive government funding for running schools, hospitals, and care homes. They assume control over the institutions and services they take over (or take back), which used to be traditionally secular bodies and roles funded and provided by the state. As this process takes place with the active cooperation of the government, we see here a state-sponsored outsourcing and de-secularisation of public goods (Szurovecz 2021). In the process, these churches also regain certain parts of the public domain that were taken away from them historically. In this sense, this is not only a process of de-secularisation of privileged religious communities, but also a reconstruction of long-lost traditional social structures.

The preamble of the Hungarian Constitution mentions Christianity's special role in the sustaining of the Hungarian nation throughout history. In line with the above-mentioned identification of the state as an entity with a clear Christian heritage, it is not surprising that the government decided to sign Comprehensive Agreements with the country's major Christian churches (Hungarian Parliament 2011). The fact that the biggest 'born-again' Christian community of the country, Hit Gyülekezete (Congregation of the Faith), also signed such an agreement is an indication that closer ties with the government are not reserved only for traditional churches, but also for those communities that have a tangible following and do not openly criticise the government (Hit Gyülekezete 2020).

However, the state can use the question of recognition and the signing of the Comprehensive Agreements as a political tool to exert influence over religious organisations. This creates an asymmetric interdependent relationship between the state as the financer of certain religious groups and the churches that perform certain public duties (education, social services) in return.

After a number of international controversies, the latest amendment to the Law on Churches in 2018 took back recognition of religious organisations from the legislature and gave it to the judicial branch. The new amended Law on Churches also allows people to form religious associations. These associations do not need to be registered as churches but they may function as faith communities nevertheless. For legal recognition as a church, the three-tier system remains in place. This three-tier recognition of churches effectively enables the state to differentiate between 'old' and 'young' (recently registered) churches, giving clear advantage to larger and historically established communities (Government of Hungary 2018). For these reasons, we consider Hungary to be moving away from formerly liberal neutralism through moderate secularism towards an increasingly identitarian form of majoritarian nationalism.

Besides, the exclusive right of the government to consider whether to enter into a Comprehensive Cooperation Agreement with a church or not gives the executive and the supporting legislative branches of power the ability to treat certain religious groups preferentially, while also enabling it to marginalise others (Government of Hungary 2018). The fact that no Muslim organisations have been able to sign such an agreement with the state thus far is likely to be seen by the Muslim community as evidence that the state prefers some communities over others. One can see an apparent preference towards Christian churches and towards those communities that remain neutral or support certain government policies. However, some of those Christian communities that dared criticise the Hungarian government have experienced persecution from state authorities. The case of the Hungarian Evangelical Brotherhood (*Magyarországi Evangéliumi Testvérközösség*) is a good example. The leader of this organisation has been a vocal critic of the current FIDESZ-led government. As a result, the organisation has been facing ongoing persecution from state authorities, including withholding state funding (Cseke 2022).

With the preferential treatment of certain 'old' churches over other organisations, as discussed above, norms linked to moderate secularism could be considered as dominant operative norms (DON). To further support this argument, the multi-tier recognition system and the government's right to decide with whom it signs a Comprehensive Agreement, and the de-secularisation of preferentially treated organisations providing certain public goods, also points in the direction of moderate secularism. Moreover, the increasing role of Christianity in the public sphere and the fact that Islamic religious organisations, although receiving the highest level of recognition, have not been able to sign a Comprehensive Agreement with the government, indicates qualifying operative norms linked to majoritarian nationalism (QON).

Slovakia

The Slovakian case represents one of the most restrictive models of state-religion relations, if not in all of Europe, certainly in the EU. Admittedly, as may be expected of an EU member state, the Constitution of Slovakia (Article 24)[2] unequivocally guarantees religious freedom and the Law on Religious Freedom and the Legal Status of Churches and Religious Organisations (Article 1) re-confirms these constitutional provisions, establishing mutual autonomy between the state and religious collectivities and their organisations.

However, as the regime of governance of religion in Slovakia operates on a one-tier principle – all registered religious organisations are treated as equal before the law (that is, there is no formal distinction into 'traditional'/'historical' religious communities and others) (Article 4.2), the state 'recognises only those churches and religious societies that are registered' (Article 4.4). The RCC has an exceptionally privileged status, as Slovakia signed a Concordat with the Holy See in 2000. Similar agreements were signed in 2002 between the state and a dozen registered Christian religious organisations (churches) representing the country's Christian minorities.

Similarly to Hungary, Slovakia has also recently amended its legislation on religions making it next to impossible for smaller faith communities to get official registration (Slovak Parliament 2017). The previously liberal Law on Religious Freedom and the Legal Status of Churches was amended in 2007, requiring any religious community seeking to register their religious organisation to have a minimum of 20,000 members 'who have a residential address in the territory of the Slovak Republic and who are Slovak citizens' (Article 11) (Slovak Parliament 2007). In 2016, in the wake of the so-called 'European refugee crisis', the legislation on religions was amended once again, tilting Slovakia's mode of governance of religious diversity clearly towards majoritarian nationalism, where the state identifies with and extends support to practically one religion – Christianity in its forms registered in the country – and includes toleration for only those faith communities that are registered. Though the president vetoed the Law, arguing that the amendments curtailed religious freedoms and rights, his veto was overturned and the amendments were passed by two-thirds in the Parliament in 2017 (The Slovak Spectator 2017). The most telling amendment to the Law was the one that raised the minimum number of members for the registration of a religious organisation from 20,000 to 50,000 members who have to be Slovak citizens permanently residing in Slovakia.

The amendments' passage has been widely seen as putting a restraint on Muslims so that they do not form a religious organisation and institutionalise Islam in the country. Some observers even have labelled the process in the Law's amendment as the 'criminalisation of Islam in Slovakia' (Werleman 2018). In fact, Slovakia is unique in the EU as it is the only member state that does not have a legally registered Muslim religious organisation. It is difficult to see one being registered any time soon given that the total population of Muslim background in Slovakia barely exceeds 5,000 (Lenc 2022).

The amendments have had devastating consequences for practically all minor faith communities that formed in the past several decades as they are forced to register according to the Law on Civic Associations of 1990 – which, incidentally, explicitly states that the Law does not cover religious collectivities (Section 1, Point 1c)[3] (Citizens Civil Law 1990) – and operate as NGOs. Being registered as NGOs and not as religious organisations, these faith communities are stripped of many of the rights that registered religious organisations have, including building and owning places of worship and other property, establishing institutions of religious education, providing pastoral care, and lobbying for rights relating to diet, religious feasts, clothing etc. As a result, as of the beginning of 2021, there were just 18 registered religious organisations in Slovakia, of which only two were non-Christian (Office of International Religious Freedom 2021).

In conclusion, on the one hand norms of moderate secularism, such as moral individualism – freedom of conscience, religion being seen as a public good in need of support but also of regulation, as well as mutual autonomy but restricted neutrality, may be considered dominant operative norms (DON) in Slovakia. On the other hand, norms associated with majoritarian nationalism – strong state identification with one religion, selective toleration for other religions – should be seen as qualifying operative norms (QON).

Russia

Even though state-religion affairs in Russia stand out in the region, they still have many similarities with the Hungarian and Slovakian cases: the postcommunist period in the Russian Federation also started with the state of liberal neutralism, which indicated a movement towards postsecularism in a Habermasian understanding (Habermas 2006, 16–17). This postsecularism and liberal neutralism were enacted by Russia's main law, the Constitution (adopted in 1993).[4] Article 14 affirms that Russia has no state religion and that people are free to follow their beliefs. This opening up of religious freedom facilitated a mushrooming of a great variety of religious collectivities who found the Russian Federation fertile soil for their activities. Such a situation was satisfactory neither for the state, which had increasing security concerns, nor for the ROC, which aimed to control and dominate the country's spiritual dimension (Anderson 2007; Koesel 2017; Marsh 2013).

The Federal law 'On Freedom of Conscience and Religious Associations' (N125-F3), which was promoted by the ROC and adopted in 1997, ended the phase of liberal neutralism and moved the state towards moderate secularism by establishing a two-tier system, which distinguished between religious organisations and religious groups.[5] The latter would need not just formal registration to operate, but were required to inform the local authorities about their existence and practice. A religious organisation had to meet much stricter criteria for registration. Initially, it was proof of 15 years of uninterrupted functioning within the borders of the Russian Federation. This requirement was later abolished, but organisation founders still had to present documents describing the basis of the religion, the way it is practised, its attitude towards family values etc. Due to the vague definition of extremism and terrorism, other Federal laws (e.g. N114-F3 'On Countering Extremist Activities' adopted in 2002 or N35-F3 'On Countering Terrorism' adopted in 2006)[6] became convenient legal tools for the state security apparatus to outlaw any religious group whenever it was deemed necessary or expedient (Shterin and Dubrovsky 2019). This judicial frame ensured the state's tight grip on religious groups and organisations and laid the groundwork for the Russian Federation to move further from moderate secularism to majoritarian nationalism. In other words, as in Hungary only even earlier, the state made a significant move towards de-secularisation.

This move towards de-secularisation required establishing a certain hierarchy among the institutionalised religions. Naturally, the top place was reserved for Orthodox Christianity, which authorities informally recognise as the state religion, even if according to strictly legal terms the state is still secular. The special position of the ROC is clear even from the content of the above-mentioned laws. For instance, the Preamble of the law

N125-F3 emphasises the role of Orthodox Christianity in constructing Russian collective identity, strengthening common values, and fostering culture. It also mentions 'other traditional religions' but does not name them, which places the Russian Orthodox Church at the top of the hierarchy of religious organisations (Koesel 2017), making it a 'de facto state church' (USCIRF 2018, 73). This position of the ROC (under the leadership of Moscow Patriarchate) is also clear from the role that it conducts in the public sphere. For instance, Orthodox teaching dominates religious education in schools, while other faiths are effectively marginalised in what was initially meant as an inclusive and comprehensive religious education curriculum (Iakimova and Menshikov 2019; Eremin and Osmachko 2017). Furthermore, Orthodox priests conventionally bless new Russian weapons and soldiers going on a mission (NYpost 2020). Even though other institutionalised religions also have this opportunity, their participation in the public sphere on the federal level is less prominent. Thus, for instance, though Muslim religious leaders are quite visible publicly in the Muslim-majority federal units, they are certainly less so on the federal level.

Since the very beginning of his tenure in office in the 2000s, Vladimir Putin realised the social and even political power of the ROC and did his best to put it into the service of the state. He increasingly utilised institutionalised religions, especially the ROC, in the state's domestic and foreign politics. By doing this, Putin sought to gain an additional legitimation tool but, at the same time, this move enabled and strengthened the position of the ROC itself (Blitt 2011; Leustean 2018). The ROC, in turn, realised the advantage of the situation and used it to become the main player on Russia's religious ground, thus contributing to the de-secularisation of the state. This symbiosis between Russian political and religious elites is still, according to Anderson (2007), 'asymmetric' due to the dominance of the political elite, which is not surprising for an officially secular country.

Furthermore, the official separation of state and religion of the majority (Orthodox Christianity) in Russia became rather nominal following the ascendance of Vladimir Putin to power in 2000. The state leadership often accentuates its belonging to the Orthodox Church (Dunajeva and Koesel 2017). The president and members of the government have their 'private churches and priests', they regularly attend religious ceremonies and celebrations such as Easter and Christmas. The leaders of the Orthodox Church are also frequently invited to official meetings or ceremonies of the government (Yakhyaev and Kamyshova 2013). Moreover, Orthodox hierarchs are actively involved in the state's domestic and foreign affairs, supporting state politics and providing diplomatic communication channels (e.g. with Georgia after the 2008 war).

In conclusion, although officially Russia is a secular country, there is significant connection between the state, politics, and religion. The exceptional position of the ROC and its importance for state politics has encouraged the thriving of majoritarian nationalism in some regions of Russia. However, the state balances its support for the ROC by redirecting funds to other religious groups including Muslims, who constitute the second-largest religious group in the country (Yakhyaev and Kamyshova 2013). The federal and regional authorities, apparently for security concerns, promote the spread of institutionalised Islam at the expense of non-institutionalised. This is especially observable in some of the 'Muslim' republics of the North Caucasus. For instance, to promote institutionalised Islam in Chechnya, the republican government even established the positions of aides to the Head of the Republic Ramzan Kadyrov, who also shapes and reshapes the religious life of the society according to his political needs.

Additionally, Russia's transition from a more liberal mode of governance of religion has been also very much tied to the state objective of preventing religious radicalisation. In the climate of the state's tightening grip on the social and political activities of religious organisations, politically active non-institutionalised groups (e.g. Salafis) and those labelled as sectarian (e.g. Jehovah's Witnesses) have experienced regular pressure and persecution from the state (Ivanenko 2020; Laruelle 2020).

Lithuania

Among the four countries under investigation in this article, Lithuania to this day continues to represent the most moderate, if not liberal, model of state-religion relations. Since the adoption of relevant legislation (the Constitution in 1992 and the Law on Religious Communities and Associations, passed in 1995), Lithuania has been and continues to represent the liberal neutralism mode of governance of religious diversity with moral individualism – freedom of conscience enshrined in them and practically all religions officially and socially tolerated.

Nonetheless, religions in Lithuania legally enjoy unequal status, as the foundational law of the country, the Constitution – besides guaranteeing religious freedom to the country's inhabitants in a number of its articles – makes an explicit distinction in Article 43 between what it refers to as a) 'traditional', b) 'state-recognised' 'churches'[7] and religious organisations, and c) those that are merely 'registered', though, admittedly, it remains silent on which ones fall under which category (Seimas of the Republic of Lithuania 1992). Article 5 of the Law on Religious Communities and Associations states: 'The State shall recognise nine traditional religious communities and associations existing in Lithuania, which comprise a part of Lithuania's historical, spiritual and social heritage: Roman Catholic, Greek Catholic, Evangelical Lutheran, Evangelical Reformed, Russian Orthodox, Old Believer, Jewish, Sunni Muslim and Karaite' (Seimas of the Republic of Lithuania 1995). This distinction and inclusion of nine denominations reveals certain features of pluralistic nationalism (difference-sensitive identity recognition and institutional accommodation of religious diversity) but also compromises the principle of the state's secular neutrality.

Article 43 of the Constitution declares that there is no state religion in Lithuania; thus, all of the traditional religious communities named in the Law on Religious Communities and Associations are formally equal, both *vis-à-vis* the state and among themselves. Non-Christian religious communities such as Karaites, Jews, and Sunni Muslims, with their share in the country's population hovering around or less than 0.1%, formally have the same rights as the Roman Catholic community, which stood at over 77% at the time of the last population census in 2011 (Department of Statistics 2013, 5).

In practice, however, the numerically dominant RCC gets preferential treatment from the state and public institutions, hence certain features of majoritarian nationalism (state identification with, and support for, one religion) are discernible. For instance, the RCC has its representative on the Council of the national TV and radio broadcaster (LRT), and Roman Catholic priests serve in state institutions (Armed Forces, Border Police) as salaried chaplains and are otherwise routinely invited to bless state property (newly opening premises, police cars) and perform rituals at military events (by blessing unit flags).

Article 14 of the Law on Religious Communities and Associations clearly prioritises 'traditional' religious communities over 'non-traditional' ones by stipulating that 'Educational and training establishments of traditional religious communities and associations providing general education of the national standard shall be funded and maintained in accordance with the procedure established by the Government or an institution authorised by it, allocating the same amount of the budget funds as allocated to state or municipal educational establishments of the corresponding type (level)' (Seimas of the Republic of Lithuania 1995). The inequality between religious communities has become evident in the practical application of the Law on Religious Communities and Associations in various other fields. As an example, for the past two decades the traditional religious communities have received, through their legal persons, annual payments from the state. The amount of these payments is divided proportionally, based on the number of believers recorded by the Department of Statistics.

The legally *de facto* unequal status of religious communities of different categories discernible in both the Lithuanian Constitution and the Law on Religious Communities and Associations, as well as a plethora of subsequent laws, was challenged at the turn of the century by a group of MPs who approached the Constitutional Court for an explanation. The Court, on two occasions in 2000 and 2007, endorsed the status quo promulgated in the Constitution (Constitutional Court 2000, 2007). There have also been attempts, thus far unsuccessful, to profoundly change the Law on Religious Communities and Associations – the draft law prepared by the Ministry of Justice has been shelved by Parliament.

Ultimately, on the one hand, certain norms of liberal neutralism, for instance moral individualism – freedom of conscience and official and social toleration of all religions, remain dominant operative norms (DON) in Lithuania. On the other hand, a number of norms of moderate secularism, such as unequal status of religions due to a multi-tiered recognition and benefits system, religion being seen as a public good in need of support, and preferred religions potentially becoming providers of certain public goods taking them over from the state, are qualifying operative norms (QON).

Discussion

As is evident from the cases presented above, the region of Central Eastern Europe and Russia is somewhat diverse in terms not only of the confessional composition of the inhabitants of different countries of the region, but also state-religion relations. Therefore, one should be careful and not see the region of Central East Europe and Russia as having identical state-religion relations. Quite the opposite, one needs to appreciate the differences in the regimes of governance of religion in the countries of the region while being able to recognise certain similarities.

Based on the analysis of the dynamics in state-religion relations, one can, however, talk of a number of dominant operative norms (DON) and qualifying operative norms (QON) common to the countries under investigation. First, the state identifies with one denomination (Roman Catholic or Russian Orthodox) of one religion (Christianity), formally or informally recognised as 'traditional', but religion is mainly seen as belonging to the private sphere with occasional instrumentalisation of it by the state. Second, one may observe a rise of religious nationalism of identitarian nature in Slovakia, Hungary, and

Russia. Third, one may also discern that religion is often seen as a public good/danger in need of support and regulation. Thus, in most of the countries analysed, only the institutionalised forms of religion (registered religious organisations) are allowed to operate freely in a public sense. Consequently, individual freedom and institutional accommodation is offered only to believers of registered religions qualified by severe diversity-restricting toleration. In Lithuania, on the contrary, moral individualism and freedom of conscience remain paramount and practically all religions are officially and socially tolerated.

One of the most striking commonalities in regard to state-religion relations among some of the Višegrad countries, most notably Hungary and Slovakia, is a recent turn by their governments towards the instrumentalisation of religion. The majoritarian Christian identity that is also tangible in the Hungarian Constitution is a political cornerstone for the government that aims to instrumentalise religion. Preserving Hungary's Christian identity has been used by the government to shape public discourse on international migration. Besides, as in Slovakia, the negative narrative on migration was also linked to Muslims and Islam, which was put into a security framework (Buzan, Weaver, and de Wilde 1998). Even though the government emphasises that Muslims in Hungary are free to practise their religion and enjoy the protection of the law and the state, the Hungarian government, like the Slovak one, is also clear about not wanting any more Muslims to settle in the country (Portfolio 2015).

The instrumentalisation of religion betrays another common trend: a turning away from liberal secularism and the secular neutrality of the state. This may be a temporary detour but it may well turn out to be an indication of a somewhat illiberal 'postsecular condition' that may lead to novel forms of state-religion relations, which might purportedly be much more selective and discriminatory. As a result, the 'traditional' religious communities and their representative organisations could receive increasing support from the state, which can be considered a process of de-secularisation. However, the 'non-traditional' faith communities could be further marginalised, stigmatised, and securitised, with some of them being either pushed underground or to extinction in a process of forced secularisation. At the same time, the spiritual administrations of the favoured 'traditional' religious communities may opt for public support of government policies (in fact, this is already observable in some of the Višegrad countries) and also seek to promote their own 'de-secularisation' agenda.

One can observe in the political elites of Slovakia and Hungary a clear turn towards populist instrumental religious nationalism, when not only fringe marginal political parties but also mainstream ones and even those in power have started resorting to rhetoric full of religious symbolism and a sense of a clash of civilisations, the latter understood almost exclusively in religious terms. As a corollary to this, the political rhetoric of top politicians (certainly in Slovakia and Hungary) increasingly contains if not manifest then certainly latent Muslimophobia or Islamophobia, something that became a new norm in the wake of the so-called 'European migrant crisis' of 2015–2016. This, however, cannot be said about Russia, the government of which has to keep in mind the need not to antagonise its significant Muslim population, not least because of fears of radicalisation. However, the instrumentalisation of religion or the way religion is treated by governments in the region may change depending on which political party leads the government. Thus, unlike in Russia, one may see dynamic changes in Central Eastern

Europe, as there is no general consensus in society on the role religion should play in the public domain.

Conclusions

Though the countries of the region of Central Eastern Europe and Russia share much common history and recent experiences, state-religion relations and modes of governance of religious diversity found in them, as shown through the cases of the countries analysed in this contribution, nonetheless differ. So, for instance, if Lithuania continues to represent the liberal neutralism mode grounded in a general freedom of religion and nine faith communities (Christian, Jewish and Muslim) recognised as 'traditional', with some features of majoritarian nationalism and pluralistic ('unity in diversity') nationalism, Slovakia has come to clearly represent the majoritarian nationalism mode grounded in a freedom of religion for only registered (state-recognised) faith communities, with some features of secularist statism. Hungary and Russia, meanwhile, represent two variants of moderate secularism. In the case of Hungary, the state plays an active role *vis-à-vis* the regulation and the utilisation of certain religious denominations and its mode features many elements of majoritarian nationalism and secularist statism. In the case of Russia, as in Slovakia, its mode is grounded in a general freedom of religion for registered (state-recognised) faith communities. It also includes many elements of secularist statism with official tolerance towards other religions and majoritarian nationalism that demonstrates favouritism towards Orthodox Christianity.

Overall, the dynamics of state-religion relations in the region of Central Eastern Europe and Russia in the foreseeable future does not look promising if viewed from the liberal secularism/secular neutrality/freedom of religion perspective. Of particular concern are state-Islam relations, which in some of the countries covered, namely Slovakia and Hungary, are already at a very low point, with Muslims (particularly of immigrant background) being increasingly securitised by the media, the public, and the national political elites.

Notes

1. In this contribution, the region of Central Eastern Europe is understood as comprising three Baltic States (Estonia, Latvia, Lithuania) and four Višegrad States (Poland, Czechia, Slovakia, Hungary).
2. Constitution of Slovak Republic [01 October 1992]. Available online at https://www.prezident.sk/upload-files/46422.pdf. Accessed 06 September 2022.
3. Citizens Civil Law Associations Act No. 83/1990, 1990-03-27. Available online at https://www.ilo.org/dyn/natlex/docs/ELECTRONIC/99932/119583/F-255803203/SVK99932%20Eng.pdf. Accessed 04 November 2021.
4. Constitution of the Russian Federation [12 December 1993]. Available online at www.constitution.ru. Accessed 12 September 2021.
5. Lower Chamber of the Russian Parliament State Duma. 1997. Federal law 'On freedom of conscience and religious associations' (N125-F3) (*Federalnyi zakon 'O svobode sovesti i o religioznykh obed"ineniiakh ot 26 sentiabria 1997'*). Available online at http://kremlin.ru/acts/bank/11523. Accessed 12 September 2021.

6. Lower Chamber of the Russian Parliament State Duma. 2002. Federal law 'On countering extremist activities' (N114-F3) (*Federalnyi zakon ot 25.07.2002 'O protivodeistvii ekstremistskoi deiatel'nosti'*). Available online at http://kremlin.ru/acts/bank/18939; Lower Chamber of the Russian Parliament State Duma. 2006. Federal law 'On countering terrorism' (N35-F3) (*Federalnyi zakon ot 06.03.2006 'O protivodeistvii terrorizmu'*). Available online at http://www.kremlin.ru/acts/bank/23522. Both accessed 12 September 2021.
7. The term 'church' used in the Constitution of the Republic of Lithuania is to be understood as a generic term synonymous to 'formalised religious hierarchy'.

Disclosure statement

No potential conflict of interest was reported by the author

Funding

The GREASE project, on which this contribution is based, has received funding from the European Union's Horizon 2020 research and innovation programme under grant agreement number 770640.

ORCID

Daniel Vekony http://orcid.org/0000-0002-7531-0447
Marat Iliyasov http://orcid.org/0000-0003-0703-4716
Egdūnas Račius http://orcid.org/0000-0001-8296-4062

References

Alkotmany.hu, 2011. *1949. Ei XX. Torveny A Magyar Koztarsasag Alkotmanya*. Accessed 9 June2019. https://alkotmany.hu/alkotmanyok/hatalyos/hatalyosalkotmany.pdf.

Anderson, J. 2007. "Putin and the Russian Orthodox Church: Asymmetric Symphonia?." *Journal of International Affairs* 61 (1): 185–201.

Antalóczy, P. 2013. "Az Alaptörvény és az egyházakra vonatkozó legújabb szabályozás dimenziói." *Jog, Állam, Politika* 4 (3): 23–38.

Berger, P. L. 2014. *The Many Altars of Modernity: Toward a Paradigm for Religion in a Pluralist Age*. Berlin and Boston: De Gruyter.

Blitt, R. C. 2011. "Whither Secular Bear: The Russian Orthodox Church's Strengthening Influence on Russia's Domestic and Foreign Policy." *Fides Et Libertas: The Journal of the International Religious Liberty Association*. University of Tennessee Legal Studies Research Paper No. 173, 89–125. https://ssrn.com/abstract=2008331.

Buzan, B., O. Weaver, and J. de Wilde. 1998. *Security: A New Framework for Analysis*. Boulder, CO: Lynne Rienner.

Chudžíková, A. 2011. "Muslims in Slovakia: Search for Identity and Status in Majority Society." In *Muslims in Visegrad*, edited by J. Bureš, 39–56. Prague: Institute of International Relations.

Coleman, H. J. 2005. *Russian Baptists and Spiritual Revolution, 1905–1929*. Bloomington: Indiana University Press.

Constitutional Court of the Republic of Lithuania. 2000. "Ruling on the compliance of Item 5 of Article 1, Paragraphs 3 and 4 of Article 10, Paragraph 1 of Article 15, Article 20, Item 2 of Article 21, Paragraph 2 of Article 32, Paragraphs 2, 3 and 4 of Article 34, Items 2 and 5 of Article 35, Item 2 of Article 37 and Items 2 and 3 of Article 38 of the Republic of Lithuania's Law on Education with the Constitution of the Republic of Lithuania." 13 June. Accessed 20 December 2017. http://www.lrkt.lt/en/court-acts/search/170/ta1161/content.

Constitutional Court of the Republic of Lithuania. 2007. "Decision on Construing the Provisions of a Constitutional Court Ruling Related with the Status of the Churches and Religious Organisations That are Traditional in Lithuania." 6 December. Accessed 19 December 2017. http://www.lrkt.lt/en/court-acts/search/170/ta1375/content

Crews, R. 2003. "Empire and the Confessional State: Islam and Religious Politics in Nineteenth-Century Russia." *The American Historical Review* 108 (1): 50–83. doi:10.1086/533045.

Crews, R. D. 2009. *For Prophet and Tsar: Islam and Empire in Russia and Central Asia*. Cambridge, Mass: Harvard University Press.

Cseke, B. 2022. "Tíz éve tart Iványi Gábor és Orbán Viktor Küzdelme." Telex.hu. Accessed 4 August 2022. https://telex.hu/belfold/2022/02/21/ivanyi-gabor-magyar-evangeliumi-testverkozosseg-nav.

Department of Statistics. 2013. *Gyventojai pagal tautybę, gimtąją kalbą ir tikybą*. Vilnius: Statistics Lithuania. Accessed 27 September 2019. https://osp.stat.gov.lt/documents/10180/217110/Gyv_kalba_tikyba.pdf/1d9dac9a-3d45-4798-93f5-941fed00503f.

Dragadze, T. 2003. "The Domestication of Religion Under Soviet Communism." In *Socialism. Ideals, Ideologies, and Local Practice*, edited by C. M. Hann, 188–198. London: Routledge.

Dunajeva, J., and K. J. Koesel. 2017. "'Us versus Them': The Politics of Religion in Contemporary Russia." *The Review of Faith & International Affairs* 15 (1): 56–67. doi:10.1080/15570274.2017.1284402.

Dunn, D. J. 2019. *Religion and Modernization in the Soviet Union*. New York: Routledge.

Eisenstadt, S. N. 2000. "The Reconstruction of Religious Arenas in the Framework of 'Multiple Modernities'." *Millenium: Journal of International Studies* 29 (3): 591–611.

Eremin, A., and S. Osmachko. 2017. "The Education Activity of the Russian Orthodox Church in the Contemporary Transcultural Space of Russia." *Procedia – Social and Behavioral Sciences* 237: 1475–1481. doi:10.1016/j.sbspro.2017.02.232.

Froese, P. 2008. *The Plot to Kill God: Findings from the Soviet Experiment in Secularization*. Berkley and Los Angeles: University of California Press.

Furman, D. 1989. *Religia, ateism i perestroika. Na puti k svobode sovesti*. Moscow: Progress.

Geraci, R. P., and M. Khodarkovsky, eds. 2001. *Of Religion and Empire: Missions, Conversion, and Tolerance in Tsarist Russia*. Ithaca, NY: Cornell University Press.

Government of Hungary. 2018. "évi CXXXII. törvény a lelkiismereti és vallásszabadság jogáról, valamint az egyházak, vallásfelekezetek és vallási közösségek jogállásáról szóló 2011". évi CCVI. törvény módosításáról. *Magyar Közlöny* 208: 36140–36154, December 21.

Habermas, J. 2006. "Religion in the Public Sphere." *European Journal of Philosophy* 14 (1): 1–25. doi:10.1111/j.1468-0378.2006.00241.x.

Habermas, J. 2008. "Notes on Post-Secular Society." *New Perspectives Quarterly* 25 (4): 17–29. doi:10.1111/j.1540-5842.2008.01017.x.

Hit Gyülekezete. 2020. "A Megállapodás Teljes Szövege." Accessed 4 August 2022. https://www.hit.hu/hirek/kormany-megallapodas-teljes-szovege.

Hungarian Parliament. 2011. *Magyarorszag Alaptorvenye*. Accessed 9 June2019. https://www.parlament.hu/irom39/02627/02627.pdf.

Iakimova, O. A., and A. S. Menshikov. 2019. "Religious Education in Russian Schools: Plans, Pains, Practices." *Changing Societies & Personalities* 3 (4): 373–387. doi:10.15826/csp.2019.3.4.083.

Ivanenko, S. 2020. "Opposition to Jehovah's Witnesses in Russia: The Anti-Cult Context. The Role of Anti-Cult Myths About Jehovah's Witnesses in the Increasing Persecution of This Denomination in the Russian Federation." *The Journal of CESNUR* 4 (6): 25–40.

Koesel, K. J. 2017. "Religion and the Regime: Cooperation and Conflict in Contemporary Russia and China." *World Politics* 69 (4): 676–712. doi:10.1017/S004388711700017X.

Konecny, P. 1995. "A Review of *Religion, State and Politics in the Soviet Union and Successor States* by John Anderson." *Canadian Journal of History* 30 (2): 356. doi:10.3138/cjh.30.2.356.

Laruelle, M. 2020. "Making Sense of Russia's Illiberalism." *Journal of Democracy* 31 (3): 115–129. doi:10.1353/jod.2020.0049.

Lenc, J. 2022. "Slovakia." In *Yearbook of Muslims in Europe*, Volume. 13, edited by S. Müssig, E. Račius, S. Akgönül, A. Alibašić, J. S. Nielsen, and O. Scharbrodt, 586–599. Leiden: Brill.

Leustean, L. N. 2018. "Eastern Orthodoxy, Geopolitics and the 2016 'Holy and Great Synod of the Orthodox Church'." *Geopolitics* 23 (1): 201–216. doi:10.1080/14650045.2017.1350843.

Levada-Center. 2013. "Rossiyane o religii." Accessed 22 June 2022. https://www.levada.ru/2013/12/24/rossiyane-o-religii/.

Malashenko, A. 2011. "Islam in Russia: Religion and Politics." In *Will Russia Become a Muslim Society?*, edited by H.-G. Heinrich, L. Lobova, and A. Malashenko, 13–38. Frankfurt am Main: Peter Lang.

Marsh, C. 2013. "Eastern Orthodoxy and the Fusion of National and Spiritual Security." In *The Routledge Handbook of Religion and Security*, edited by C. Seiple, D. Hoover, and P. Otis, 22–32. Oxford: Routledge.

NYpost. 2020. "Russia's Orthodox Church Wants Priests to Stop Blessing Nuclear Weapons." *New York Post*. 5 February.https://nypost.com/2020/02/05/russias-orthodox-church-wants-priests-to-stop-blessing-nuclear-weapons/.

Office of International Religious Freedom. 2021. *2020 Report on International Religious Freedom: Slovak Republic*. https://www.state.gov/reports/2020-report-on-international-religious-freedomesskiaa/.

Parmaksız, U. 2018. "Making Sense of the Postsecular." *European Journal of Social Theory* 21 (1): 98–119. doi:10.1177/1368431016682743.

Pew Research Center. 2017. *Religious Belief and National Belonging in Central and Eastern Europe*. https://www.pewforum.org/2017/05/10/religious-belief-and-national-belonging-in-central-and-eastern-europe/.

Portfolio, H. 2015. *Orbán elárulta, mi lesz a menekültkérdés végső tétje*. Accessed 13 January 2020. https://www.portfolio.hu/gazdasag/20150907/orban-elarulta-mi-lesz-a-menekultkerdes-vegso-tetje-219172.

Račius, E. 2020. "The Legal Notion of 'Traditional' Religions in Lithuania and Its Socio-Political Consequences." *The Journal of Law and Religion* 35 (1): 61–78. doi:10.1017/jlr.2020.9.

Raj, T. 1996. *Az Izraelita vallás egyenjogúsítása és a zsidó szervezetek*. Accessed 29 October 2021. https://www.szombat.org/archivum/az-izraelita-vallas-egyenjogusitasa-es-a-zsido-szervezetek.

Ramet, P. 1989. "The Interplay of Religious Policy and Nationalities Policy in the Soviet Union and Eastern Europe." In *Religion and Nationalism in Soviet and East European Politics*, edited by P. Ramet, 3–41. Durham: Duke University Press.

Ramet, S. 2002. "Politics and Religion in Eastern Europe and the Soviet Union." In *Politics and Religion in the Modern World*, edited by G. Moyser, 67–95. London: Routledge.

Roy, O. 2019. *Is Europe Christian?* London: Hurst & Company.

Seimas of the Republic of Lithuania. 1992. "Constitution of the Republic of Lithuania". https://e-seimas.lrs.lt/portal/legalAct/lt/TAD/TAIS.21892.

Seimas of the Republic of Lithuania. 1995. "Law on Religious Communities and Associations of the Republic of Lithuania". https://e-seimas.lrs.lt/portal/legalAct/lt/TAD/TAIS.385299?jfwid=16j6tpgu6w.

Shterin, M., and D. Dubrovsky. 2019. "Academic Expertise and Anti-Extremism Litigation in Russia: Focusing on Minority Religions." *The Soviet and Post-Soviet Review* 46 (2): 211–236. doi:10.1163/18763324-04602006.

Slovak Parliament. 2007. "Act No. 201/2007 of 29 March 2007 Amending Act No. 308/1991 on Freedom of Religious Belief and the Status of Churches and Religious Societies as Amended by Act No". 394/2000. https://www.noveaspi.sk/products/lawText/1/65138/1/2#c_42. Accessed 04 November 2021.

Slovak Parliament. 2017. "Act No. 39/2017 of 31 January 2017 Amending Act No. 308/1991 on Freedom of Religious Belief and the Status of Churches and Religious Societies". Accessed 4 November 2021. https://www.noveaspi.sk/products/lawText/1/88029/1/2.

The Slovak Spectator. 2017. "Registration of Churches to Become Stricter." 2-1. Accessed 4 November 2021. https://spectator.sme.sk/c/20448220/registration-of-churches-to-become-stricter.html.

Smolkin, V. 2018. *A Sacred Space is Never Empty. A History of Soviet Atheism*. Princeton and Oxford: Princeton University Press.

Sulok, S. 2010. *Muslim Minority in Hungary*. Budapest: Organisation of Muslims in Hungary.

Szurovecz, I. 2021. "Kiss-Rigó Lászlóék veszik át a budapesti állami nevelőszülői hálózatot". 444.hu, Accessed 4 August 2022. https://444.hu/2021/05/28/kiss-rigo-laszloek-veszik-at-a-budapesti-allami-neveloszuloi-halozatot.

USCIRF. 2018. "United States Commission on International Religious Freedom Annual Report." Accessed 25 April 2018. https://www.uscirf.gov/sites/default/files/USCIRFannual2018_tagged508.pdf.

U.S. Department of State. 2017. "2016 Report on International Religious Freedom: Hungary". Accessed 9 June 2018. https://www.state.gov/reports/2016-report-on-international-religious-freedom/hungary/.

Werleman, C.J. 2018. "Slovakia's Deplorable Move to Criminalise Islam." *The New Arab*, September 18. Accessed 4 November 2021. https://www.alaraby.co.uk/english/comment/2018/9/18/slovakias-deplorable-move-to-criminalise-islam.

Yakhyaev, M., and E. Kamyshova. 2013. "Vlast i religiya v sovremennoy Rossii: metamorfozy zaimodeistviya." *Islamovedenie* 15 (1): 6–19.

Negotiating religion-state relations in the MENA region: actors' dynamics, modes, and norms

Georges Fahmi and Mehdi Lahlou

ABSTRACT

Religion-state relations in the MENA region have been shaped by two main dynamics. First is the modern political elites' interest in shaping their own versions of Islam to legitimise their rule. Second is the desire of religious actors to use modern state structures to impose their religious norms on society. Despite moments of tension, political and religious leaders have often reached a compromise on regulating the relationship between Islam and the state. In different cases, different agreements that reflect the different balances of power between political and religious actors have been reached. These agreements between political and religious authorities have been contested twice, leading in some cases to a renegotiation of their terms: the first time with the religious revival in 1970s, and the second after the 2011 popular uprisings known as the Arab Spring. This contribution seeks to unpack these dynamics between political and religious elites, their impact on the rules governing religion-state relations, how they have been renegotiated over time, and how these different institutional arrangements have created their own norms, policies, and practices, highlighting the gaps between formal mechanisms and informal practices.

Introduction

The nineteenth century witnessed the formation of modern nation-states in different parts of the MENA region. Agreements with the state elite were imposed on religious actors, and the role of religion in both state and society was regulated by a new modern elite. However, there is internal variation in the historical pathways through which religious authorities were subjected to the new governments in the region. Each of these agreements between the political and the religious authorities reflects a different power dynamic between the two authorities and their claims for political and religious legitimacy. This contribution looks at five cases in the MENA region (see Figure 1) that each represent a different historical path.[1] At one end of the spectrum, Morocco represents a case where the political regime itself, in the shape of the king, enjoys claims to religious legitimacy. On the opposite end of the spectrum, the cases of Turkey and Tunisia

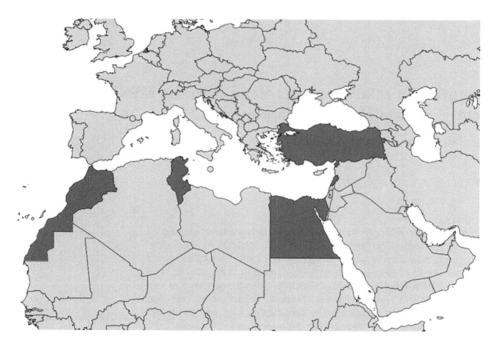

Figure 1. MENA countries covered in this contribution: Morocco, Tunisia, Egypt, Lebanon, and Turkey.

represent modes where the secular political regimes (at least under Ataturk and Bourguiba) fully controlled religious authorities. The case of Egypt is one where political regimes have maintained the upper hand, while it could not ignore the religious legitimacy of Egypt's historical and deeply rooted religious establishment (al-Azhar).[2] Within this pattern of religion-state relations, the case of Lebanon seems to be the exception. Lebanon follows a confessional system, structured within the framework of consociationalism and based on the existence of an extremely politicised and polarised religious diversity. In order to analyse these different cases, the contribution has relied on secondary sources, content analysis of official documents and newspaper articles, as well as fieldwork in Morocco, Tunisia, and Egypt.

Religion-state agreements in the region have been contested twice, leading in some cases to a renegotiation of their terms. The first time was due to changes in the religious landscape in the 1970s, with a religious revival in many countries of the region. Political regimes responded to the return of religion by allowing more space for both religious ideas and religious actors in the public sphere. The second was due to changes in the political landscape after the 2011 popular uprisings known as the Arab Spring, leading in some cases to Islamist groups rising to power, as in Egypt and Tunisia.

This contribution seeks to analyse dynamics between political and religious actors during these shifts and how they have influenced both the modes and norms of governance of religion-state relations in the region. It focuses on five cases: Turkey, Egypt, Tunisia, Morocco, and Lebanon.

Historical review

Modern nation-state formation

The rise of the nation-state, as a new ruling structure in the region to govern the relationship between the ruling elites and their societies, created tensions between traditional religious actors and the new modern elite in MENA societies. The transition from dynasty to nation-state had a deep impact on the role of the religious actors and their religious claims. While dynastic rule could co-exist with religious actors' claims, the nation-state is by its very nature intolerant of any competing claim for authority. After the nation-state became an institutional reality, state elites and Islamic religious actors had to negotiate agreements to decide on religion-state relations in the new institutional environment. Religious actors first refused to be subservient to the new state and insisted on an important role for religious values in shaping these new modern institutions. Such claims often clashed with the interests of new modern elites. Country by country, different agreements were reached between the state elite and religious actors, through which the role of religion in both state and society was institutionalised.

When Mohammad Ali came to power in Egypt in 1805, he initiated the first steps towards Egypt's modernisation with the aim of having a modern army that could help expand his rule. Mohammad Ali's modernisation both inspired and threatened the Ottoman elite, especially after they witnessed the performance of the Egyptian army in the battle against Greek rebels in 1825 (Ahmad 1993). In 1839 the Ottoman elite adopted the Hatt Şerif of Gülhane (Noble Edict of the Rose Chamber) that introduced a radical programme of reforms. These reforms became also known as the *Tanzimat*, including the reorganisation of the Ottoman state structure, of civil, territorial, and trade laws, and of the judiciary. Tunisia witnessed a process of modernisation similar to that of both Egypt and Turkey, starting in the nineteenth century with its first reforming monarch, Ahmad Bey (1837–1855). As with Egypt's Mohammed Ali, while the modernisation project aimed mainly at modernising the Tunisian military, these reforms also impacted on education and the judiciary, reducing the influence of religious actors in these two spheres.

In 1922 Britain unilaterally accorded Egypt its independence, and in 1923 Ataturk established the Turkish Republic after the implosion of the Ottoman Empire. For both polities, a debate over the constitutional basis of the state commenced. Egypt adopted its first constitution in 1923, which recognised Islam as the state religion but also stated that all powers emanated from the nation. After a group of young military officers staged a military coup and took control of power in 1952, a new constitution was adopted in 1956 and the same status of Islam as a state religion was retained. After he assumed power, Anwar Sadat adopted a new constitution in 1971 and, besides declaring Islam the state religion, Islamic law (Sharia) was specified as one of the sources of legislation. The 1971 Constitution was amended again after a referendum in 1980, making the principles of Islamic Sharia 'the' main source of legislation. However, as Hisham Hellyer has argued, 'the Sharia Article acts as a restraining mechanism in terms of legal precedent, rather than an active, positive law-making mechanism that then results in further legislation one way or another' (Hellyer 2021, 221).

As for Turkey, the 1924 Constitution made Islam the state religion. However, only four years later the Turkish Constitution was amended so that Islam was no longer recognised as the state religion. Moreover, in 1937, the adjective *'laik'* (secular) was added to the Constitution to define the nature of the Turkish state. According to Serif Mardin, despite the extensive secularisation of the nineteenth century, birth, education, culture, marriage, death, and inheritance still required the services of the *ulama* (Islamic scholarly authorities) during this period. From 1937, however, these practices were secularised (Mardin 2006, 233–34).

In July 1957 the Tunisian republic was declared, and one of the most prominent figures in the struggle for independence, Habib Bourguiba, became Tunisia's first president. The Tunisian Constitution adopted in 1959 stated Islam as Tunisia's religion.

Unlike the paths followed by Turkey, Egypt, and Tunisia, Morocco has been ruled since the sixteenth century by a dynasty claiming to be descended from the Prophet Muhammad. This dynasty initiated certain modernisation attempts in the nineteenth century, and in 1912 it accepted the French protectorate under pressure from the colonial system. Lahlou and Zouiten argue that 'while the king's authority was exerted only partially throughout the territory, he used this new political context to establish his legitimacy over the entire territory' (Lahlou and Zouiten 2021, 241).

Since its independence in 1956, Morocco's ruling elites have chosen a version of a nationalised and territorialised Islam. In 1962 Islam was declared the official state religion, but the state maintained full religious freedom for Christians and Jews. Moroccan law is based on Sharia law as rooted in the legal system of Sunni Islam. Sharia law is assured through the constitutional provisions which name the king 'Commander of the Faithful' (*Amir Al-Mouminin*), tasked with ensuring respect for Islam throughout the legal system. Since the 1962 Constitution, the Moroccan monarch bears the additional title of Commander of the Faithful, indicating his status as a leader not only on political but also on spiritual grounds. This does not make Morocco a theocratic state, since legal codes vary and include secular French law, while an elected parliament has legislative power up to a certain extent. Rather, Morocco represents until now a case where the regime of the king is the only political institution that is constitutionally allowed to combine both political and religious powers (El-Katiri 2013, 55).

The religious revival

Starting in the 1970s, an Islamic religious resurgence has been occurring in every Islamic society in the region regardless of size and political, economic, and cultural environment (Dekmejian 1980, 1–2). In both Turkey and Egypt, incumbent regimes used religion and religious actors as tools to deal with domestic challenges, namely, the Islamic insurgence in Egypt and the Kurdish insurgence in Turkey. During the 1980s and 1990s, both regimes faced armed insurgencies and neared civil war. For both regimes, religion became an important tool with which to face these challenges.

The Egyptian regime responded to the radical Islamic threat by adopting a strategy which treated the various groups differently, depending on their threat to or support for the regime. This distinction was a part of the regime's strategy for allowing non-violent Islamic voices space within the state and civil society (Bianchi 1989). In Turkey, meanwhile, the military regime established by the 1980 coup responded to the Kurdish separatist movement, as well as to the polarisation between the left and the right, by adopting an ideological project stressing the relationship between Turkish nationalism and Muslim identity, called the 'Turkish-Islamic synthesis'. This ideology was based on three pillars: the family, the mosque, and the military (Yavuz 2003, 73). These strategies have expanded the public and political space for Islam in Egypt and Turkey, including a larger role for Political Islam as is the case with the Egyptian Muslim Brotherhood (*al-Ikhwān al-Muslimīn*), and the Refah (Welfare) and Justice and Development (*Adalet ve Kalkınma Partisi*, henceforth AK party) parties in Turkey.

In Tunisia, the regime tied a secularisation process into the struggle for independence in the 1950s. However, the situation started to shift in the 1960s as the regime faced economic difficulties that impacted its political legitimacy. To face this legitimacy crisis, the regime relied on religious claims to bolster its position (Dell'Aguzzo and Sigillo 2017, 512). As in Egypt and Turkey, these new policies created a favourable environment for Islamic forces, mostly inspired by the doctrine of the Muslim Brotherhood in Egypt, to reappear in the public sphere (Fahmi 2021).

As for Morocco, the 1960s and 1970s witnessed a central role of religion in state formation (Tozy 2009, 64), while the 1980s were decisive in the organisation of the religious sphere. In fact, in 1984 the regime initiated the reorganisation and control of the religious field. These religious policies aimed to prevent the spread of Islamic militant ideologies. Morocco has seen, since the end of the 1970s and the beginning of the 1980s, a growing Salafist presence influenced by Salafism in Saudi Arabia. The banned Islamic movement Al-Adl wa Al-Ihssan (Justice and Benevolence) is one of the most important Islamist groups, and has openly criticised the monarchy, as well as many government policies. Al-Adl wa Al-Ihssan has maintained its stance on boycotting all elections in order to convey its disagreement with the regime and the current political system in place. Taking a very different approach, Morocco's Islamist party PJD (*Hizb al Adala wal Tanmia* the Justice and Development Party) opted for political participation from the mid-1990s accepting the political rules of the game, including the executive role of the monarchy (El-Katiri 2013).

The Arab Spring

After the 25 January 2011 uprising in Egypt, the idea of writing a new constitution led to a debate between Islamists and secularists over the place of Sharia in this new constitution. As this debate increased the level of tension within society, the 2012 Constitution kept the same article (Article 2) from the old constitution according to which 'Islam is the religion of the state and Arabic is its official language. The principles of Islamic Sharia are the principal source of legislation'.[3] To allay the concerns of religious minorities regarding the application of Islamic Sharia, the 2012 Constitution added Article 3, stating that 'the principles of Christian and Jewish laws are the main source of legislation for followers of Christianity and Judaism in matters pertaining to personal status, religious affairs and nomination of spiritual leaders'. In turn, al-Azhar has managed to take advantage of the new political environment to lobby for inclusion of an article strengthening its institutional indepen-dence. Article 4 of the 2012 Constitution states that 'Al-Azhar's Grand Sheikh is independent and cannot be dismissed'. Even after the ousting of the Muslim Brotherhood from power in July 2013, the current Egyptian Constitution – adopted in 2014 – has kept these same articles (as Articles 2, 3, and 7).

As in Egypt, after the Tunisian revolution in January 2011, debate over the place of religion in the new republic of Tunisia has reopened. As polarisation reached worrying levels, Ennahda (the Renaissance Party) leadership reached the conclusion that there was no need to explicitly refer to Islamic Sharia in the Tunisian Constitution and that it would be enough to keep the pre-existing first clause of the 1959 Constitution, which states that 'Tunisia is a free, independent and sovereign State. Its religion is Islam, its language is Arabic and its type of government is the Republic'.[4] The Tunisian Constitution also declares the country to be a 'civil state'. Hence, the Tunisian Constitution does not mention Sharia as a source of legislation. The Constitution designates the government as the 'guardian of religion' and obligates the state to disseminate the values of 'moderation and tolerance'. It prohibits the use of mosques and other houses of worship to advance political agendas or objectives and guarantees freedom of belief, conscience, and exercise of religious practice.

As for Morocco, the youth protests that took place in Morocco in 2011 led the king to take several reformist steps to prevent the Arab Spring from reaching his kingdom. A new constitution was proposed in March, and adopted in July 2011. The constitutional reforms transferred some of the king's prerogatives to the elected government and the parliament but retained exclusive authority in the person of the king in all matters relating to religious affairs as well as in other spheres. Thus, according to Article 41 of the Constitution, 'The King, Commander of the Faithful ("Amir al- Mu'minin"), sees to the respect for Islam. He is the Guarantor of the free exercise of beliefs'.[5] He presides over the Superior Council of the Ulama (*Conseil supérieur des Oulémas*), which reviews questions submitted to it by the king (Lahlou and Zouiten 2021, 243–244).

The Lebanese exception

Lebanon offers a different mode of religion-state relations, given its ethnic composition with the presence of three main religious communities, Sunni, Shia, and Christian, none of which form a majority. This demographic situation has made it difficult for the Lebanese state to follow the mode of the other cases, where the state identifies with one religion. In that sense, 'Lebanese confessionalism can be considered as an improvised form of the Ottoman *millet* system based on a hierarchy of religions' (Taşkın 2021, 207).

There are four historical turning points in the formation and development of the Lebanese confessional system: the making of the 1926 Lebanese Constitution, the 1943 National Pact, the 1989 Ta'if Accord that ended a 15-year-long civil war, and the October 2019 uprising calling for an end to this sectarian regime.

Lebanon wrote its constitution in 1926 when the country was still under French control. Although the Constitution claimed to follow the secular French model, it embraced a political system based on the representation of sects, including five Islamic sects (Sunni, Shia, Druze, Alawite, and Ismaili); the Maronites and 11 other Christian sects; and the Jewish community (Henley 2016).

The Constitution envisioned the separation of state and religion in line with the French notion of *laïcité* and the introduction of a secular civil law as well. Yet religious leaders opposed infringement of their authority and, on many occasions, forced the state to retreat (Taşkın 2021, 213).

Lebanon's sectarian political regime was consolidated through an unwritten agreement that became known as the National Pact in 1943 (Bahout 2016). According to the National Pact, 'Maronite and Sunni leaders distributed executive, legislative, and judicial powers based on a corporate confessional power-sharing arrangement' (Taşkın 2019, 3). According to this arrangement, the president would be a Christian Maronite, the prime minister is to come from the Muslim Sunni community, and the speaker of the parliament would come from the Muslim Shia community.

As noted by Joseph Bahout, although the Lebanese civil war (1975–1990), erupted partly due to calls to end political sectarianism, these arrangements of the National Pact survived the civil war (Bahout 2016). The Ta'if agreement of 1989 put an end to this civil war, but at the same time consolidated the sectarian regime. The agreement did however shift the balance of the executive from the president to the prime minister.

Since 17 October 2019 Lebanon has been witnessing unprecedented popular protest calling for the abolition of the sectarian power-sharing regime. These protests bring together people from different sects, regional backgrounds, ages, and social classes (Karam and Majed 2022). Although it has so far failed to bring change to the rules governing the sectarian regime, the legislative elections held in May 2022 have seen the victory of a number of voices that identify with the October 2019 uprising.

Applying the modes of governance framework

This analytical part divides the cases into two groups to elaborate on the modes and norms that characterise them as shown in Table 1, while following the distinction

Table 1. Modes and norms for the governance of religious diversity.

Majoritarian Nationalism (Turkey, Egypt, Tunisia, and Morocco).	<ul><li>Strong state identification with one religion; but not usually theocratic</li><li>May or may not include toleration for other religions</li><li>May or may not include personal laws</li><li>In radical cases the state takes over or controls the institutions and followers of one or more religions (e.g. Diyanet)</li><li>The state may come to be controlled by religious parties (e.g. AKP, Muslim Brotherhood)</li></ul>
Secularist Statism (Turkey under the CHP rule, and Tunisia under Bourguiba)	<ul><li>State control of religion</li><li>The state excludes religion from the political and the civic, confining religious freedom largely to the private sphere</li><li>This mode of secularism may be self-defined as part of the national identity</li><li>May include some support of some religions, but religion mainly seen as belonging to the private sphere</li></ul>
Pluralistic Nationalism (Lebanon)	<ul><li>Multiculturalising moderate secularism</li><li>Difference-sensitive identity recognition</li><li>Institutional accommodation of religious diversity</li><li>'Respect All, Positive Cooperation, Principled Distance'</li><li>Active and present in public and political life</li><li>Policy cooperation – religious reasons in political sphere</li><li>Accommodative of differentiated legal status, religious personal laws</li><li>Primacy of group autonomy and social support for deep diversity</li></ul>

between a 'dominant operative norm' (DON), a dominant feature of state-religion relations, and a 'qualifying operative norm' (QON), a provision that limits, adjusts or modifies the dominant norm in a way that tempers (or exacerbates) the state's approach to religious diversity (see Modood and Sealy in this collection).

Majoritarian nationalism

Four of our countries represent a mode of majoritarian nationalism, comprising their dominant norms: Morocco, Tunisia, Egypt, and Turkey. All four countries feature strong state identification with one religion, where Sunni Islam is an integral part of their national identity. These four cases have experienced an overwhelming dominance of the common heritage of Sunni Islam with varying levels of tolerance accorded to Christian and Jewish communities on the one hand and a lack of tolerance for what Sunni *ulama* typically classify as 'heretical' or 'deviant' groups (as is the case with Bahá'í and Shia Muslims) on the other.

This pattern has been common in four cases despite differences in how their respective constitutions draw the relation between religion and state. In Turkey, although the Constitution describes Turkey as 'secular' (*laik*, after the French *laïcité*), the reality is quite different. Sunni Islam is practically the official religion of the state, and Turkish national identity is closely tied to Islam (Gülalp 2021, 193). Non-Muslim citizens of Turkey, moreover, are considered 'step-citizens', with restricted citizenship rights (Ekmekcioglu 2014).

The Egyptian state, too, identifies with a particular religion, Sunni Islam. The Egyptian state does have a particular kind of identitarian nationalism, which relies mainly on Islam, while acknowledging the Coptic contribution to the establishment of the modern state in Egypt and Copts' role in the struggle for independence against the British occupation. As Vivian Ibrahim argues, 'narratives of Muslim – Coptic unity have played an important role in the imagination of the nation' (Ibrahim 2015, 2589). This is particularly the case after the 1952 military coup. However, these sorts of narratives have limited Coptic discourse on the Copts' religious and political rights as a minority, as demands for such rights have been framed as a threat to national unity. This is not unique to the case of Copts in Egypt. A similar situation can also be observed in the case of Alevis in Turkey (Tambar 2014). While the Alevis are recognised as an important component of the struggle for the establishment of the Turkish republic, any call for Alevi rights perceived as potentially harming Turkish national unity is not tolerated. According to the Turkish Constitutional Court in 1994, any expression of Alevi cultural differences will be criminalised if it is perceived as 'destroying the unity of the nation [. . .] by means of creating minorities on the land of the Turkish Republic' (Ibrahim 2015, 2590).

However, in both cases, Copts and Alevis have contested this state narrative. Alevi groups have mobilised against the state's imposition of its version of Sunni Islam. Their mass demonstrations have gone as far as to call for the abolishment of the Directorate of Religious Affairs (*Diyanet İşleri Başkanlığı*) as the state institution that supports this Sunni narrative of Turkish religious identity. In Egypt too, since 2011, Coptic groups have moved beyond a debate over equality of citizenship to defend specific minority rights (Ibrahim 2015, 2585).

Likewise in Tunisia, the Constitution (both of 1959 and 2014) states that Islam is the religion of the state. Despite the secular discourse of Bourguiba, Islam has remained an integral part of Tunisian national identity since its independence.

As for Morocco, Islam has been, and remains, a unifying element of Moroccan society, a society that is characterised by cultural, ethnic, and intellectual diversity, but united by common adherence to the Sunni branch of Islam (El-Katiri 2013, 55). The Moroccan state considers Islam one of its three major pillars. In this sense, according to Article 3 of the Constitution, 'Official religion, Islam, is the religion of the State, which guarantees to all the free exercise of beliefs'; and according to Article 4, 'The motto of the Kingdom is God, the Country, the King'.

Another dominant norm is that all four countries recognise toleration for other religions, particularly Christianity and Judaism. However, it is mainly because these two religious traditions are recognised by the official state religion, Sunni Islam. Insofar as the legitimacy of any religion is based on an Islamic interpretation of acceptable practice, ultimately this serves to exalt the religion of the majority (Islam) over that of any minority (Ibrahim 2015, 2586). While all these countries insist on freedom of conscience in their legal norms, these official norms as stated in legal documents are not in fact operative norms in these countries. In practice religions do not enjoy equal status and are not all officially and socially tolerated. All four states restrict the ability of other Muslim communities that don't follow their official version of Islam to freely practise their religion, as this would challenge state control over religious institutions and narratives.

The Turkish Constitution protects 'the freedom of conscience, religious belief and conviction'. However, this is not the case for all religious communities in Turkey. The non-recognition of the Alevi community, which amounts to at least 15 million people, represents a clear violation of this constitutional principle. Turkish official religious discourse considers Alevis to be a heretical religious group, despite several judicial decisions in their favour (Gülalp 2021, 195). The Directorate of Religious Affairs has been often accused by the Alevis of only representing the Sunni version of Islam, while as a republican institution it should serve all religious communities.

Likewise, in Egypt, freedom of religion is specifically guaranteed under the Egyptian Constitution of 2014. Both Christian and Jewish communities are entitled to refer to their own religious canon law. However, the state puts more restrictions on Shia and Bahá'í communities, as they challenge the state-sponsored Sunni narrative. The law does not recognise the Bahá'í faith or Shiism. However, on the whole the government continues to allow Bahá'ís and Shia Muslims to worship privately in small numbers but refuses requests for public religious gatherings (U.S. Department of State 2021a).

The Tunisian Constitution also insists on freedom of conscience. According to Article 6 of the Constitution, the state guarantees freedom of conscience and belief. However, the only minorities recognised are the Christian and Jewish communities, as both are considered by Islam as 'people of the book'. According to the founder of the Tunisian republic, Habib Bourguiba, in a speech to a large Jewish audience in 1957, 'the Tunisian government has never known any racial discrimination and [. . .] we have always considered the Tunisian nation as including Muslims and Jews as well as Christians' (Laskier 1994, 288). However, Bahá'ís remain unrecognised by the Tunisian state. Bahá'í groups took advantage of the post-2011 democratic political environment to lobby for their cause, but they have so far failed to gain official recognition. Although in February 2020 an administrative court ruled in favour of allowing them to establish an association, the general prosecutor presented an appeal to the court referencing a non-public fatwa issued by the grand mufti in 2016, which stated that Bahá'í faith members were apostates and infidels and therefore should not be permitted to practise their faith (U.S. Department of State 2021b, 8).

In Morocco, the Constitution says the state guarantees everyone 'the free exercise of beliefs'. However, in practice Sunni Muslims and Jews are the only religious groups recognised as native to the country. A separate set of laws and special courts govern personal status matters for Jews, including functions such as marriage and inheritance. However, the Moroccan state denies Christian citizen groups the freedom to worship in churches, the right to Christian or civil marriage and funeral services, and the right to establish churches (U.S. Department of State 2021c, 8). Expat Christians, however, may worship freely as long as they do not evangelise, a crime that is punishable by up to three years in prison (El Haitami 2021, 6). Although the government acknowledges the existence of a Shia minority who mostly live in the North of Morocco, the political authorities refuse to allow Shia groups to register as associations and prevent them from gathering for public religious observations. Moroccan Christian, Bahá'í, and Shia faiths report that fear of government surveillance leads them to refrain from public worship and to meet discreetly to practise their faith privately instead (El Haitami 2021, 6).

The four countries (Turkey, Egypt, Tunisia, and Morocco) strongly control religious institutions, narratives, and followers. In the cases of Turkey and Tunisia there have been phases in the past where state authorities excluded religion from the political and the civic, confining religious freedom largely to the private sphere. This was the case under one-party rule in Turkey, from the establishment of the Republic in 1923 until 1950 when the Republican People's Party (*Cumhuriyet Halk Partisi*, CHP) established by Ataturk lost their majority to the Democratic Party (*Demokrat Parti*), as well as in Tunisia under the rule of Bourguiba, particularly during the 1950s and 1960s. Hence, during these historical periods, one might consider the state exclusion of religion from the political and the civic as a qualifying norm for both Turkey and Tunisia.

After the formation of the Republic of Turkey, the new Turkish government abolished the Ministry of Religious Affairs, on the grounds that religion and religious services should be kept out of politics. The Ministry was replaced with the Directorate of Religious Affairs (DRA). According to its legal status, the DRA is an administrative unit established to execute services regarding Islamic faith and practices, to 'enlighten' society about religion, and to carry out the management of places of worship (Gözaydın 2008, 216). It decides matters concerning the beliefs, worship, and ethics of Islam, administers places of worship, and appoints and dismisses religious officials. In other words, the DRA was designed as an administrative tool to 'regulate' Islam within Turkish society (Gözaydın 2008, 216). Over the last three decades, the DRA's responsibilities have been further extended. Nowadays, it is one of the largest institutions in Turkey. It employs 104,000 people (2019 DRA estimation), many of them prayer leaders, preachers, and legal scholars. It also oversees more than 89,000 mosques (2019 estimation). The share of the DRA in the national budget has steadily increased since the AK party came to power, from 0.6% in 2002, to 0.9% in 2008, and to 1.1% in 2017. The DRA 2017 budget ranks above that of the Ministry of Foreign Affairs and of the Interior Ministry. Under the rule of the AK party, the

DRA's role shifted from ensuring state control over religion to the state's religious control over society (Gülalp 2021).

In Egypt, after regime change in 1952, the core of the 1952 regime policies was to bring all religious organisations under state control either by banning them or integrating them into the state structure. Through this process, the Egyptian regime aimed to have a version of Islam that would serve the goals of Arab nationalism. Starting with religious endowments, *Awqaf*, all the different *Waqf* types (personal, public, and mixed), were either abolished or brought under the control of the Ministry of Endowment (Law 18 of 1952, and Law 152 of 1957). Moreover, in 1960, President Gamal Abdel Nasser issued Law 157 stating that the Ministry of Endowment should supervise all mosques. Traditionally, Egyptian mosques had remained outside state control; but under Nasser, the government increasingly took charge of their administration. As for voluntary associations, they were either closed or incorporated into the regime's organisations. Al-Azhar too, Egypt's oldest religious organisation, did not escape state control, and in 1961 the government adopted Law 131 to reform al-Azhar. The reform reduced the Sheikh of al-Azhar to a mere figurehead, and placed al-Azhar's various administrations into the hands of laymen appointed by the government. According to the new law, al-Azhar was attached to the Presidency of the Republic, and the minister of al-Azhar affairs was to be appointed by the president. However, the Arab Spring weakened state control over the religious sphere. Between 2011 and 2013 the Egyptian state was effectively controlling and supervising fewer than half of Egypt's mosques. The post-2013 political regime, like its predecessors, consequently sought to acquire an absolute monopoly over the religious sphere. It issued decision no. 64 in 2014 to bring all mosques in Egypt under its control and promulgated Law 51 in the same year, which prohibited people without official authorisation from delivering sermons (Fahmi 2014). However, when it comes to the Coptic Orthodox Church, the Egyptian state has respected its independence both in terms of its authority over Coptic personal affairs, as well as the Church's own institutional independence, as is the case with its budget for example. While many Islamist voices have asked the state to oversee the Church's budget, the regime has refrained from making such a move. This reflects the pact between the regime and the Coptic Orthodox Church, according to which the regime guarantees the Church independence, and the latter offers its political support in exchange (Fahmi 2015).

Following the paths of Egypt and Turkey, President Bourguiba adopted several measures to ensure all religious institutions in the country were dependent on and subordinate to the political institutions of the new Republic of Tunisia. However, unlike the approach of Nasser towards al-Azhar, Bourguiba dismantled Al-Zaytouna University, founded in 737 CE. He closed its primary and secondary schools and moved its higher education faculty to a faculty of theology at the then newly established University of Tunis (Ghozzi 2002, 326).

After the second president of Tunisia, Zine al-Abidine Ben Ali, was toppled in 2011, the security apparatus lost control over the religious sphere. For example, during the Friday prayers that followed Ben Ali's flight, Islamists, whether proponents of Political Islam or Salafists, took over mosques and expelled imams appointed by the state. Estimates point to approximately half of the mosques in the country having had their imams expelled during this period (Donker 2019, 507). However, as state institutions have started to regain their strength and legitimacy, since 2013 successive ministers of religious endowments have been working to extend the Ministry's control over all mosques and imams and to close all illegal mosques. The current Tunisian Constitution, adopted in 2014, declares that the state is 'the guardian of religion', and it 'undertakes to disseminate the values of moderation and tolerance and the protection of the sacred, and the prohibition of all violations thereof'.[6]

In Morocco, the Ministry of Endowments and Islamic Affairs (MEIA) remains the principal government institution responsible for shaping the country's religious sphere and promoting its interpretation of Sunni Islam. It employed 1852 *morchidines* (male preachers) and 804 *morchidates* (female preachers) in mosques or religious institutions throughout the country. The MEIA also monitors the content of sermons in mosques, Islamic religious education, and the dissemination of Islamic religious material by broadcast media. The construction of new mosques, including those constructed using private funds, requires authorisation from the MEIA (U.S. Department of State 2021c, 9).

Some of these states came under the control of religious parties, as is the case with the AK party in Turkey (2003 to date), the Muslim Brotherhood in Egypt (2012–2013) and Ennahda in Tunisia (2011–2014). However, this shift from secular to Islamic ruling regimes has not influenced the nature of the norms governing the relationship between religion and state as already discussed.

Lebanon: pluralistic nationalism

Lebanon forms somewhat of an exception from the majoritarian nationalism of the region. The closest mode to describe the case of Lebanon is that of pluralistic nationalism. Lebanon represents a case of frozen identities defined at the point of foundation of the state of Lebanon, which neither the state nor political actors dare to touch. The Lebanese political mode institutionalises the representation of various religious sects and grants their leaders broad powers over religious affairs, including personal-status courts, religious endowments, and education (Henley 2016), what Habib (2009, 63) has called 'the tyranny of confessionalism'. The Lebanese case shows how deep religious diversity entrenched by a religiously based consociational system prevents the establishment of a democratic non-confessional political system, in particular with the absence of a strong state (Bray-Collins 2016).

Difference-sensitive identity recognition would apply to the Lebanese case, as citizens are indeed classified according to their (officially recognised) religious identities. Institutional accommodation of religious diversity is another relevant concept, as the confessional system is precisely based on the granting of political rights to the institutional structures of (officially recognised) religious communities.

The Lebanese model includes also Respect All, Positive Cooperation, Principled Distance among the different religious communities. These groups are often active and present in public and political life. The three main centres of powers: the presidency (led by a Christian Maronite), the parliament (led by a Shia Muslim), and the government (led by a Sunni Muslim) are likely to cooperate to reach political compromises in order to avoid repeating the experience of the civil war. The Lebanese regime has managed to survive primarily because of its elites' willingness to remain and work within the framework of confessionalism and consociational democracy (Taşkın 2021, 208). The Lebanese regime is accommodative of the differentiated legal status of the different religious communities. The regime guarantees religious groups' autonomy, and it does not threaten social diversity.

However, while these characteristics might be framed as 'positive' features of a regime of governing religious diversity, in Lebanon this system has led to political tensions that even developed into a 15-year civil war.

The Lebanese model shows that with a lack of state power and an acceptance of existing regimes as politically legitimate, a sense of common citizenship and individual rights cannot be guaranteed. Instead, group identities are used to control members, in a communalistic way, rather than to give everyone a sense of belonging together, in a series of sub-national majoritarianisms. This model has been challenged over the past few years with a strong popular mobilisation movement, known as the October 2019 uprising (Karam and Majed 2022). The last legislative elections held in May 2022 saw the victory of 13 candidates known for their support for the October 2019 uprising and its agenda to change this sectarian regime in favour of non-sectarian democratic regime.

Conclusion

Religion-state relations in the MENA region have been shaped by two main dynamics. The first is the modern state elites' interest in shaping their own versions of Islam that legitimise their rule. The political elites in Turkey, Egypt, Tunisia, and Morocco led a process of modernisation in all sectors, including in terms of religion-state relations. However, these political figures understood this modernisation process not as a separation of religion and the state, but rather as placing religion under the strict control of state institutions. The project was framed as not an attempt to suppress Islam, but rather to build what they considered an enlightened version of Islam.

The second dynamic at play is the religious actors' desire to use modern state structures to impose their religious norms on society. In four cases (Egypt, Morocco, Tunisia, and Turkey) the political authorities have sought to ensure their full control over the official religious institutions. However, the religious revival that started in the 1970s broke the monopoly of these religious establishments over Islam, and similarly weakened state control over the religious sphere. In these different cases, the ruling elite had to renegotiate its rules to allow religious actors access to both the political arena and civil society, giving rise to the religiously inspired political parties. These political parties have ended up being in power, totally or partially, in these four countries. This proved possible in the cases of Egypt and Tunisia only due to the Arab Spring that brought down the old regimes and changed the rules of the political game.

However, despite these shifting dynamics between state elites and religious actors, the core of the rules governing the relationship between the state and religion remained unchanged. The cases of Turkey, Egypt, Tunisia, and Morocco belong to what we defined as majoritarian nationalism mode where the dominant operative norms (DON) include strong state identification with one religion, Sunni Islam. These DONs also include tolerations for other religions recognised by Sunni Islam but not what Sunni Islam considers heretics, such as Shia and Bahá'í communities. In radical cases the state takes over or controls the institutions and followers of one or more religions as is the case with the

Directorate of Religious Affairs in Turkey. The state may come to be controlled by religious parties, as is the case with the AK party in Turkey, the Muslim Brotherhood in Egypt, Ennahda in Tunisia, and the PJD in Morocco, although the PJD's level of control continued to be limited by the palace.

Even when Islamic political groups came to power in Turkey, Egypt, and Tunisia, they kept the same rules of the game and tried to use them to their advantage. Historically, both Turkey and Tunisia have experienced phases where state authorities excluded religion from the political and the civic spheres altogether. This was the case under one-party rule in Turkey, from the establishment of the Republic in 1923 until 1950, as well as in Tunisia under the rule of Bourguiba, particularly during the 1950s and 1960s. Hence, during these historical periods, one might consider the state exclusion of religion from the political and the civic as a qualifying operative norm (QON) for both Turkey and Tunisia.

While all these four cases have sponsored one official religion, Sunni Islam, Lebanon represents an exception to this trend in the region. While these four cases have restricted the rights of religious groups not recognised by the official religious narrative, Lebanon represents a case where there is no singular, dominant religious narrative, and where religious and ethnic groups have their own parties and compete for political power.

However, both modes failed to guarantee pluralism in the region. Suppression of religious groups has only led to further fragmentation of societies, as is the case in Turkey. Meanwhile, institutionalisation of the various religious and ethnic communities has led to the creation of new religious and ethnic centres of power that do not necessarily represent the interests of their own communities. Both models failed to deal with the challenge of governing the relation between equal citizens who adhere to different religious and ethnic groups.

Notes

1. This contribution is largely based on published as well as unpublished materials of the GREASE project, in addition to many discussions among the GREASE team. The authors would like to thank in particular Hisham Hellyer, Mounir Zouitien, Haldun Gülalp, and Yüksel Taşkın for their invaluable help with this contribution.
2. Founded in 973 CE, al-Azhar represents a pillar of mainstream Islam in Egypt today. Through its different committees, al-Azhar guides many Muslim lives by defining what is and is not Islamic. Through its religious faculties, al-Azhar trains Islamic preachers and teachers, who go on to take up positions throughout the country and abroad.
3. The full text of the 2012 Egyptian Constitution is available at https://www.constituteproject. org/constitution/Egypt_2012.pdf and the current Egyptian Constitution is available at https:// www.constituteproject.org/constitution/Egypt_2014.pdf
4. The full text of the 1956 (revised 2008) Tunisian Constitution is available at https://www. constituteproject.org/constitution/Tunisia_2008.pdf. The current Tunisian Constitution is available at https://www.constituteproject.org/constitution/Tunisia_2014.pdf.
5. The full text of the Moroccan Constitution is available at: https://www.constituteproject.org/ constitution/Morocco_2011.pdf.
6. The full text of the Tunisian Constitution is available at https://www.constituteproject.org/ constitution/Tunisia_2014.pdf.

Disclosure statement

No potential conflict of interest was reported by the author(s).

Funding

The GREASE project, on which this article is based, has received funding from the European Union's Horizon 2020 research and innovation programme under grant agreement number 770640.

References

Ahmad, F. 1993. *The Making of Modern Turkey*. London: Routledge.
Bahout, J. 2016. *The Unraveling of Lebanon's Taif Agreement: Limits of Sect-Based Power Sharing*. Beirut: Carnegie Middle East Center.
Bianchi, R. 1989. *Unruly Corporatism: Associational Life in Twentieth-Century Egypt*. New York: Oxford University Press.
Bray-Collins, E. 2016. "Sectarianism from Below: Youth Politics in Post-War Lebanon." PhD diss., University of Toronto.
Dekmejian, R. H. 1980. "The Anatomy of Islamic Revival: Legitimacy Crisis, Ethnic Conflict and the Search for Islamic Alternatives." *The Middle East Journal* 34 (1): 1–12.
Dell'Aguzzo, L., and E. Sigillo. 2017. "Political Legitimacy and Variations in State-Religion Relations in Tunisia." *The Journal of North African Studies* 22 (4): 511–535. doi:10.1080/13629387.2017.1340841.
Donker, T. H. 2019. "The Sacred as Secular: State Control and Mosques Neutrality in Post-Revolutionary Tunisia." *Politics and Religion* 12 (3): 501–523. doi:10.1017/S1755048318000597.
Ekmekcioglu, L. 2014. "Republic of Paradox: The League of Nations Minority Protection Regime and the New Turkey's Step Citizens." *International Journal of Middle East Studies* 46 (4): 657–679. doi:10.1017/S0020743814001007.
El Haitami, M. 2021. "Religious Diversity at the Contours of Moroccan Islam." *The Journal of North African Studies*. doi:10.1080/13629387.2021.1978291.
El-Katiri, M. 2013. "The Institutionalisation of Religious Affairs: Religious Reform in Morocco." *The Journal of North African Studies* 18 (1): 53–69. doi:10.1080/13629387.2012.712886.
Fahmi, G. 2014. *The Egyptian State and the Religious Sphere*. Beirut: Carnegie Middle East Center.
Fahmi, G. 2015. *The Coptic Church and Politics in Egypt*. Beirut: Carnegie Middle East Center.
Fahmi, G. 2021. "Tunisia: Governing the Religious Sphere After 2011." In *Routledge Handbook on the Governance of Religious Diversity*, edited by A. Triandafyllidou and T. Magazzini, 228–237. London: Routledge.
Ghozzi, K. 2002. "The Study of Resilience and Decay in Ulema Groups: Tunisia and Iran as an Example." *Sociology of Religion* 63 (3): 317–334. doi:10.2307/3712472.
Gözaydın, İ. B. 2008. "Diyanet and Politics." *The Muslim World* 98 (2/3): 216–227. doi:10.1111/j.1478-1913.2008.00220.x.

Gülalp, H. 2021. "Turkey: Whither Secularism?" In *Routledge Handbook on the Governance of Religious Diversity*, edited by A. Triandafyllidou and T. Magazzini, 193–205. London: Routledge.

Habib, C. 2009. "Lebanese Politics and the Tyrany of Confessionalism." *Confluences Méditerranée* 70 (3): 63–70. doi:10.3917/come.070.0063.

Hellyer, H. 2021. "Egypt: Religious Diversity in an Age of Securitization." In *Routledge Handbook on the Governance of Religious Diversity*, edited by A. Triandafyllidou and T. Magazzini, 217–227. London: Routledge.

Henley, A. 2016. *Religious Authority and Sectarianism in Lebanon*. Washington, DC: Carnegie Endowment for International Peace. https://carnegieendowment.org/files/CP_295_Henley_Lebabon_Final.pdf.

Ibrahim, V. 2015. "Beyond the Cross and the Crescent: Plural Identities and the Copts in Contemporary Egypt." *Ethnic and Racial Studies* 38 (14): 2584–2597. doi:10.1080/01419870.2015.1061138.

Karam, J. G., and R. Majed, eds. 2022. *The Lebanon Uprising of 2019: Voices from the Revolution*. London: I.B. Tauris.

Lahlou, M., and M. Zouiten. 2021. "Morocco: Governing Religious Diversity." In *Routledge Handbook on the Governance of Religious Diversity*, edited by A. Triandafyllidou and T. Magazzini, 238–252. London: Routledge.

Laskier, M. 1994. *North African Jewry in the Twentieth Century: The Jews of Morocco, Tunisia and Algeria*. New York: New York University Press.

Mardin, Ş. 2006. *Religion, Society, and Modernity in Turkey*. Syracuse, NY: Syracuse University Press.

Tambar, K. 2014. *The Reckoning of Pluralism: Political Belonging and the Demands of History in Turkey*. Redwood City: Stanford University Press.

Taşkın, Y. 2019. "Lebanon." *GREASE Country Reports*. http://grease.eui.eu/publications/country-reports-and-profiles/#Lebanon.

Taşkın, Y. 2021. "Lebanon : Confessionalism and the Problem of Divided Loyalties." In *Routledge Handbook on the Governance of Religious Diversity*, edited by A. Triandafyllidou and T. Magazzini, 206–216. London: Routledge.

Tozy, M. 2009. "L'évolution du champ religieux marocain au défi de la mondialisation." *Revue internationale de politique comparée* 16 (1): 63–81. doi:10.3917/ripc.161.0063.

U.S. Department of State. 2021a. "Egypt 2020 International Religious Freedom Report." https://www.state.gov/reports/2020-report-on-international-religious-freedom/egypt/.

U.S. Department of State. 2021b. "Tunisia 2020 International Religious Freedom Report." https://www.state.gov/reports/2020-report-on-international-religious-freedom/tunisia/.

U.S. Department of State. 2021c. "Morocco 2020 International Religious Freedom Report." https://www.state.gov/reports/2020-report-on-international-religious-freedom/morocco/.

Yavuz, H. 2003. *Islamic Political Identity in Turkey*. USA: Oxford University Press.

🔓 OPEN ACCESS

South and Southeast Asia: deep diversity under strain

Thomas Sealy ⓘ, Zawawi Ibrahim ⓘ, Pradana Boy Zulian ⓘ
and Imran Mohd Rasid ⓘ

ABSTRACT
South and Southeast Asia is characterised by an historic and deep
religious diversity and countries in the region have also been
shaped by colonialism. Focusing on the cases of India, Indonesia,
and Malaysia, this contribution explores the governance of religious
diversity and conceptions of secularism influenced by – but quite
distinct from – those found in the West. It assesses how, upon
independence from colonial rule, a core concern in all three was
a settlement that reflected the history and presence of deep religious diversity. The contribution then explores how these settlements have since come under strain as majorities in each country
have more aggressively asserted their dominance. Since independence, settlements that aimed to secure rights for the multiple
religious groups in each country have been tested. A trend in all
three countries is a rise in forms of more exclusive majoritarian
nationalisms tied to the dominant religion. This trend presents
serious implications for minority faiths as well as for ideas of freedom of religion and the place and role of religion in society and
politics. The contribution suggests that we might be witnessing an
erosion of the post-independence settlements such that the mode
of governance itself is shifting.

Introduction

South and Southeast Asia is characterised by an historic and deep religious diversity and
there is not a dominant religious tradition that covers the region in the same way that
Christianity is associated with Europe (Adeney-Risakotta 2015). This contribution comparatively analyses the governance of religious diversity in India, Indonesia, and Malaysia
(see Figure 1), and recent trends affecting how that governance takes shape.[1] Indonesia
and Malaysia are majority-Muslim countries, and Indonesia has the largest Muslim population in the world. India is majority Hindu but has the largest Muslim population of non-
Muslim-majority countries (in fact the second largest of all countries), and significant
minority religious populations are present in all three countries. All three have at times
been held up as exemplars of pluralism; Indonesia has been praised for its multicultural

---

This is an Open Access article distributed under the terms of the Creative Commons Attribution License (http://creativecommons.org/
licenses/by/4.0/), which permits unrestricted use, distribution, and reproduction in any medium, provided the original work is properly
cited.

Figure 1. Countries covered in this contribution: Indonesia, Malaysia, and India.

tolerance (Hefner 2000), India as the world's largest democracy, and Malaysia for its 'moderation' (Saat 2020b).

As well as the character of religious diversity in the region, the countries being discussed here have been shaped by European colonialism. Having gained their independence in the mid-twentieth century, the governance of religious diversity was a core concern and the frameworks that emerged are marked by the deep diversity of the region as well as by the colonial periods of rule. Yet, the settlements reached at independence have come under strain as majorities in each country have more aggressively asserted their dominance. Whereas previous characterisations of the governance of religious diversity have emphasised deep diversity and pluralism in these three countries, we seek to also account for this majoritarian turn.

Based on extensive research of secondary material, relevant data, legal and policy measures, and interviews with figures from key institutions (both governmental and civil society), this contribution first provides an overview of our three country cases, outlining important historical dynamics with regard to religious diversity and paths to secularism. We then present the mode and norms of governance of religious diversity from our framework (see Modood and Sealy, this collection) and assess the implications of current trends and challenges for this mode.

Historical overview

Significant numbers of people of different religions have lived in territories that have become India, Indonesia, and Malaysia over the centuries. Indigenous religious traditions,

Hinduism, Buddhism, and Islam have all asserted themselves and vied for dominance, often linked to trade routes.

In what is now Indonesia, Hinduism and Buddhism evolved during the rise and fall of the ancient Nusantara Kingdoms, before Islam, emergent from the fourteenth century, had become the dominant religion by the end of the sixteenth century, incorporating many local customs in a process of syncretism. Malay polities were influenced by a fusion of Hindu and Buddhist concepts at the state and local level prior to the spread of Islam, when from the twelfth century onwards Islamic law began to be incorporated into the pre-existing state and customary law (see, for example, Hussain 2011; Lukito 2012). What is now India is the home of both Buddhism and Hinduism, and Islam has been present since the seventh century. Significant parts of the landmass were under Muslim rule from as early as the twelfth century but the Mughal period between the sixteenth and eighteenth centuries marks the peak of Muslim rule in the territory (see Fisher 2012).

The impact of European colonial rule changed the power balances and structural features of the governance and place of religion in public and political life. For instance, Dutch colonisation in Indonesia and its impositions in the politics of religious life meant a diverse range of Islamic movements emerged to respond to and confront the socio-economic position of Muslims. In Malaysia, the relationship between the legal precepts derived from Islam and the common law tradition that arrived with colonialism created a complicated nexus of competing jurisprudence, in which Islamic laws were applicable only to Muslims and relegated to the realm of personal law, which remains salient to this day. It was during the colonial period, moreover, that secularisation – in terms of enforced state-religion separation – became pronounced. Upon independence, all three countries faced questions over secularism and the relations between the state, politics, law, and religion as part of new constitutional settlements that also involved grappling with the diversity of the countries as well as the legacy of the structures of colonial rule that remained – although Hefner cautions that we should not over-emphasise colonial carry-overs when it comes to religious freedom Hefner (2021).

The following section now turns to outline these settlements in more detail and relate them to our framework of modes of governance of religious diversity.

Secularism and freedom of religion

In all three emerging states the issue of managing the deep religious diversity of the populations meant grappling with ideas of secularism. These ideas were partly influenced by, but in some ways very different from, those of the former European colonial powers and their bases in principles of separation, neutrality, and an emphasis on freedom of religion as freedom of conscience. Each country came to its own settlement drawing on influences both local and national, as well as transnational (Six 2021).

One of the most important challenges following the Indonesian Declaration of Independence in 1945 was formulating a state philosophy where the diversity of religious groups was accommodated. Nationalist leaders like Sukarno as well as both moderate Muslim leaders and non-Muslims saw a pluralistic and more secular state as a suitable model, whereas other Muslim leaders aspired for Indonesia to be an Islamic state. Through prolonged debate a middle position was taken. The term 'secular' in Indonesia comes with its specific meaning and the claim that Indonesia is neither a state of religion nor a secular state, adopting a consensus between the two (Mahfud 2019; Sjadzali 1993); the first, and fundamental, principle of the state philosophy of *Pancasila* is '*Ketuhanan Yang Maha Esa*' ('unity of God'), and professing a religion is a key aspect of Indonesian citizenship.

In Malaysia, 11 of the 13 British colonial entities in the region attained independence in 1957 and signed a constitution for governing a newly independent Federation of Malaya that would eventually culminate in the formation of Malaysia in 1963. In the Federal Constitution, the principles and provisions enshrined are mostly inspired by the incorporation of the two historical legacies: pre-colonial Islamic laws and traditional customs, and the colonial administrative system introduced during British rule (Aishah 1993). The formulation of Malaysia's mode of governance in managing religious diversity is predicated upon the spirit and principles of the national philosophy, the *Rukun Negara*, which was formulated in 1970. The *Rukun Negara* calls for all citizens to be sensitive to and respectful of the concerns of other religious communities, to embrace 'a liberal approach towards her [Malaysia's] rich and varied cultural traditions', but it also asserts 'belief in God' as a core principle. Islam was made the 'religion of the federation', but this was conceived as primarily ceremonial and within a secular conception of the state (Shad 2005; Fernando 2006; Ibrahim and Ahmad Fauzi 2017; Abdul Rahman 1977; Mohamed Suffian 1962; Ahmad 1985).

India gained independence from British rule in 1947 but independence came with Partition and unprecedented communal violence. In this context, the question of religion, and the anxieties of the religious minorities, particularly Muslims who had remained in India, were key debates for members of the Constituent Assembly. Despite its contrastingly more secular settlement, India steered away from the liberal secular framework and permitted greater mingling of state and religion. The Indian Constitution accepted the 'no-establishment' principle and gave equal rights to all citizens. Yet, premised on the belief that living with diversity required something more than granting the same basic rights to all citizens, it instituted formal measures for recognition of diversity and supplemented these with several informal measures of accommodation (Mahajan 2013): politically, all persons were treated as undifferentiated citizens, but in the cultural and religious domain the population was seen as heterogeneous, and citizens were differentiated on the basis of their community membership, in part to provide safeguards to shield minorities from the threat of majority dominance. In these different ways then, each sought to create a national unity whilst respecting and recognising the pluralistic makeup of the country, for which religion was central.

In these countries, negotiating a model to respond to the circumstances and challenges of newly independent and religiously heterogenous states meant quite different 'innovative formulas of accommodation' from those found in the West (Stepan 2011, 140). Derived from three cases, India and Indonesia and Senegal, Stepan (2011) outlined what he called the 'respect all, positive cooperation, principled distance' model to capture a more pronounced form of religious diversity occupying a more emphasised position in the public sphere. This is distinguished by three main features: respect for minority and majority religions in the public sphere, positive political and policy cooperation, and principled distance, which he borrows from Rajeev Bhargava (Bhargava 2009).[2] An alternative conceptualisation has been 'covenantal pluralism' (Stewart, Seiple, and Dennis 2020) which emphasises legal equality along with recognition and respect for cultural difference. Covenantal pluralism, however, remains a normative aspirational idea,

Table 1. Modes and norms for the governance of religious diversity.

Pluralistic ('unity in diversity') Nationalism	• Difference-sensitive identity recognition • Institutional accommodation of religious diversity • 'Respect All, Positive Cooperation, Principled Distance' • Active and present in public and political life • Policy cooperation – religious reasons in political sphere • Accommodative of differentiated legal status • Primacy of group autonomy and social support for deep diversity

whereas our typology and analysis is built around what governance looks like in the countries under consideration (see Hefner 2020, who applies covenantal pluralism and assesses the gaps between this ideal and the case of Indonesia).

Our own approach is to outline the mode of governance evident from a contextualised account (see Modood and Sealy, this collection), and analyse norms of governance at legal, institutional, and practical levels. The region of South and Southeast Asia is captured by what we call *pluralistic nationalism*, and which forms the dominant operative norms (DONs) for the governance of religious diversity (Table 1). In terms of freedom of religion, what we observe is an emphasis on groups and what has been called 'institutional religious freedom' (Hefner 2021) and a pronounced presence and influence of religion in the public and political spheres.

There are, however, two stories to tell, and these two stories relate to two different modes of governance. The first two sections below focus on the types of recognition and accommodations in the three country cases in relation to how they reflect the dominant mode of pluralistic nationalism. The third section then discusses trends of majoritarianism that undermine and directly challenge this deep diversity, and have come to represent important qualifying operative norms (QONs) in the region.

Legal frameworks and institutional accommodation

As discussed above, constitutional settlements following independence from European colonial rule sought to navigate between an idea of the secular, on the one hand, and deep religious diversity, on the other hand. The resulting settlements established pluralistic nationalism as the DONs. Following these constitutional principles, the legal systems also reflect a plural entanglement as well as the colonial legacy.[3]

The legal system in Malaysia follows the plural legal system that the British had established during the colonial era (see Hussain 2011). Its court system is based on the UK legal system but incorporates distinct characteristics in the form of Sharia courts and two separate High Courts for the Peninsula and for the Borneo states. The Malay rulers, who retain their positions as heads of Islam in their respective states, are responsible for overseeing the Sharia courts and appointing judges, a provision which allows for each state to have the freedom to enact its own interpretation of Islamic law and establish its own state Islamic courts to adjudicate disputes.

In Indonesia too the legal picture is a complex mixture, based on some old Dutch as well as modern statutes, *adat* (customary) rules which continue to exist alongside the formal legal system, and Islamic law (see Hussain 2011). In contrast to Malaysia, nevertheless, there is no formal parallel system of religious courts; Sharia courts are part of the state system and adjudicate in matters of family law for Muslims (Hussain 2011; Lukito

2012). Some regions have greater autonomy, where Sharia courts also encompass broader laws and regulations; for instance, Aceh (Hussain 2011; see also Salim 2010, 2015).

In India, differentiated legal statuses were accommodated for matters relating to family law, where all persons were to be governed by the personal laws of their community. Nevertheless, courts assert a certain competence in religious affairs. When conflicts emerge between practices, the Supreme Court applies an 'essential practice' test (Mahajan 1998, 2013; Sen 2010), interpreting religious doctrine to determine if a practice is an essential part of that religion, or a kind of cultural accoutrement. When a group seeks recognition as a separate and new religion, it is again the Supreme Court that decides whether a particular system of beliefs constitutes a separate religion or merely a sect or denomination of another religion. Nevertheless, successive governments have, by and large, been reluctant to intervene in religious practices even when these clash with the principle of gender equality or personal autonomy. Moreover, when conflict has arisen between rights as a result, on balance, resolutions have tended towards religious (institutional) rather than individual liberty (Mahajan 2013, 2015).

Aside from legal frameworks, in all three countries formal accommodations are made in the public sphere as part of the overall framework for the governance of religious pluralism. Major religious festivals or events from all religions have been included in the list of public holidays, for instance (Mahajan 2017; Stepan 2011). In terms of institutional accommodations and state-religion connections, these have also occurred across spheres covering education, places of worship, and other issues. In India, community institutions have considerable autonomy to regulate their religious affairs and are formally recognised as the representative organisations of their respective communities. Although the Indian Constitution affirmed that no religious education would be provided in any educational institution 'wholly maintained out of State funds' (Article 28[1]), religious groups can establish educational institutions to impart the 'education of their choice' (Article 30[1]), and are eligible for some state funding.[4] A plural network of community educational and charitable institutions, some exclusively for the community and others open to the rest of society, can therefore be found. As well as the formal institutional framework, informal accommodative measures relating to religious practices and observances have played a critical role in nurturing a sense of being counted and treated as equal (Mahajan 2021).

In the Malaysian Constitution, Article 11 stipulates that every religious group has the right '(a) to manage its own religious affairs; (b) to establish and maintain institutions for religious or charitable purposes; and (c) to acquire and own property and hold and administer it in accordance with law'.[5] There is no legal obligation for a religious group to formally register with the state, yet many, especially of non-Muslim background, do register as non-profit charitable organisations or companies to avoid being harassed by the religious authorities and to gain better access to funding and working opportunities with the government. Matters pertaining to Islam come under the purview of the states, and federal Islamic institutions like the Department of Islamic Development Malaysia (*Jabatan Kemajuan Islam Malaysia*, JAKIM) were established.

As for religious education, Islamic education is compulsory for Muslims in Malaysia (Bouma, Ling, and Pratt 2010; Abdul Hamid 2018). The federal government and state's administrations are also responsible for funding religious teachers. Islamic Departments both at the federal and state level are heavily funded by the government. Other religions can set up private educational centres providing they are kept within their own religious community.

In Indonesia, the Department of Ministry of Religious Affairs is responsible for regulating all issues related to the religious life of religions formally acknowledged by the state, including rituals such as almsgiving (*zakat*) and pilgrimage to Mecca. Semi-governmental institutions also act as the representative interlocutors with government and are responsible for regulating the religious activity and doctrine for each of the recognised religions. Religious instruction is a core and compulsory feature of Indonesia's education system, where pupils have the right to be taught this subject by a teacher from their faith group as part of a 'mono-religious' model (Yusuf and Sterkens 2015).

Religion and politics

Another of our features of pluralistic nationalism is a pronounced and integral presence in politics and policy cooperation between state and religious actors. This can promote the multivocality of religions, which in turn provides scope for religious reasons and religious arguments in public debates (Stepan 2011). Religions *and religious reasons* are thereby valued as a public good, as a source of that good, and as dialogical partners and shapers in policy.

In India no formal role is accorded to religious communities in public policy and decision-making bodies, and no separate or special representation is given on grounds of religious identity.[6] On the one hand, the Indian Constitution allows the government to regulate secular affairs – financial matters, matters related to property, management of trusts, etc., – of religious institutions, whilst on the other hand, religious groups mobilise, lobby, and are actively present in the public domain. In terms of religion and politics in Indonesia, there are Islamic organisations that play a significant role as pressure groups in politics and policy development, although formally they are not political organisations or parties. Groups such as Muhammadiyah and Nahdlatul Ulama ('Revival of the Ulama', NU) play defining roles in many state political processes (see, for example, Hefner 2021). In Malaysia, the federal government allocates two ministerial positions under the Prime Minister's Department to govern religious affairs: the Ministry of National Unity and Ministry of Religious Affairs, the latter being tasked to administer various religious bodies and institutions. Through these two departments, the government conducts various engagements and programmes to improve the relations between differing religious communities in the country and to foster 'dialogues' and unity between different religious communities. In theory, religious-based political parties are free to have their organisation registered and to run their activities, as long as this organisation upholds the principle of the Federal Constitution of Malaysia and does not go against state laws.

A further strong connection between politics and religion is how the state relates to citizens, where citizens are seen first and foremost as members of an ethno-religious group and primacy is given to group, rather than individual, autonomy.

In Indonesia and Malaysia national identity cards are designed to specify the religious affiliation of the card holder, which must be one of the officially recognised religions. In this way, ethnic and religious characteristics tend to be conflated in the realms of politics, cultural expressions, and everyday social norms. In both countries, Islam is the religion of the majority and atheism is not formally recognised; a religious identity will instead be assigned based on the ethnic community the person belongs to. Other religious groups can register as social or cultural organisations or as companies but are not recognised as official religions, meaning that members of other religions (or none) must choose a religion to misrepresent themselves on their ID cards (Bouma, Ling, and Pratt 2010). In Malaysia, the Federal Constitution (Article 160) in fact dictates that all ethnic Malays (the majority population) are Muslim and it has been argued by some high officials that atheism is anti-patriotic as it is in contradiction with the first principle of the *Rukun Negara* that every citizen is expected to believe in God. In Indonesia six religions are recognised: Islam, Christianity (Protestantism and Catholicism), Hinduism, Buddhism, Confucianism, and following the acceptance of a petition by the Constitutional Court in 2017, adherents to indigenous religions – long unrecognised as 'religions' – are able to complete the 'religion' column of their identity card with the name of their belief system (Hefner 2021). While institutional religious freedom might be emphasised, individual freedom of conscience, including conversion for instance, is thus circumscribed.

In these ways, through constitutional settlements, differentiated legal codes, institutional arrangements, policy cooperation, and state-citizen relations, DONs in relation to the governance of religious diversity strongly reflect a mode of pluralistic nationalism.

Majoritarian challenges

Since independence, the settlements and DONs that aimed to secure rights for the multiple religious groups in each territory have been tested. Trends in all three countries show a rise in forms of more exclusive majoritarian nationalisms that are tied to the dominant religion, with serious implications for minority faiths as well as for ideas of freedom of religion. Despite the seeming guarantees of religious freedom in the constitutional settlements, what appeared to be settlements of pluralism have turned out to be 'fairly easy to misinterpret or abuse' (Sofjan 2016, 58; also Bajpai 2017). Therefore, alongside the inclusive and peaceful settlements founded in our country cases, and those models that emphasise them, we also need to account for growing, although in many ways not wholly new, trends of majoritarianism that qualify the pluralistic arrangements put in place. For this, it is necessary to consider another mode of governance of religious diversity in addition to pluralistic nationalism. As well as pluralistic nationalism, as discussed above, these three countries also show significant features of *majoritarian nationalism* (Table 2), which represent notable QONs. This section outlines how we see features of this second mode operating in our country cases and how these norms are having significant qualifying effects on the pluralistic nationalism in our three country cases.

In Malaysia, the passage of time has blurred the initial secular and pluralistic intentions of the framers of the Federal Constitution, and the constitutional statement that 'Islam is the religion of the Federation' has come to provide a basis for those who push for

Table 2. Modes and norms for the governance of religious diversity.

Majoritarian Nationalism	• Strong state identification with one religion; but not usually theocratic
	• May or may not include toleration for other religions
	• May or may not include personal laws
	• In radical cases the state takes over or controls the institutions and followers of one or more religions
	• The state may come to be controlled by religious parties

Malaysia to become a more explicitly Islamic state. Official or preferential status for Islam can be seen, for example, in that the right to propagate any religious doctrine or belief is reserved for Muslims, and the Sharia courts rarely allow religious conversion (see, for example, Sofjan 2016). This primacy of Islam, moreover, relates only to officially orthodox Sunni Islam. Other forms of Islam, especially Shia, are deemed heretical and deviant, and are subject to action by religious authorities. In practice then, despite norms of pluralism, non-Islamic or 'deviant' Islamic groups are often restricted from organising any activities that may be deemed a threat to the superiority of the majoritarian Islam in the country.

Forms of majoritarian nationalism have in fact been a consistent feature of Malaysian politics. Majoritarian pressure towards greater Islamisation imposed by state and non-state actors since the 1960s has increased the scale of restrictions on religious expression in public and non-public spaces (Farid 2014). During the 1980s, Prime Minister Mahathir Mohammed strengthened Islamic values in government and the Shariah courts (Bouma, Ling, and Pratt 2010) and in recent decades, proponents who interpret Islam as the religion of the federation and push for an enlargement of the judicial powers along Islamic lines have found greater political purchase. The United Malays National Organisation (*Pertubuhan Kebangsaan Melayu Bersatu*, UMNO), the lead partner in government coalitions from independence to 2018, has long had ethnonationalism as a leading strand of its politics and policies, found in the idea of defending Malay supremacy (*ketuanan Melayu*). Furthermore, there has been an increasingly conservative interpretation of Islam as both UMNO and the Malaysian Islamic Party (*Parti Islam Se-Malaysia*, PAS) have competed in an 'Islamisation race' in order to maintain political legitimacy and vie for Malay electoral support since the 1980s (Ibrahim and Rasid 2021).

Moreover, in contrast to successive governments' rhetoric of moderate Islam (*Islam Wasattiyah*) and multiculturalism, especially on the international stage, progressive Islamic voices have been increasingly restricted (Saat 2020a). Most recently, following the 2018 general election won by the Pakatan Harapan coalition on a proclaimed reformist and inclusive agenda, UMNO and PAS cooperated to form a Malay Islamic bloc and force a government turn towards greater Islamic conservativism (Saat 2019). Following the government's political crisis, which saw former Minister of Home Affairs Muhyiddin Yassin taking over as prime minister in March 2020, UMNO has been brought back to power and PAS is represented in the cabinet for the first time since the 1970s (Ibrahim and Rasid 2021).

These trends have raised serious questions about religious freedom for both Muslims (if not part of the mainstream) and non-Muslims alike. Much state-sponsored Islamisation has been conducted in a manner that directly challenges the existing constitutional rights and religious freedoms that are granted to citizens. Organisations and commentators have complained, for instance, that the reach of JAKIM has extended and marginalises alternative viewpoints and voices (Saat 2020a). Measures have also included the banning of books, prosecution of individuals or groups for their involvement in practising 'deviant teachings', raiding private premises to enforce Sharia for 'violations' such as indecent dress, alcohol consumption, or *khalwat* (close proximity to a non-family member of the opposite sex). Interfaith dialogues have also frequently been blocked 'due to Islamist intimidation of the Federal government' (Bouma, Ling, and Pratt 2010, 77; Sofjan 2016).

There has also been a growing 'sharia-isation' – understood here as the institutionalisation of Sharia-based values, norms, and categories in the discourse and practice of the country's legal corpus (Ibrahim and Ahmad Fauzi 2017). A series of constitutional amendments has given Sharia courts increased autonomy and states have begun to aggressively increase the scope of their powers to regulate the affairs of Muslims located within their boundaries. Although attached to the larger secular judicial framework, this has raised concerns over the practice of secularism in Malaysia, in part also precipitated by a flurry of rulings following the 2001 High Court ruling in *Lina Joy v Majlis Agama Islam Wilayah and Anor*. In this landmark case Lina Joy, who had converted from Islam to Christianity, lost her case to change her officially assigned religion on her identity card to reflect her conversion. Beneath these tensions is the creeping narrative that Malaysia has always been an Islamic state and that the alleged 'ambiguity' of the Federal Constitution must be interpreted in ways that prioritise Islamic principles above all else; indeed, a Pew survey in 2013 found that 86% of Malays support Sharia becoming the official state law (see Zaman 2020). Saat (2018) has argued that *ulama* (Islamic religious leaders) have been able to effectively 'capture' parts of the state, that is, that they have been able to capitalise on their co-optation by the state and push their own agendas. This is something Saat finds is relevant to Indonesia too.

Turning to Indonesia, Hefner (2013) notes that religious disputes have been a feature of each of Indonesia's political transitions and that the proper place of religion in society has been a constant debate since independence. In Indonesia, too, we can see the secular and pluralistic principles in the Constitution and pluralistic principles of the national philosophy of *Pancasila* aimed at uniting Indonesia's various groups being eroded by a majoritarian and more exclusionist interpretation which holds that the 'spirit' of the country is Islamic (Rahardjo 2010; Husaini 2005, 2006; Thaha 2005; Maarif 2006).[7] Official political parties tend to subscribe to *Pancasila*, even though strong trends challenge it in the social sphere and leading figures in the political and legal spheres appear unable (Schneier 2016; Hefner 2021) or unwilling (Sofjan 2016) to prevent the trend of Islamisation and erosion of the more pluralistic principles of *Pancasila*.

The New Order period (1966–1998) tended to limit the participation and expressions of Islam in the public sphere with strong insistence on the adoption of *Pancasila* as organisations' sole philosophical basis (Ramage 2010; Jurdi 2010), something accepted at the time by the two main Indonesian Islamic organisations, the NU and Muhammadiyah. In the last quarter of the New Order regime, nevertheless, strong manifestations of religious revivalism and a strongly politicised Islam directly challenging the government were evident (Hasan 2017; Schneier 2016). Following the collapse of the New Order regime, diverse Islamic groups and religion-based political parties came to the fore. This marked a new dynamic in the relationship between the state and religion with Islamic symbols and concepts more assertively expressed in politics and increased pressure for the government to Islamise the country.

A 'conservative turn' then took place in the 2000s, especially in the upper echelons of Indonesia's Muslim organisations, such as the Indonesian Ulama Council (*Majelis Ulama Indonesia*, MUI), with 'anti-vice' militias imposing their morality in ways not always checked by the government (Hefner 2013, 2020, 2021; also Saat 2018). This resulted in, for example, the forced closure or targeting of places of worship, attacks on those deemed heretical, the introduction of local Sharia regulations, and *fatwa* issued by the MUI declaring secularism, 'liberal Islam', 'deviant' Islamic groups, and pluralism incompatible with Islam and condemning interfaith marriage and activities (Bagir and Fachrudin 2020;

Bouma, Ling, and Pratt 2010; Hasan 2017; Hefner 2013, 2021; Sofjan 2016). The most striking development has been the emergence of politically radical and fundamentalist Islamic movements such as Front Pembela Islam, Jamaah Islamiyah, Salafi Jihadist, and those represented by Partai Keadilan Sejahtera and Hizbut Tahrir Indonesia. One of the most visible consequences of this development is the growth and strengthening of support for enforcing Islamic morality in the public sphere. These groups are generally hostile to any type of contemporary discourse that they perceive as western constructs such as democracy, gender equality, and pluralism, which are seen as un-Islamic 'secular' systems incompatible with Islam (Yunanto 2003).

When Joko Widodo (Jokowi) became president in 2014, he did so on pledges of moderation and pluralism. He assembled a coalition made up of secular nationalists, non-Muslims, and moderate Muslims through aligning himself closely with NU, disbanded Hizbut Tahrir Indonesia, and in a series of events between 2014 and 2017 served to restate *Pancasila* as the state philosophy. Yet, rather than the conservative turn halting, these voices and organisations have remained influential in a pluralised and democratised public and political arena (Bagir and Fachrudin 2020). As a result, restrictions on institutional religious freedoms have in fact intensified since Indonesia's return to democracy in 1998 (Hefner 2021).

The majoritarian turn has continued, along with discriminatory treatment of minority religious groups and non-mainstream Muslim groups (Wahid Foundation 2017). More, and stricter, regulations have been introduced for publications, dress codes, social media, and interfaith commissions, all of which have been used to enforce majoritarian control as part of an Islamisation drive. Moreover, in some cases, regulations designed to ensure peaceful coexistence can play into majoritarianism and 'undercut a more robustly pluralistic commitment to religious freedom' (Hefner 2013, 22; Hefner 2020, 6). For example, building places of worship in Indonesia is regulated by the Ministerial Decree on the Construction of Houses of Worship, which stipulates that a certain number of signatures is needed from locals of other religions. In practice this can mean that some religious communities are unable to build a place of worship or, as noted above, are forced to close their places of worship. In this climate, the Law on Religious Defamation and Blasphemy – dating back to the New Order period but reaffirmed in 2010 by the Constitutional Court – is particularly problematic, and minorities have become increasingly targeted. More than 150 people, mostly religious minorities, including Muslim minorities (Hasan 2017), have been convicted under the Law. Yet, Hefner (2021) also observes that despite these significant challenges and erosions, institutional religious freedom and a sense of Indonesia as plural does still hold, suggesting its embeddedness in society and politics; and this also perhaps marks a difference between Indonesia and Malaysia in its strength. Indeed, from a different angle, considering the political repression of ethnic Chinese communities in both countries, Chin and Tanasaldy (2019) have also argued that Indonesia's institutional framework has proven more inclusive and resistant to majoritarian pressures in comparison to Malaysia.

When we turn to India we can also see a rising majoritarian nationalism that is having severe consequences for religious diversity, especially for India's Muslims, resulting in greater state support for the majority as well as cases of interreligious violence that the state seems unable or unwilling to curb. Since the 1990s we see greater assertion of 'Hindu culture' – identified as 'Indian' culture – and a homogenising drive pushing for greater space for it in the public domain. This is reflected politically in rising voter support for the Bhartiya Janata Party (BJP), which in 2019 increased to 37.4% and 303 of the 542 seats in the Lower Chamber.

There are a few elements important to the narrative that has accompanied this majoritarian shift. The first is the allegation that the majority has been wronged and treated unfairly. These allegations are based on the perception that past governments have, on the one hand, interfered in the affairs of the majority – through reform of Hindu Personal Law in the late 1950s, setting up of management boards for major temples, and so on. On the other hand, however, so the allegations go, similar interventions did not take place in the life of minority communities. On this account, the government has tried to 'appease' the Muslim minority in various ways, such as by not reforming Muslim Personal Law (despite demands from women in the Muslim community to do so to afford them more equality and protection in areas such as divorce procedures, polygamy, and custody of children). According to this narrative then, the affairs of the majority, Hindu community have been unfairly interfered with in ways that have not also occurred for minorities, particularly Muslims. The second is that Hindus suffer discrimination in neigh-bouring countries, where they form a minority, whereas in India the Muslim minority enjoys a better status. In effect this signals that Hindus are neglected in India and discriminated against in the region (Mahajan 2021). To rectify these perceived wrongs, the BJP has usurped aspects of the liberal agenda to demand the formulation of a Uniform Civil Code and eliminate community-based personal laws, and simultaneously question the rationale for community/group differentiation.

Partition, subsequent wars with Pakistan, political turmoil in Kashmir valley, and recurrent terror attacks have also made national security concerns paramount. The Right has owned the security agenda more stridently and supported a muscular nation-alism that in its view should correct the wrongs done to the Hindus. By constructing a narrative around 'invasions' by Mughal rulers, oppression of Hindus in the past, terrorist attacks by members of various Islamic groups in contemporary India, alongside extolling the virtues of Hinduism as a tolerant and peaceful religion (something previously a part of the pluralistic idea), the BJP has cast a shadow over the Muslim presence as a 'hostile other' (see also Shani 2021; Bajpai 2017).

Conclusion

All three countries profess some degree or kind of secularism and freedom of religion, albeit in different ways and in ways that are different from the liberal secular paradigm of freedom of religion. Instead, the emphasis is on moral groupism and institutional religious freedom.

In so far as South and Southeast Asia (on the basis of the three cases considered here) can, on the whole, be considered an example of a region that reflects pluralistic nation-alism, we can identify two important starting points for all these three countries which bear on how freedom of religion is conceived. One is recognition of the presence of many different religions. The other is that the state operates with the notion of an embedded individual (not an abstract individual), with individuals being seen as members of a religious and ethnic community, and thereby based in the primacy of group autonomy, moral groupism, and toleration.

However, religion and its connections to state and recognition might also be an aspect of its management by the state and a vehicle for majoritarian nationalism that introduces strong currents of diversity-limiting ethno-religious nationalism. This might operate through the legal system and political processes, including policymaking, and be argued to have constitutional grounding. Schneier has suggested that studies of democracy in Indonesia 'divide into two camps: those who see the glass as half empty and those who describe it as half full' (Schneier 2016, 220), and this perhaps captures something of how our three country cases sit on overlapping currents of, on the one hand, DONs from a pluralistic nationalism respectful of deep diversity, accommodating of religious pluralism, and concerned with 'religious harmony', and on the other hand, trends of majoritarian nationalism that are seeking dominance and eroding these pluralistic elements. What we see in the region, then, is that while pluralistic nationalism can be considered to operate as a dominant set of norms, this has been in constant tension with QONs of majoritarian nationalism. While these have always been present, we might note a shift in how these might be moving from more qualifying norms to a second set of dominant norms as the tensions between the two sets increasingly plays out in political and legal spheres.

Whether this proves to be a sequential shift from one mode and set of DONs to another, or a rebalancing of the simultaneity between the two modes, and whether the strengthening majoritarian QONs will continue to operate more prominently or will wane in any or all three cases, only time will tell. In the cases here, where religion and accompanying ideas of what is sacred are so pervasive, there are thus two contrasting situations: on the one hand, an enormous degree of religious and cultural diversity and, on the other, conflicts around religious issues, which can be fuelled by sectarianism (Saleem 2021; Arifianto 2021), and conflicts which play out in the political life of the countries. A key question for the country cases considered, therefore, is whether and to what extent pluralistic nationalism, and its norms of recognition, and of institutional and legal accommodation, will be able to hold back the tides of diversity-limiting majoritarian nationalism.

Notes

1. We remember with affection our GREASE colleague Zawawi Ibrahim, who contributed to this collection but unfortunately passed away on 18 May 2022 and so did not live to see its publication.
2. In brief, Bhargava's conception of Principled Distance is one where separation between state and religion is established at the levels of ends and of institutions, but not in policy and law. The state may legitimately interfere and support religions in a differentiated way to ensure equalities and freedoms.
3. Although Fisher (2012) also notes in relation to India the legacy of Mughal rule on British colonial rule.
4. The Indian Constitution can be accessed online (in a variety of language versions including English) at: https://legislative.gov.in/constitution-of-india, and for a PDF version in English see https://legislative.gov.in/sites/default/files/COI.pdf.
5. The full text of the Federal Constitution of Malaysia can be accessed here: https://www.wipo. int/edocs/lexdocs/laws/en/my/my063en.pdf.
6. A deliberate effort was made, however, to have members from all communities in the highest decision-making bodies (the Central Cabinet) and other prestigious public positions.

7. Some have argued that *Pancasila* has always been a screen for majoritarian authoritarianism (see, for example, Sofjan 2016). The full text of the Indonesian Constitution can be accessed here: http://www.humanrights.asia/indonesian-constitution-1945-consolidated/.

Acknowledgments

We are grateful to two anonymous reviewers and the journal editors for their comments on this contribution. We are indebted to our GREASE partner Gurpreet Mahajan, whose work greatly informed the discussion of India.

Disclosure statement

No potential conflict of interest was reported by the author(s).

Funding

The GREASE project, on which this article is based, has received funding from the European Union's Horizon 2020 research and innovation programme under grant agreement number 770640.

ORCID

Thomas Sealy ⓘ http://orcid.org/0000-0002-3211-6900
Zawawi Ibrahim ⓘ http://orcid.org/0000-0001-9751-2659
Pradana Boy Zulian ⓘ http://orcid.org/0000-0003-0087-6232
Imran Mohd Rasid ⓘ http://orcid.org/0000-0003-0756-8128

References

Abdul Hamid, A. F. 2018. "Islamic Education in Malaysia." In *Handbook of Islamic Education*, edited by H. Daun and R. Arjmand, 745–761. Cham: Springer International.

Abdul Rahman, P.-A.-H.-T. 1977. *Looking Back: Monday Musings and Memories*. Kuala Lumpur: Pustaka Antara.

Adeney-Risakotta, B. 2015. "Pendahuluan: Mengelola Keragaman." In *Mengelola Keragaman di Indonesia: Agama dan Isu-isu Globalisasi, Kekerasan, Gender, dan Bencana di Indonesia*, edited by B. Adeney-Risakotta, 19–43. Bandung: Mizan.

Ahmad, I. 1985. "The Position of Islam in the Constitution of Malaysia." In *Readings on Islam in Southeast Asia*, edited by A. Ibrahim, S. Siddique, and Y. Hussain, 213–220. Singapore: Institute of Southeast Asian Studies.

Aishah, B. 1993. "The Historical and Traditional Features of the Malaysian Constitution." *Jebat: Malaysian Journal of History, Politics and Strategic Studies* 21 (3): 20.

Arifianto, A. R. 2021. "From Ideological to Political Sectarianism: Nahdlatul Ulama, Muhammadiyah, and the State in Indonesia." *Religion, State & Society* 49 (2): 126–141. doi:10.1080/09637494.2021.1902247.

Bagir, Z. A., and A. A. Fachrudin. 2020. "Democracy and the 'Conservative Turn' in Indonesia." In *Alternative Voices in Muslim Southeast Asia Discourses and Struggles*, edited by N. Saat and A. Ibrahim, 139–155. Singapore: ISEAS Publishing.

Bajpai, R. 2017. "Secularism and Multiculturalism in India: Some Reflections." In *The Problem of Religious Diversity: European Challenges, Asian Approaches*, edited by A. Triandafyllidou and T. Modood, 204–227. Edinburgh: Edinburgh University Press.

Bhargava, R. 2009. "Political Secularism: Why It is Needed and What Can Be Learnt from Its Indian Version." In *Secularism, Religion and Multicultural Citizenship*, edited by G. B. Levey and T. Modood, 82–109. Cambridge: Cambridge University Press.

Bouma, G. D., R. Ling, and D. Pratt. 2010. *Religious Diversity in Southeast Asia and the Pacific*. London: Springer.

Chin, J., and T. Tanasaldy. 2019. "The Ethnic Chinese in Indonesia and Malaysia: The Challenge of Political Islam." *Asian Survey* 59: 959–977. doi:10.1525/as.2019.59.6.959.

Farid, S. S. 2014. "The Islamic Legal System in Malaysia." *Pacific Rim Law & Policy Journal* 21 (1): 85–113.

Fernando, J. M. 2006. "The Position of Islam in the Constitution of Malaysia." *Journal of Southeast Asian Studies* 37 (2): 249–266. doi:10.1017/S0022463406000543.

Fisher, M. 2012. "Mughal Empire." In *The Ashgate Research Companion to Modern Imperial Histories*, edited by J. Marriott and P. Levine, 161–186. London: Routledge.

Hasan, N. 2017. "Religious Diversity and Blasphemy Law: Understanding Growing Religious Conflict and Intolerance in Post-Suharto Indonesia." *Al-Jāmi'ah: Journal of Islamic Studies* 55 (1): 105–126.

Hefner, R. W. 2000. *Civil Islam: Muslims and Democratization in Indonesia*. Oxford: Princeton University Press.

Hefner, R. W. 2013. "The Study of Religious Freedom in Indonesia." *The Review of Faith and International Affairs* 11 (2): 18–27. doi:10.1080/15570274.2013.808038.

Hefner, R. W. 2020. "Islam and Covenantal Pluralism in Indonesia: A Critical Juncture Analysis." *The Review of Faith & International Affairs* 18 (2): 1–17. doi:10.1080/15570274.2020.1753946.

Hefner, R. W. 2021. "Islam and Institutional Religious Freedom in Indonesia." *Religions* 12: 415. doi:10.3390/rel12060415.

Husaini, A. 2005. *Pluralisme Agama Haram: Fatwa MUI Yang Tegas Dan Tidak Kontroversial*. Jakarta: Pustaka al-Kautsar.

Husaini, A. 2006. *Pluralisme Agama: Parasit bagi Agama-agama: Pandangan Katolik, Protestan, Hindu, dan Islam*. Jakarta: Dewan Dakwah Islamiyah Indonesia.

Hussain, J. 2011. "More Than One Law for All: Legal Pluralism in Southeast Asia." *Democracy and Security* 7 (4): 374–389. doi:10.1080/17419166.2011.617621.

Ibrahim, Z., and A. H. Ahmad Fauzi. 2017. "Governance of Religious Diversity in Malaysia: Islam in a Secular State or Secularism in an Islamic State." In *The Problem of Religious Diversity: European Challenges, Asian Approaches*, edited by A. Triandafyllidou and T. Modood, 169–203. Edinburgh: University of Edinburgh Press.

Ibrahim, Z., and I.M. Rasid. 2021. "Malaysia: A Secular Constitution Under Siege?" In *Routledge Handbook on the Governance of Religious Diversity*, edited by A. Triandafyllidou and T. Magazzini, 282–295. London: Routledge.

Jurdi, S. 2010. *1 Abad Muhammadiyah: Gagasan Pembaruan Sosial Keagamaan*. Jakarta: Kompas.

Lukito, R. 2012. *Legal Pluralism in Indonesia: Bridging the Unbridgeable*. London: Routledge.

Maarif, A. S. 2006. *Islam dan Pancasila sebagai Dasar Negara: Studi tentang Perdebatan dalam Konstituante*. Jakarta: LP3ES.

Mahajan, G. 1998. *Identities and Rights: Aspects of Liberal Democracy in India*. Oxford: Oxford University Press.

Mahajan, G. 2013. *India: Political Ideas and the Making of a Democratic Discourse*. London: Zed Books.

Mahajan, G. 2015. "Contextualising Secularism: The Relationship Between State and Religion in India." In *Secularism, Religion, and Politics: India and Europe*, edited by P. Losonczi and W. Van Herck, 36–56. London: Routledge.

Mahajan, G. 2017. "Living with Religious Diversity: The Limits of the Secular Paradigm." In *The Problem of Religious Diversity: European Challenges, Asian Approaches*, edited by A. Triandafyllidou and T. Modood, 75–92. Edinburgh: Edinburgh University Press.

Mahajan, G. 2021. "India: The Challenge of Being Plural and Multicultural." In *Routledge Handbook on the Governance of Religious Diversity*, edited by A. Triandafyllidou and T. Magazzini, 255–266. London: Routledge.

Mahfud, M. D. 2019. "Indonesia Bukan Negara Agama Dan Bukan Negara Sekuler." 10 June. https://www.republika.co.id/berita/dunia-islam/islam-nusantara/19/01/10/pl49ek320-mafhud-md-indonesia-bukan-negara-agama-dan-bukan-sekuler

Mohamed Suffian, H. 1962. "The Relationship Between Islam and the State in Malaya." *Intisari* 1 (1): 7–21.

Rahardjo, M. D. 2010. *Merayakan Kemajemukan, Kebebasan dan Kebangsaan*. Jakarta: Penerbit Kencana.

Ramage, D. E. 2010. *Politics in Indonesia: Democracy, Islam, and the Ideology of Tolerance*. London: Routledge.

Saat, N. 2018. *The State, Ulama and Islam in Malaysia and Indonesia*. Amsterdam: Amsterdam University Press.

Saat, N. 2019. "A Complicated Political Reality Awaits the Malays." *Perspective* No.40, Yusof Ishak Institute.

Saat, N. 2020a. "Mainstreaming Alternative Islamic Voices in Malaysia." In *Alternative Voices in Muslim Southeast Asia*, edited by N. Saat and A. Ibrahim, 118–136. Singapore: ISEAS-Yusof Ishak Institute.

Saat, N. 2020b. "The Politics of Islamic Discourse in Malaysia." In *Alternative Voices in Muslim Southeast Asia*, edited by N. Saat and A. Ibrahim, 3–8. Singapore: ISEAS-Yusof Ishak Institute.

Saleem, S. 2021. "Constructing the 'Liberal' Muslim Other: Ethnic Politics, Competition, and Polarisation in Malaysia." *Religion, State & Society* 49 (2): 109–125. doi:10.1080/09637494.2021.1877992.

Salim, A. 2010. "Dynamic Legal Pluralism in Indonesia: Contested Legal Orders in Contemporary Aceh." *The Journal of Legal Pluralism and Unofficial Law* 42 (61): 1–29. doi:10.1080/07329113.2010.10756640.

Salim, A. 2015. *Contemporary Islamic Law in Indonesia: Sharia and Legal Pluralism*. Edinburgh: Edinburgh University Press in association with The Aga Khan University.

Schneier, E. 2016. *Muslim Democracy: Politics, Religion and Society in Indonesia, Turkey and the Islamic World*. Abingdon: Routledge.

Sen, R. 2010. *Articles of Faith: Religion, Secularism and the Indian Supreme Court*. Delhi: Oxford University Press.

Shad, S. F. 2005. "The Malaysian Constitution, the Islamic State and Hudud Laws." In *Islam in Southeast Asia: Political, Social and Strategic Challenges for the 21st Century*, edited by K. S. Nathan and M. H. Kamali, 256–277. Singapore: Institute for Southeast Asian Studies.

Shani, G. 2021. "Towards a Hindu Rashtra: Hindutva, Religion, and Nationalism in India." *Religion, State & Society* 49 (3): 264–280. doi:10.1080/09637494.2021.1947731.

Six, C. 2021. "The Transnationality of the Secular: Travelling Ideas and Shared Practices of Secularism in Decolonising South and Southeast Asia." *Religion and Politics* 2 (1): 1–74.

Sjadzali, M. 1993. *Islam Realitas Baru dan Orientasi Masa Depan*. Jakarta: UI Press.

Sofjan, D. 2016. "Religious Diversity and Politico-Religious Intolerance in Indonesia and Malaysia." *The Review of Faith & International Affairs* 14 (4): 53–64. doi:10.1080/15570274.2016.1248532.

Stepan, A. 2011. "The Multiple Secularisms of Modern Democratic and Non-Democratic Regimes." In *Rethinking Secularism*, edited by C. Calhoun, M. Juergensmeyer, and J. Van Antwerpen, 114–144. Oxford: Oxford University Press.

Stewart, W. C., C. Seiple, and R. H. Dennis. 2020. "Toward a Global Covenant of Peaceable Neighborhood: Introducing the Philosophy of Covenantal Pluralism." *The Review of Faith & International Affairs* 18 (4): 1–17. doi:10.1080/15570274.2020.1835029.

Thaha, A. M. 2005. *Tren Pluralisme Agama: Tinjauan Kritis*. Jakarta: Penerbit Perspektif.

Wahid Foundation. 2017. *Laporan Tahunan Kemerdekaan Beragama/berkeyakinan (KBB) di Indonesia 2017*. Jakarta: The Wahid Foundation.

Yunanto, S., ed. 2003. *Militant Islamic Movements in Indonesia and South-East Asia*. Jakarta: Freiderich-Ebert-Stiftung.

Yusuf, M., and C. Sterkens. 2015. "Analysing the State's Laws on Religious Education in Post-New Order Indonesia." *Al-Jāmi'ah: Journal of Islamic Studies* 53 (1): 105–130.

Zaman, D. 2020. "Civil Society–state Engagements on Religion in Malaysia." In *Alternative Voices in Muslim Southeast Asia*, edited by N. Saat and A. Ibrahim, 9–16. Singapore: ISEAS-Yusof Ishak Institute.

∂ OPEN ACCESS

Diversities and dynamics in the governance of religion: inter-regional comparative themes

Thomas Sealy ⓘ and Tariq Modood ⓘ

ABSTRACT
Debates and controversies over the governance of religious diversity are important features of the social and political landscape in all five regions covered in this collection. All have historical as well as contemporary forms of these debates that have had a significant impact on not just the structures and forms of governance but also on the very identity of each state as it has grappled, and continues to grapple, with religious diversity and the issues it raises. This final contribution presents an inter-regional comparative analysis and findings of different modes of state-religion connections between our different regions, following on from the discussions in the individual contributions of the collection focused on intra-regional analyses. Moreover, central to state-religion relations is the idea of political secularism and so we offer a definition of political secularism from which we can compare countries and regions. We assess the idea of political secularism against our typology of modes of governance of religious diversity and explore convergences and divergences between our regions along three conceptual lines: the idea of secularism, the idea of freedom of religion, and the relationship between national identity and religion.

Introduction

Debates and controversies over the governance of religious diversity are important features of the social and political landscape in countries across the world. To elucidate some of the key challenges and responses, and what these debates look like, the contributions to this collection have focused on selected country cases in five regions: Western Europe and Australia, South and Southeastern Europe, Central Eastern Europe and Russia, MENA, and South and Southeast Asia. They have shown how all these country cases have historical as well as contemporary forms of these debates that have had a significant impact on not just the structures and forms of governance but also on the very identity of each state as it has grappled, and continues to grapple, with religious diversity and the issues it raises. Each of the contributions has sought to identify what might be said at a regional level as well as intra-regionally, and what is shared along with important differences, when it comes to the governance of religious diversity.

This is an Open Access article distributed under the terms of the Creative Commons Attribution License (http://creativecommons.org/licenses/by/4.0/), which permits unrestricted use, distribution, and reproduction in any medium, provided the original work is properly cited.

In this final contribution, we take some stock of this and summarise some key features. We also, however, go further and develop an inter-regional comparison based on the separate intra-regional analyses of the contributions. As such, we also address how the core ideas and concepts of political secularism and freedom of religion 'travel' between the different regions, not least as the issues of contextualism and travelability have been at the heart of scholarly debates and innovations in studies of secularism and state-religion relations (for example, Bhargava 1998, 2009; Modood 2012, 2019; Burchardt 2020).

This concluding contribution begins with comparative summaries of the separate contributions of this collection. We first outline different paths to secularism between our different regions, based on differing historical trajectories, and which bear on contemporary forms of governance of religious diversity, before outlining contemporary challenges that have emerged from and across our separate regional contributions. The second part of the contribution then turns to our inter-regional comparison and discussion of political secularism and freedoms of religion.

Establishing religion and paths to secularism

Secularism is a contested concept, as we have seen throughout the contributions to this collection. While for some it is the best, or only, way of guaranteeing important freedoms and equalities in diverse societies (especially pronounced in liberal secular societies), for others it is an alien concept, perhaps even a (western) imposition that has limited purchase in non-western contexts. Secularism can be 'top down' and statist, or it can emerge from social currents below, and both of these directions might push or pull at each other. Secularism, contrary to (western) popular opinion, can even be advocated by religions themselves. It can evolve gradually or be imposed forcibly and quickly. What secularism means and what it looks like in terms of state-religion relations is also at issue. This section provides brief overviews of each region and how secularism came to salience as a form of governance, whether it has endured, and where it has receded.

We can point to three 'pasts' from which these various countries in the regions have developed, and through which we can trace three broad and distinct paths in relation to secularism. Their formation from these three points of origin into modern nation-states is at the heart of otherwise quite different paths to (or even out of) secularism.

One is a Christian-majority past, which has resulted in separation between church and state (of different characters). Here, a dominant form of Christianity was the main religious tradition followed by the population, notwithstanding religious minorities and diversity, and also closely entwined with government and state apparatus. This is particularly reflected in countries in Western and Southern Europe. The path of secularisation and tolerance of religious diversity in these countries has, on the whole, been a gradual affair, albeit one which has accelerated since the latter half of the twentieth century.

A second is from a colonial past on top of a Hindu- or Muslim-majority past, again diversity notwithstanding. This came to be marked by the imposition of Western European colonial rule and subsequent independence, where religion has assumed a central role in society and politics. This is particularly reflected in South and Southeast Asia and in the MENA region. (Western European countries of course have colonial pasts, but as colonisers rather than colonised, this is rather different.) On the path we can trace here, aspects of secularism were codified by colonial powers, before constitutional settlements following independence in the latter half of the twentieth century saw debates and struggles over secularism play out between those seeking control over the religious sphere for a particular religion and those seeking pluralistic settlements.

A third is a communist past layered on top of a Christian/Muslim/multi-confessional imperial (Austro-Hungarian/Ottoman/Russian) past. The path of secularism in countries coming out of this past saw a staunchly atheistic secularism initially forced, before the fall of communism led to new negotiations over the place of religion in public and political life. This is particularly reflected in Central and Eastern Europe.

These pasts all mark the present forms of secularism and freedom of religion and their challenges in important ways as they combine with more recent trends. The different paths sketched here have all set the contexts for diverse contemporary challenges to the governance of religious diversity across the regions. Nevertheless, whilst taking account of the importance of historical context, we have been guided by Modood and Thompson's (2018) 'iterative contextualism' to avoid an overly deterministic path dependency, and to assess how ideas of secularism and freedom of religion 'travel'. The following section outlines the main contemporary challenges to and for the governance of religious diversity in each region.

Contemporary challenges

Western Europe and Australia

In Western Europe and Australia we focused on the cases of Belgium, France, Germany, and the UK, along with Australia (which shares many key characteristics as a result of its history as a British penal colony). Since the late 1980s debates about the proper place and role of religion have resurfaced and have come to be marked by two characteristics: fears of threat to the liberal secular order and security concerns associated with (violent) radicalisation. There have been high-profile legal cases involving Christians, particularly around sexuality and Christian symbols in public buildings. Yet, the issue of public religion in Western Europe has largely been a result of extra-Christian religious diversity that developed in the region following the end of the Second World War. Accommodations and exemptions have been claimed, at times made, at times refused or revoked for certain aspects of dress, funeral practices, religious buildings, ritual slaughter, and educational provision, for instance. Questions over the ability of Islam to be accommodated in Western European countries have been a particular issue for the far right, which has often come to define itself in opposition to Islam and Muslims. Nevertheless, some liberals and those on the left, far more comfortable with anti-racism than religion, have also expressed scepticism about certain practices and values seen to be out of step with liberal society, especially around issues of gender equality and sexuality. This has produced, in some instances, renewed thinking and attention to how accommodation and inclusion might be achieved, or in other instances, a contraction in pro-diversity arrangements and policies.

The issue of freedom of religion has thus become a significant debate. Freedom of religion as (privatised) freedom of conscience remains assured, but beyond this there are important distinctions, the clearest being between on the one hand, a more multiculturalist and moderate secularism for most of the region, and on the other hand, the assimilationist secularist statism of France. Across both of these, pressures towards reassertions of 'neutrality' and liberal secularism have increased, yet to different extents, with different intensities, and with different legal and policy outcomes.

Southern and Southeastern Europe

Here we focused on the country cases of Italy, Spain, Greece, Bosnia and Herzegovina (BiH), Albania, and Bulgaria. A key issue in these countries is the relation between national identity and religion, which can provide a barrier to inclusion of diversity. Overall, in this region moderate secularism is clearly evident. Yet, in contrast to some of our Western European cases, this is balanced much more strongly by forms of majoritarian nationalism and sometimes by liberal neutralism, an implication of which is that there is less institutional accommodation of diversity.

Despite moves to open up to diversity in recent decades, contemporary challenges revolve around the inclusion of long-standing religious minorities. BiH is probably the most acute case as ethnic and religious identities are fused; the divisions created during the war (1992–1995) remain and the religious institutions revived after the fall of communism continue to be involved, often controversially, in political and public life. In Albania, the state maintains a tight collaboration with major religious denominations and the Albanian Muslim Community (*Komuniteti Mysliman i Shqipërisë*) plays an important role in supporting state supervision. Differential treatment by the state towards religious communities remains a significant challenge. In Bulgaria, although denominations have equal rights and equal standing, the Constitution of the Republic of Bulgaria declares the majority Orthodox denomination 'traditional', which puts it in a favourable position with regard to the other denominations, who must register to be allowed to operate. In recent years, we can find similarities between Bulgaria and Greece in the way in which religion has remained an important marker of identity and state-religion relations have been fraught with tensions over further separating church and state and accommodating native religious minorities as well as recent migrant populations; while the legal protections might be comprehensive, their practical application is still not always effective.

While long-standing minority populations have been one source of challenge, more recent migrant populations have also given rise to debates and challenges. For Spain and Italy, controversy arose as formal agreements were reached with representatives of minority religions from the early 1990s. The number of religious minorities recognised by the Italian State continued to widen in the 2000s but left out religions perceived to be at odds with Italian law, namely Islam and Sikhism. A further dimension, one which Italy in particular shares with Greece and some Southeastern states, has been the rise of far-right political groups on anti-diversity and anti-immigrant platforms, exacerbated by the economic crisis in 2010 and so-called 'refugee crisis' (2014–2016). Spain here might be seen to diverge from the other two southern countries, although in the face of a similar economic crisis and immigration concerns we should be cautious of underestimating the risk of a rise of far-right forces or of anti-immigrant rhetoric.

Central Eastern Europe and Russia

Throughout Central Eastern Europe, the first decade after the collapse of communist rule witnessed very liberal regimes of governance of religion and the securing of religious freedoms, and led to a large number of groups seeking recognition as faith communities. Yet, there are questions of equality between groups. Alarmed by these large numbers, the governments in the region gradually introduced tougher regulations on the registration and operation of religious organisations, and increasingly reoriented policies to ensure the state's control over religion.

Looking at the cases of Lithuania, Slovakia, Hungary, and Russia, we can see how some of the countries in the region appear to be turning away from the liberal secularism cherished in the immediate aftermath of the fall of the Iron Curtain – ties with dominant churches are tightening and minority religions are facing greater barriers to inclusion in the face of more assertive majoritarian nationalisms. These kinds of measures have, as elsewhere on the continent, been related to anti-diversity and anti-immigrant platforms and the rise of the far right in politics in response to the 2014–2016 refugee crisis. There has been a clear turn in the political elite towards populist nationalism emphasising Christian heritage. This is not restricted to fringe political parties, but also mainstream parties have started resorting to a rhetoric full of religious symbolism and the sense of a clash of civilisations understood almost exclusively in religious terms. As a corollary to this, the political rhetoric of the region's top politicians increasingly contains if not manifest, then certainly latent anti-Muslim sentiment, something that became a new norm in the mid-2010s. Whereas this trend and challenge can be seen in Russia, Hungary, and Slovakia, Lithuania represents a more moderate case, where characteristics of liberal neutralism are more pronounced than in the other country cases in this region.

MENA

The Arab Spring in some MENA countries has given way to challenges about the idea of religion's separation from politics and the reflection of the dominant religion in areas such as law has raised issues of minority religions and the religious identities of the states, and debates between secularists and political Islamists have often been fraught. These concerns have been exacerbated by violent radicalisation, which has become a significant challenge across the region. By focusing on the country cases of Egypt, Tunisia, Morocco, and Turkey we see how some political figures in the MENA region have understood secularism not as separation between religion and the state, but rather as placing religion under the strict control of state institutions. The modernisation projects in the region prior to the 1970s were originally framed as an attempt to build what leaders considered an enlightened version of Islam. However, the religious revival that started in the 1970s broke state control over the religious sphere and the ruling elite had to renegotiate its rules to give access to religious actors in both political and civil spheres of society. Religious political parties have ended up being in power, totally or partially, in the four countries. Prevailing in the region are forms of majoritarian nationalism where Islam is the dominant religion, and where minorities, including Muslim minorities not fitting with state norms, are highly circumscribed even allowing for features such as personal law.

The case of Lebanon, however, differs from our other country cases in the region. Here there is an ongoing and intense political and intellectual debate on whether the confessional system is a working solution or source of enduring political, cultural, and economic problems (Taşkın 2021). A further dimension to this has been the vast number of Sunni Muslim refugees that have arrived in Lebanon as a result of the war in Syria.

South and Southeast Asia

In South and Southeast Asia we focused on the country cases of India, Indonesia, and Malaysia. Despite settlements in recognition of deep diversity and the need to promote a sense of national unity as pluralistic, since these countries gained independence these settlements have been tested. Trends in all three countries show a rise in more exclusive majoritarian nationalisms that are tied to the dominant religious group, with serious implications for minority faiths as well as for ideas of freedom of religion and the place and role of religion in society and politics. This trend represents a major political and state challenge to deep diversity and ideas of secularism.

In Malaysia and Indonesia, the most striking development has been the emergence of politically radical and fundamentalist Islamic movements, giving way to a majoritarian turn that has created issues of discriminatory treatment of minority groups including non-mainstream Muslim groups (Chin 2022; Tanasaldy 2022). In this sense we can see trends of what has been called 'Islamisation' and 'Sharia-isation' of the state and legal apparatuses, trends which seek to strengthen the idea that the state is Islamic and that forms of governance should reflect this. In India, majoritarian pressures come from the Hindu majority, facilitated and encouraged by the ruling Bharatiya Janata Party (BJP). These pressures have particularly targeted India's Muslim population, who are subject to increasingly restrictive and aggressive measures. The exemptions and accommodations secured following independence, which aimed to provide institutional freedoms and the right of India's different religious communities to live according to systems of personal law, are especially under pressure.

Regional summary

Taking the contributions together, the challenges across the regions are diverse and contextually dependent on domestic and wider events steeped in historical relations. Yet despite these considerable differences, there are a number of shared themes. Old and new populations continue to pose challenges, leading to debates and controversies about privilege, equality, and inclusions. Issues of nation, state, and identity loom large and give rise to difficulties in inclusion, even when concerted efforts are made towards this challenge. When they are not, there are sharp exclusions through forms of majoritarianism (and majoritarian backlash) and even violence; and these exclusionary forces might be state-backed and/or from sub-state groups. Moreover, we do see that overall, and notwithstanding exceptions, our regional configurations do make sense. There is enough commonality within each, which also distinguishes each region from others, that it is meaningful to talk about these regions as regions. We can and should point to exceptions (Lebanon, Lithuania, France, BiH, for example), but these do not serve to disturb this claim. This will be further elaborated below.

Table 1 presents a visual summary of the findings in the contributions. It returns to the table of modes set out in the first contribution to this collection, mapping our regions and

Table 1. Comparison of modes and norms by region.

Majoritarian Nationalism	Secularist Statism	Liberal Neutralism	Moderate Secularism	Pluralistic Nationalism
Western Europe and Australia				
			Belgium ↑	
	France ↑			
			Germany ↑	
			UK ↑	(UK)
			Australia ↑	
Southern and Southeastern Europe				
Greece ↑		(Greece)	(Greece)	
(Italy)		Italy	Italy ↑	
(Spain)		Spain	Spain ↑	
(BiH) ↑		BiH	BiH	
Bulgaria ↑		(Bulgaria)	Bulgaria	
Central Eastern Europe and Russia				
Hungary ↑				
(Lithuania)		Lithuania ↑		(Lithuania)
Slovakia ↑	(Slovakia)			
Russia ↑	Russia			
	(Albania) ↑	Albania	Albania	
MENA				
(Lebanon) ↑				Lebanon
Turkey ↑				
Egypt ↑				(Egypt)
Morocco ↑				
Tunisia ↑				
South and Southeast Asia				
(India) ↑				India
(Indonesia) ↑				Indonesia
(Malaysia) ↑				Malaysia

countries against this framework and also indicating movement in modes and norms of governance. The *dominant operative norms* are shown for each country, with significant *qualifying operative norms* shown in brackets (where not already covered). The arrows indicate the direction of travel, i.e. which mode is most pronounced in the current challenges regarding religious diversity in each case, and so which are headed towards neutrality, moderate secularism, or greater restrictions, for instance.

It is important to note that in adopting this analytical approach we are not saying that there is a causal connection between our modes and the shifts and changes that we observe. We are not suggesting, for example, that pluralistic nationalism necessarily leads to majoritarian nationalism. Our concepts are non-causal but provide us with tools to describe and explain, and to account for patterns and shifts. Things can move in different directions, and we are able to capture this through tracing convergences and divergences. The 'moving parts' aspect of our framework also lends itself to thick description of cases whilst avoiding the trap of path dependency, and is an important aspect of a more dynamic 'iterative contextualism'.

Convergence and divergence: inter-regional

Having briefly summarised the main findings from the contributions, we now address inter-regional points of convergence and divergence. The discussion here will draw out in more detail some of what can be seen in Table 1 and present a comparative conceptual analysis of key terms and how they travel between our regions.

There are a few conceptual commonalties across the different regions considered here and on which this section further elaborates:

(1) Countries in all five regions have grappled with secularism and many, although not all, have professed and continue to profess some form of secularism.

(2) The notion of freedom of religion is professed in all cases but comes to look quite different in different contexts and under different modes. A significant aspect of this relates to the dimensions of freedom of conscience and freedom of worship or practice. A further dimension to this is an often-marked difference between freedom of religion *de jure* and *de facto*, where the gap between formal measures, such as constitutional provisions, and practice can reflect diversity-restricting approaches.

(3) The relationship between national identity and religion is something present across the cases, although in markedly different ways, and in many it is intensifying in diversity-restricting ways. Indeed, one of the analytical strengths of our approach is that it brings out, as in Table 1, how important nationalism is in some states; in MENA this particularly means majoritarian nationalism, and with South and Southeast Asia it currently means a movement in that direction from an older pluralistic nationalism sustained by an historic deep diversity. This is a feature of contemporary dynamics missing from political theory discussions of secularism.

In the first contribution in this collection we drew attention to, first, a minimalist definition of political secularism, where the core idea of political secularism is that of political autonomy; namely that politics or the state has a *raison d'etre* of its own and should not be subordinated to religious authority, religious purposes, or religious reasons. This minimalist definition represents a one-way type of autonomy, and so we then added that we also need to recognise that secularism can additionally be supportive of autonomy of organised religion and freedom of religion, which is consistent with some government control of religion, some interference in religion, some support for religion, and some cooperation with (selected) religious organisations and religious purposes providing it does not compromise the autonomy of politics (Modood 2012).

So here we have a minimalist definition of political secularism, premised on one-way autonomy, and what we might call a minimalist+ definition which preserves the minimalist insistence on political autonomy but includes state-religion connections (SRCs) and mutual autonomy in its scope. This, moreover, helps us avoid what Maclure and Taylor (2011) have referred to as a 'fetishism of means', where measures to achieve political secularism, such as church-state separation, become ends in themselves. This allows us to shift from foregrounding the idea of separation and its extent to instead foregrounding connections and their character. If we accept that connections are a feature of all secular societies, what becomes important, and what our disaggregated norms allow us to explore and assess, is the character and extent of these connections. Thus, rather than focusing on whether connections are 'properly' secular, we can explore how they affect the governance of religious diversity and the inclusion or accommodation of religion in the public and political spheres.

However, here we want to take this thinking about political secularism further for the purposes of our comparative approach. The different modes of governance of religious diversity we identify relate the different expressions that political secularism takes in different contexts. From the above, therefore, we can begin to indicate what we refer to as *dimensions of secularism*: namely, freedom of religion (as conscience and worship), national identity in relation to religion, how a state relates to its citizens (individuals or groups), and autonomy (one or two way). We can begin now to outline these dimensions and characteristics of political secularism and SRCs in more detail, and to characterise our modes of governance of religious diversity against them in a way that allows us to assess how the core notions of political secularism and freedom of religion travel, compare, and contrast between our cases. Table 2 presents the dimensions outlined above against our modes of governance from Table 1.

The inter-regional discussion that follows draws upon these dimensions to highlight points of convergence and divergence between our five regions and assess how the core ideas of political secularism and freedom of religion contrast between them. It also recaps some of the principal intra-regional dynamics as it relates its discussion to Table 2. It is worth highlighting at this stage that this is a necessarily limited number of regions and country cases within them. The comparative discussion and analysis we present here could be usefully expanded to include further cases, and indeed we would welcome its wider application, and the comparative implications of doing so. This, however, would not serve to bring the approach itself into question. As it stands, we argue that our approach is useful in providing observations and insights into the cases we discuss. This general point of analytic utility and understanding, we suggest, could only expand and develop as did the number of cases considered by working with it.

Inter-regional comparative discussion

For the purposes of our comparative analysis, we can start in Western Europe and Australia. All our country cases in this region fit the minimalist definition of political secularism. The UK, Belgium, Germany, and Australia also fit our minimalist+ definition, while the balance in France tips towards a more one-way autonomy. These countries also all have relatively weak ties between nation and religion, in so far as the influence of religion in political life has declined significantly as religious diversity has grown. While

Table 2. Dimensions of political secularism and modes of governance.

Modes → Dimensions ↓	Majoritarian Nationalism	Secularist Statism	Liberal Neutralism	Moderate Secularism	Pluralistic Nationalism
National Identity	ethno-religious	secular-national	'neutral'	'neutral' or 'weak multi'	ethno-religious or 'strong multi'
Mutual autonomy	Low	Low	Medium	Medium	High
Freedom of religion (conscience)	Low	High	High	High	Medium
Freedom of religion (practice)	Low	Low	Medium	Medium	High
State's relation to citizens	ethno-religious	Individual	Individual	Individual (+ ethnic/ ethno-religious)	Ethnic/ethno-religious (+ individual)

they undoubtedly identify with a Christian past in ways significant for religious diversity, this is not identarian in a strong sense in that it is not an exclusive identity where religion and ethnicity are tied together, and might also recognise minority identities in important ways. We might say, nevertheless, that France is distinct in having stronger ties between nation and secularism, where public identity and how the state relates to citizens is more strongly secularist in identity terms. This is not just a feature of the French state but regarded as central to the country, France; for some it is what it means to live in France and to be French.

They also all have important connections between state and religion, even in France there is no 'absolute separation'. The key difference here is in the quality of these connections; the balance between religion treated as a public good or danger and between state control of or autonomy for religions. In terms of SRCs, the former comes, albeit in often limited ways, to reflect the diversity of the polity in key public ways, such as in education or welfare, while the latter leans towards a uniform conception of identity and assimilation.

A further point of difference relates to freedom of religion, where this is based in moral individualism and freedom of conscience, but where in the case of moderate secularism this is the basis for public religion and for France it is individualised and confined to the private sphere to a greater degree. As a result, while all states guarantee freedom of conscience as an absolute right, freedom to practise is a qualified right, and qualified in different ways.

Starting with Western Europe and Australia already gives us differing perspectives on secularism, split by the balance of 'autonomies' and thereby levels of control/regulation, and also by the form that freedom to practise takes and thus the extent of the public presence of religion, while freedom of conscience is significant in all the states. There is also a distinction with regard to identity and its relation to state, albeit this is in France's strong insistence on a secularist identity tied to the idea of nation and state.

Turning to Southeastern Europe, again the country cases fit our minimalist definition of political secularism. Here, however, the ties between nation and religion are stronger, state regulation is higher, and the types of recognition associated with moderate secularism are lower. Where moderate secularism does form the DONs, these are qualified by QONs that distinguish the governance of religious diversity. Freedom of religion is based in moral individualism and freedom of conscience, but with more prominent features of majoritarian nationalism in some cases or secular statism in other cases, the mutual autonomy of state-religion relations and accommodative character of SRCs is weaker. To differing degrees, features of majoritarian nationalism qualify and curtail the public character of religious diversity. This is perhaps weaker in Spain and Italy, and Albania has a comparatively stronger presence of secularist statism and the links between nation and religion are weaker. In all three cases, SRCs are mediated by features of moderate secularism, and thereby of public religious diversity. In Bulgaria and Greece majoritarian nationalism forms significant dominant norms, with the Orthodox churches and national identity more closely linked. BiH, as something of an outlier in its more multi-confessional arrangement is, nevertheless, perhaps also characterised as akin to a form of sub-state majoritarian nationalism, where these features operate within differently dominant confessional regions rather than in one overarching state-wide way. A further feature in the region, especially perhaps Spain, Italy, Greece, and Bulgaria, is the trend of increased scrutiny and regulation of countries' Muslim populations or exclusion of them from standard SRC routes in the contexts of fears over radicalisation and an increased immigrant presence.

Taking this to Central Eastern Europe and Russia, we again find the common factor of freedom of religion grounded in moral individualism and freedom of conscience, and again the countries here fit the minimalist definition of political secularism. Considering the cases in this region, however, begins to draw out more clearly two main points of contrast with other European regions. The first pertains to identity, and the second to majoritarian nationalism.

The practice of freedom of religion, and particularly its public character, distinguishes how secularism operates in the region. We can begin with the exception, Lithuania, which is more strongly grounded in liberal neutralism with features of moderate secularism. Elsewhere, however, majoritarian nationalism, with a close identification between state and dominant church, is an increasingly strong feature of SRCs. One aspect of this that stands out in the region is pronounced tiered systems, where 'traditional' religions are privileged above those which are 'registered' or just 'associations'. This tiered system of recognition is not novel to the region and is consistent with moderate secularism (see also for example Lægaard 2012; on Denmark; Thompson and Modood 2022 on Finland and Alsace-Lorraine); we might in fact say that tiered systems within a supposed neutralism are the status quo of SRCs across Europe. Nevertheless, the types of privileging prominent in, for example, Slovakia, Hungary, and Russia are marked by majoritarian nationalism in producing close ties between the state and the dominant form of Christianity. This type of privileging, moreover, works in practice to deprivilege minorities, older and newer, including Christian minority denominations. This is also a relationship where the state exerts strong influence over the dominant church, restricting two-way autonomy. An important point of identification is that we are not merely talking about the *use* of religion by political elites without identification. A more straightforward utilisation would be more compatible with secularist statism but what we are witnessing here is more consistent with the type of identification that is a feature of majoritarian nationalism.

A result of these features is that there are, at times, severe restrictions placed on non-recognised religions or denominations which – especially if critical of the government – face high levels of interference and control; we might think of Jehovah's Witnesses banned as an extremist group in Russia or the Methodists in Hungary. In contrast to the role majority churches can sometimes play in Western Europe, the role of the majority Orthodox Church can be a barrier rather than support or ally to minority faiths (Sarkissian 2010). This particularly but by no means exclusively affects 'new' religions, that is those of more recent populations, and is reminiscent of how NRMs were targeted in some states in Western Europe in the 1980s and 1990s (see Richardson 2004). A further comparative point we might make here, although this time looking towards Southeast Asia (see below), is that following regime change an initial period of more openness to diversity came in before a more majoritarian turn, even if in postcommunist countries it was short lived.

In thinking about the picture of secularism in Europe, we can begin to see certain patterns. All countries meet the minimalist definition of political secularism and across Europe there is a common grounding in freedom of religion based in moral individualism and freedom of conscience. This is in common, however, only in so far as it is limited to the private sphere. Key differences come in relation to how this freedom operates in practice and in public, as well as the current direction of travel of SRCs and religious diversity governance. That is, the key differences arise when looking at our minimalist+ definition of political secularism. While in some parts of Europe the influence of the church and church-state bond has receded gradually as religious diversity, including importantly non-belief, have risen, in other areas of the continent, connections have intensified in identarian ways. As some nation-states have sought to consolidate following imperial and communist rule, the positions of dominant churches have entrenched, creating problems for minorities, particularly in the context of the refugee crisis a number of these countries have found themselves at the centre of. In countries characterised by majoritarian nationalism the relation of religion to national identity is coloured by an imagined ethnos to a greater extent and thereby more likely restrict the public presence of minorities. Notably, however, this is not simply about ethnic identification, as Christian denominations that are not part of the dominant church – and especially those critical of the government or that openly proselytise – also face the same restrictions. Those country cases that are more characterised by secularist statism, such as France and to perhaps a lesser degree Albania and Slovakia, similarly restrict public roles and have a national identity strongly tied to a secularist ideal where ethnic or religious identities take a back seat, at least in a public sense.

Moving beyond Europe, we can begin to see how these modes and norms compare with other regions. Looking first to the MENA region, it is less certain if the minimal definition of secularism can be applied. Recent challenges have directly addressed the state of secularism across the region, where secularists and Islamists have clashed over the role of the state and its relation to religion, and a rise in extremism has entrenched a relationship between the governance of religion and security. While the region is not without a discourse of freedom of religion, this is divorced from practice at legislative, institutional, and practical levels. Freedom of religion is more closely tied to citizenship status through ethno-religious identification.

Identitarian majoritarian nationalism grounded in one religion is pronounced. In contrast to the observations made above, here majoritarian nationalism forms the dominant operative norms, which are then qualified in some cases by some limited features of other modes; that is, features of majoritarian nationalism are the qualified rather than the qualifiers. National identity is closely entwined with religious identity such that the state, in different ways and through different instruments, controls and constitutes itself as the head of Islam and Islam is protected and supported in ways not available to minorities. There are exceptions where this is mediated by toleration for a couple of historical minorities, but this is often restrictive for these minorities in terms of participation outside of their communities and discrimination remains widespread. Moreover, these minorities might be effectively forced to downplay their religious identity in the service of national unity (as has been argued about Egypt and the Coptic minority, Yefet 2019; Ibrahim 2015) rather than their religious identity being included in the national identity. These trends are also apparent in Turkey, which although previously perhaps more consistent with secularist statism has, under Erdoğan, increasingly come to represent majoritarian nationalism. Freedom of religion (as conscience) is stated in constitutional documents, yet in practice this is restricted. Indeed, according to Pew research, the region has the highest government restrictions on religion globally and has also seen the greatest rise in these restrictions in the last decade.[1] In Tunisia Islam is the religion of the state with some recognition for Christian and Jewish minorities, and the state, as the 'guardian of religion', exerts high levels of control. Lebanon is an exception in formally recognising a multi-confessional polity, and in this reflects aspects of the pluralistic nationalism found in Southeast Asia. This, however, entrenches sectarian lines between groups and sectarian identities. In this it shares features with BiH of sub-state majoritarianism, and would perhaps make for an interesting comparison between the two in its own right.

Finally, we turn to South and Southeast Asia. On the whole, being characterised by pluralistic nationalism, we can say that the minimalist+ definition applies. Yet, these understandings of a secular state are markedly different from that in European polities, with religion featuring much more prominently and in much more entangled ways with politics, legal codes, and statecraft. These are also expressed through the national philosophies of Indonesia and Malaysia, with the unity of God one of the five principles of *Pancasila* in Indonesia, and the *Rukun Negara*, which calls for all citizens to be sensitive to and respectful of the concerns of other religious communities in Malaysia.

When it comes to freedom of religion, there is a striking contrast between how freedom of worship and practice are conceived and operate between Europe and South and Southeast Asia. While freedom of worship and practice (in public) are often guaranteed in European states, this is a qualified right, in contrast to the absolute right of freedom of conscience. In more secularist countries religion is regarded primarily today as an 'inner life', a 'belief', a private matter and is a much more socially restricted set of activities, relationships, and forms of authority than was the case before secularism's rise to ascension. This looks very different in South and Southeast Asia, where the character of support and recognition is a more embedded feature of governance and religion's place in the public and political spheres. The foundations of freedom of religion can properly be said to be based in the primacy of group autonomy and moral groupism, and what Hefner has referred to as 'institutional religious freedom' (Hefner 2021).

This difference gives religion a distinct public presence, such as recognition of multiple religious holidays and direct government assistance for public worship, forms of legal pluralism that recognise personal laws of religious communities, and is a characteristic of the historic 'deep diversity' of the region. It also means that the government is more involved in religion and autonomy becomes a blurrier concept. The legal pluralism in India, for example, has meant the Supreme Court applying an 'essential practice' test, with which it interprets religion to determine if the said practice is an essential part of that religion when resolving issues of tension between individual and group rights. It also means that the balance of rights is adjudged differently, where group rights can trump individual rights, and this can serve to limit the freedom of religion of groups within communities, such as women or 'minorities within minorities' (Eisenberg and Spinner-Halev 2005).

Yet, these settlements and the forms of pluralism and two-way autonomy are being put under strain with regard to current trends. Identities and how these relate to the state are tied and fixed to ethno-religious categories and citizens are religiously differentiated. This becomes extremely problematic when other norms, which strongly reflect aspects of majoritarian nationalism, become increasingly operative and the state comes to closely align with one ethno-religious identity and a sense of 'unity in diversity' becomes eroded, affecting the status and practice of citizenship of minorities. In these cases, as with our Central Eastern Europe cases, an initial period of greater openness and accommodation following independence has been eroded by majoritarian pushes.

While on the one hand then, pluralistic nationalism can be seen to represent formal mechanisms for the recognition of religious diversity, the ethno-religionisation of identities creates its own forms of restriction as ethno-religious identities become fixed by the state and limited in number. This also has an impact on freedom of conscience. When one's citizenship or political status relies on group membership, the resulting moral groupism can lead to individual beliefs being misrecognised or to some belief perspectives or life decisions (such as religious conversion) being formally proscribed. This type of recognition has also not curtailed the privilege of the majority against minorities. Rather than some religious minorities in some European states being alienated and marginalised from the state on secular bases, minorities instead face marginalisation from a majority ethno-religious group that is increasingly assertive in the political sphere.

Concluding remarks

Political secularism as we have presented it is then compatible with a weak identification of a state with a particular religion and even a stronger secularist statist mode of public identity. It is less compatible with a strong majoritarian identification with a particular ethno-religious group, however; where this is strongly associated with national identity along ethnic or ethno-religious lines to the exclusion of minorities. This in turn significantly impacts on freedom of religion (principally practice but conscience to a degree also) and affects how the state does or does not relate to citizens and vice-versa. This contrasts with modes marked by civic forms of identity. Here, nevertheless, we can point to two trends. The first is the stronger, assimilationist neutrality of secularist statism, which can have an equally restrictive pressure on public religion and religious diversity, albeit one that stresses a denuded public sphere and secularist public identity for citizens that affects all religions, rather than majoritarian nationalism's promotion of one religion to the exclusion of others. The second contrast is with, for instance, moderate secularism, where a weak identification with a religious tradition does not necessarily result in exclusionary nationalist identities (except for peripheral far-right currents) and state-citizen relations.

The discussions above have suggested the usefulness of disaggregating each mode into its constituent norms as a way of conceptualising state-religion religions and approaches to the governance of religious diversity. In so doing we are able to provide an analytically nuanced reading that points to similarities as well as allowing us to account for important differences and developing trends, and what is often significant is the balance, interaction, and direction of travel between dominant norms (DONs) and qualifying norms (QONs).

Freedom of religion is a common phenomenon but we can observe two directions of travel. Parts of Europe are largely moving in the direction of 'levelling up' or at least reducing the gap between the historic religion(s) and the minorities, albeit unevenly between and within country cases. In MENA the majority religion is being pushed upwards by the new religio-political actors, and this is also occurring to a lesser extent in Malaysia and in Indonesia; and in India a different kind of majoritarianism has been on the rise (Dhanda 2022; Sikka 2022).

What the more restrictive pathways alert us to, of whatever stripe and character, is that pro-diversity arrangements are always projects, subject to political contingency and restrictive forces that can tip the balance of norms. One can create formal space for accommodation of diversity, whether of a moderate secularism or pluralistic nationalism for instance, but after that, trust between communities and a common sense of citizenship has to be nurtured assiduously by the government and civil society.

The experiences here show, moreover, that neither the realisation of freedom of religion nor accommodation of diversity is, by itself, enough. Both these ends need to be pursued side-by-side. Instead of seeing them as alternatives from which we must choose, they must be seen as parallel concerns that should coexist. When diversity is accommodated, the state and community need to ensure that the basic right of equality is protected for the vulnerable groups in a community and inter-community conflict is swiftly curbed and dealt with. When basic rights are protected for all individuals, one needs also to ensure that the dominant majority culture does not disadvantage or shrink opportunities for minorities. For these reasons, we have developed analytical frameworks able to account for such dynamics, and have argued that this is of great significance for understanding the governance of religious diversity and for addressing the challenges that it gives rise to.

Note

1. See: https://www.pewresearch.org/fact-tank/2018/06/21/key-findings-on-the-global-rise-in-religious-restrictions/.

Acknowledgments

We are grateful to two anonymous reviewers and the journal editors for their comments on this contribution. We are also indebted to GREASE team members, upon whose work on the different regions and country cases the discussion in this contribution relies.

Disclosure statement

No potential conflict of interest was reported by the author(s).

Funding

The GREASE project, on which this contribution is based, has received funding from the European Union's Horizon 2020 research and innovation programme under grant agreement number 770640.

Notes on contributors

ORCID

Thomas Sealy http://orcid.org/0000-0002-3211-6900
Tariq Modood http://orcid.org/0000-0001-8712-5508

References

Bhargava, R. 1998. "What is Secularism For?" In *Secularism and Its Critics*, edited by R. Bhargava, 486–542. New Delhi: Oxford University Press.

Bhargava, R. 2009. "Political Secularism: Why It is Needed and What Can Be Learnt from Its Indian Version?" In *Secularism, Religion and Multicultural Citizenship*, edited by G. B. Levey and T. Modood, 82–109. Cambridge: Cambridge University Press.

Burchardt, M. 2020. *Regulating Difference: Religious Diversity and Nationhood in the Secular West*. New Brunswick: Rutgers University Press.

Chin, J. 2022. "Racism Towards the Chinese Minority in Malaysia: Political Islam and Institutional Barriers." *The Political Quarterly* 93 (3): 451–459. doi:10.1111/1467-923X.13145.

Dhanda, M. 2022. "The Concurrence of Anti-Racism and Anti-Casteism." *The Political Quarterly* 93 (3): 478–487. doi:10.1111/1467-923X.13147.

Eisenberg, A. I., and J. Spinner-Halev. 2005. *Minorities Within Minorities: Equality, Rights and Diversity*. Cambridge: Cambridge University Press.

Hefner, R. W. 2021. "Islam and Institutional Religious Freedom in Indonesia." *Religions* 12: 415.

Ibrahim, V. 2015. "Beyond the Cross and the Crescent: Plural Identities and the Copts in Contemporary Egypt." *Ethnic and Racial Studies* 38 (14): 2584–2597.

Lægaard, S. 2012. "Unequal Recognition, Misrecognition and Injustice: The Case of Religious Minorities in Denmark." *Ethnicities* 12 (2): 197–214. doi:10.1177/1468796811431273.

Maclure, J., and C. Taylor. 2011. *Secularism and Freedom of Conscience*. London: Harvard University Press.

Modood, T. 2012. "Is There a Crisis of Secularism in Western Europe?" *Sociology of Religion* 72 (2): 130–149.

Modood, T. 2019. *Essays on Secularism and Multiculturalism*. London: Rowman-Littlefield and European Consortium of Political Science.

Modood, T., and S. Thompson. 2018. ""Revisiting Contextualism in Political Theory: Putting Principles into Context"." *Res Publica* 24 (3): 339–357.

Richardson, J. T., ed. 2004. *Regulating Religion: Case Studies from Around the Globe*. New York: Springer.

Sarkissian, A. 2010. "Religious Reestablishment in Post-Communist Polities." *Journal of Church and State* 51 (3): 472–501.

Sikka, S. 2022. "Indian Islamophobia as Racism." *The Political Quarterly* 93 (3): 469–477.

Tanasaldy, T. 2022. "From Official to Grassroots Racism: Transformation of Anti-Chinese Sentiment in Indonesia." *The Political Quarterly* 93 (3): 460–468. doi:10.1111/1467-923X.13148.

Taşkın, Y. 2021. "Lebanon : Confessionalism and the Problem of Divided Loyalties." In *Routledge Handbook on the Governance of Religious Diversity*, edited by A. Triandafyllidou and T. Magazzini, 206–216. London: Routledge.

Thompson, S., and T. Modood. 2022. "The Multidimensional Recognition of Religion." *Critical Review of International Social and Political Philosophy*. Advance Online. doi:10.1080/13698230.2022.2115228.

Yefet, B. 2019. "Defending the Egyptian Nation: National Unity and Muslim Attitudes Toward the Coptic Minority." *Middle Eastern Studies* 55 (4): 638–654. doi:10.1080/00263206.2019.1573365.

Afterwords: Normative vs. Actual Secularism(s)

Haldun Gülalp

Introduction

Privileged with the opportunity to contribute an Afterword to this impressive collection of essays that presents part of the results of several years of collaborative research, in which I also participated, I endeavor to offer in this short piece some general thoughts on the question of secularism. I do so, inspired partly by the empirical findings reported in these essays and partly by the theoretical debates that took place during the research project. My views diverge from the broad theoretical framework that informs this collective work but are developed in an engagement with it and so are also indirectly informed by it.

The framework in question has been built and expounded over the years by Tariq Modood (2013, 2017, 2019a), with key and closely interlinked concepts of "moderate secularism," "state-religion connections" (SRCs), and "multiculturalism." Not every participant in the project necessarily endorses these controversial concepts as normatively preferable features of the governance of religion, and here I critically address them in a general discussion that compares competing "normative" concepts of secularism with the observed "actual" experiences.

Actual Secularisms

Two common features across all cases covered in the project stand out for recognition and are so noted by Tariq Modood and Thomas Sealy, the editors of this volume: (1) Directly or indirectly, implicitly or explicitly, religion constitutes a (if not *the*) core dimension of national identity. (2) The state is always directly involved in the regulation of religion(s) and religious affairs and is often very particular about it, just as it should be in my judgment, with all kinds of detailed legislation, policy debates about modes of intervention, and so on.

The first feature challenges the often-unquestioned claims of nationalisms to be secular, as well as the literature that takes these claims seriously. This feature exists even in France, where national identity is presumably based on "*laicité*" (see, e.g., Marx, 2003; Balibar, 2004; Klausen, 2005). It follows that the dominant religious identity in a nation has a differential cultural status over the minority ones, whether of the historically established or newly arrived immigrant populations, which are then treated with some measure of apprehension and generally suffer from discrimination and exclusion.

Similarly, we see that across all cases, regardless of which of the five specified categories the country falls into and whether there is more freedom of religion or less, the role of the state is central, exercising power over religious organizations, either to regulate them according to some presumably democratic criteria or to manipulate them for authoritarian political ends. This fact alone should lead us to question a notion that has been prevalent in recent literature, distinguishing between "passive" and "assertive" secularisms and associating the former with democracy (see, e.g., Yavuz, 2003; Kuru, 2009). Indeed, the implication that the political visibility of religion correlates with democracy is not supported by the evidence (Gülalp, 2017). One may argue, on the contrary, that more religion and/or religious reasoning in politics implies less flexibility and negotiation, and more threats and imposition, as we see in the use of religious identity and/or ideology by authoritarian regimes. Finally, the observation that states intervene across the board should also lead us to question the received definition of secularism as the separation between state and religion. There is no meaningful *degree* to which the state should be involved; what rather matters is the quality or character of state involvement, a point to which we shall return.

Given these two observations, the question then is, how do these commonly found features compare to the *normative* concept of secularism?

Normative Secularism

In their opening chapter, the editors quote what Modood (2017, p.52) has called the "minimalist" definition of political secularism: "… politics or the state has a *raison d'etre* of its own and should not be subordinated to religious authority, religious purposes or religious reasons." This is a comprehensive definition that seems incontrovertible. But Modood also qualifies it by introducing other concepts, noted above, such as "moderate secularism," "SRCs," and "multiculturalism," which create complications that I address below. But first, I would like to propose a more substantive definition of secularism that aims to reveal its foundations as a normative political principle.

In my assessment, secularism is a political-institutional arrangement that aims to guarantee citizens the right to freedom of "thought, conscience and religion," as spelled out in international human rights documents (*Universal Declaration of Human Rights*, Article 18; *European Convention on Human Rights*, Article 9), and thus entails the existence of a political space separate from and independent of religions for the purpose of negotiating common issues and areas of concern, so that the social and political needs of all religious and nonreligious members of society may be met. Secularism in this sense is indifferent to the question of private religiosity. It is not concerned with praising or rebuking religion(s) but with the protection of the freedom of *all* citizens, religious or not. The point of this protection is not to allow religion(s) to occupy the political space but to enable citizens to have the right to believe or not as they wish, and to fulfil the requirements of their beliefs individually or collectively, provided they do not infringe on the rights of others. It therefore implies the existence of a segregated area free of state interference where individuals and groups can enjoy their freedom of belief and conscience, so long as they do not disturb the public order or violate anyone else's rights. Likewise, the secular state is responsible for creating a political space free of religion(s), where all persons can negotiate their common problems as a civic community. As a normative principle, secularism aims to promote and maintain peace in a religiously diverse society.

This definition already sheds light on some common misconceptions. For instance, no distinction may be made between "freedom of" and "freedom from" religion, although the latter characterization is sometimes used to describe secularism in France, including by the editors of this volume. In fact, they are, by definition, the two sides of the same coin and cannot be separated from each other. This misconception, I suspect, derives from another confusion, that between "freedom of" and "freedom for" religion(s). By the former I mean the freedom granted to individual citizens, which is the essence of secularism as a liberal principle, whereas the latter refers to the notion that at least *some* freedom ought to be granted to religious organizations and communities, whether in the name of "mutual autonomy" between state and religion, or SRCs, or multiculturalism, which may readily lead to a violation of secularism by turning these corporate entities into political actors with authority that may very well restrict the freedom of belief and conscience of individual citizens.

Another common misconception concerns the notion of the "neutrality" of the secular state and the complaint that the modern state violates neutrality by regulating religious affairs. In normative secularism, as I have defined it, the state is not neutral *vis-à-vis* religion(s) per se, it is neutral *between* religions, meaning it does not favor one (or several) over others. If for any reason there is need for intervention in religious affairs, it does not (or *should* not) discriminate between religions by allowing more leeway to some than to others. But this principle is precisely violated by the notion of "multiculturalism" because the latter implies the upholding of some specific religious communities, necessarily at the expense of others, as "multi" does not denote an unlimited number. Secularist "neutrality" *between* religions is the means to allow for religious diversity in society, rendering void the concept of (or the need for) multiculturalism. If the state did not concern itself with the variety of beliefs in society, real diversity would be achieved not only among different religious communities but also among individual believers within each community. The liberal-democratic state should clearly opt for the protection of the freedom of the individual citizen and not of the whole community as an entity, even if the individual citizen voluntarily identifies with it and feels embedded in it, because a religious community typically has its own system of hierarchy and limits to internal diversity.

Finally, the concept of "separation" between church and state is misleading, as also noted by Modood and Sealy in their contributions. Indeed, even the famous (or, according to some, infamous) French law of 1905, the so-called "Law on the Separation of Church and State," proclaims in its first article that the Republic guarantees freedom of conscience and worship, but only within limits spelled out in the law in the interest of public order. In other words, the state, though separate, may intervene in order to ensure both the freedom of conscience and the public order, which are obviously symbiotic. The question is, what is preferable as a form of state intervention: regulation or manipulation of religion and religious organizations? A democratic state is answerable to *all* citizens, whether religious or not, or whether adherent of this religion or that, whereas religious communities and their organizations are not. It is therefore the democratic state's responsibility to ensure that all persons and institutions, including the religious ones, operate within limits set by the requirements of human rights and social peace. There is no reason why religious institutions should have any kind of immunity or any differential status, as may be implied by the notion of "mutual autonomy" between church and state. Beyond activities that pertain to matters of belief and conscience, such as organizing collective worship, teaching doctrine, and so on, a religious organization cannot have any special autonomy concerning this-worldly affairs that are the remit of the democratic state.

The French law is often presented as an extreme form of secularism, in the sense of suppressing religion and religiosity, but in fact similar provisions exist in the *Universal Declaration of Human Rights* and the *European Convention of Human Rights*. Using nearly identical language, these two documents declare: "Everyone has the right to freedom of thought, conscience and religion…," but then go on to add that

> Freedom to manifest one's religion or beliefs shall be subject only to such limitations as are prescribed by law and are necessary in a democratic society in the interests of public safety, for the protection of public order, health or morals, or for the protection of the rights and freedoms of others.

It may be noted that these two documents place conscience and religion on a par with *thought* (on the significance of which, see Bielefeldt, 2013). Put simply, it implies that one is entitled to hold any belief that one may wish, but that belief does not occupy a higher plane than any thought that anyone else may have, all of which are protected, but only within limits specified by the democratic state.

Here we have two alternative conceptions of normative secularism, the difference between which can best be examined by reference to their respective positions regarding the two features noted above as being present in all actual cases. Strikingly, they take opposing position in relation to both features.

Divergences between the Normative and the Actual

Regarding the centrality of religion in national identity as seen in all actual cases, it must be clear from the discussion so far that this feature takes us away from my conception of normative secularism. This is an issue that exists within the broader context of conceiving citizenship in general. To make good on its promise of cutting ties with traditional or primordial identities, the modern state must separate citizenship from nationality, whatever may be the latter's origins, be it religion, race, or ethnicity, through a regime of universal human rights (Gülalp, 2006). This is akin to Jürgen Habermas' formula for "constitutional patriotism" (Habermas, 1994, 2001; see also Calhoun, 2002). In this conception, the only meaningful way to create equal citizenship is to discard the myth, and hence the presumed requirement, of national homogeneity and liberate citizenship rights from any primordial/communal identities.

Modood's normative concept, however, has the exact opposite projection. His proposal for a "multicultural nationalism" seeks to not only retain the majority's primordial identity but also bring primordial identities of the minorities into the mix (Modood, 2019b). He describes this project as "equalizing upward" through "thickening" national identity, as opposed to "equalizing downward" through "thinning" it. It must also be noted that in Modood's conception, the multiple cultural groups in society essentially consist of religious communities. Thus, creating a multicultural national identity in this framework means "multiculturalizing secularism" (Modood, 2019a, Ch.11).

The question of how this is to be achieved brings us to the second universal feature, that is, state involvement in religious affairs. While both conceptions agree on both the inevitability and desirability of the state's role, the normative projections move in opposite directions. Describing religion as a "public good," that is, as beneficial to public life, Modood seeks to go beyond the model of "mutual autonomy" and assign mutually *supportive* roles in a collaboration between the state and religious organizations (or communities). His SRCs work both ways: In his view, the state ought to support religion and religious organizations and allow them to contribute to society by taking over some of the tasks of the state and offer services in such areas as education, welfare, health care, and so on. This arrangement, which he believes is not only desirable but also already prevalent in most of Europe, is described as "moderate secularism." Multiculturalizing moderate secularism, then, takes place by extending SRCs to all (recognized) religions in society beyond the one that is historically dominant.

Testing Modood's normative idea against the actual findings, however, must give us pause. The empirical observations reported in this book reveal the actual existence of the potential problems pointed out in the previous section. Some examples will show this to be the case.

In their chapter on Western Europe and Australia, Sealy and Modood observe that there are strong SRCs in these countries despite differences between their forms of religious establishment:

> Through this kind of cooperation, the norms in these states go beyond a privatised view of religion in society as merely a matter of individual conscience. Religion is seen as a public good … [particularly in] education and welfare service provision.

They add that also "a large degree of mutual autonomy is assured." But then a problem appears: "There are, for instance, some exemptions from equalities legislation (particularly on gender and sexuality) as applied to the labour market for some positions [in the religious organizations] where doctrinal specifications are in conflict."

In their concluding chapter, Sealy and Modood observe that the Central Eastern European countries and Russia "fit the minimalist definition of political secularism." But in these countries, except for Lithuania,

> majoritarian nationalism, with a close identification between state and dominant church, is an increasingly strong feature of SRCs. One aspect of this that stands out in the region is pronounced tiered systems, where 'traditional' religions are privileged above those which are 'registered' or just 'associations'.

The problem is more clearly articulated in the chapter on Central Eastern Europe and Russia, by Daniel Vekony *et.al.*, particularly through the case of Hungary. In the authors' assessment, "Even though religion plays a steadily decreasing role in people's lives, … the current government's policy returns some aspects of religion and religious organisations from the private to the public sphere." Hungary's new constitution, adopted in 2011, "allows the government to cooperate with religious organisations for certain public interests or goals," although it still defines the state as secular and guarantees freedom of religion. Certain religious organizations are consequently "allowed to take over certain responsibilities from the state … and receive financial assistance in return." This arrangement "not only erodes the idea of secular neutrality, but essentially de-secularises certain religious communities and the providing of certain public goods," such as education and social care. These religious organizations "assume control over the institutions and services they take over (or take back), which used to be traditionally secular bodies and roles funded and provided by the state." This, I would argue, is hardly a desirable outcome and shows that "moderate secularism" is hardly a type of secularism.

Regarding the question of multiculturalism, we may turn to the situation in South and Southeast Asian countries. These countries are described as having "deep diversity," meaning religious diversity that exists historically rather than caused by recent immigration as is the case in Europe, and display features of "multiculturalism," which Europe is urged to adopt. The question is how well do they fare regarding religious freedoms. Not very well, it seems. Modood and Sealy note that "recent events in India, Indonesia, and Malaysia show trends of increasing majoritarianism, even state and communal persecution, which is putting religious diversity and freedom of religion in the region under severe strain" (Chapter 1, this volume).

According to Sealy *et.al.*, in their chapter on South and Southeast Asia, the multicultural model is historically present in the following institutional structures of these countries: "In terms of freedom of religion, … [there] is an emphasis on groups … and a pronounced presence and influence of religion in the public and political spheres." Thus, "citizens are seen first and foremost as members of an ethno-religious group and primacy is given to group, rather than individual, autonomy." Additionally, "Religions *and religious reasons* are … valued as a public good, … and as dialogical partners and shapers in policy." But the authors also point out that, for example, in both Malaysia and Indonesia, citizens are obligated to identify with a religion that is officially recognized by the state and have it inscribed in their identity cards; and while the institutional structure may appear to be favoring religious diversity and freedom, in reality "individual freedom of conscience, including conversion for instance, is circumscribed." In explaining the turn from "pluralistic nationalism" to "majoritarian nationalism" in these countries, the authors perceptively point out that "religion and its connections to state and recognition might also be an aspect of its management by the state and a vehicle for majoritarian nationalism that introduces strong currents of diversity-limiting ethno-religious nationalism."

Lebanon is another example where politics and citizenship rights are organized around confessional lines. Religious diversity is recognized and institutionally structured, but political authority is vested in the leaderships of the officially recognized religious communities. In the Lebanese system of power-sharing, political positions are distributed between religious communities, with a Christian president, a Sunni prime minister, and a Shiite speaker of the house, and a proportional representation along confessional lines in the parliament. The proportional representation has been based on the religious composition of the population as counted in the 1932 census and, disturbingly, "Since then no census has been held due to the fragile nature of the political balance among different confessions" (Taşkın, 2021, p.216, fn.1). This political system has led to continuous tension and turmoil, including a prolonged civil war (1975–1990) and a seemingly permanent economic and political crisis, but a persistent popular demand for secularism that transcends the current structure of recognizing religious diversity. It appears, therefore, that the multicultural model is not exactly stable. Where there is a majority religion, there is also a tendency for it to claim the state as its own. But where a numerical majority does not materialize to claim ownership of the state, civil war may very well ensue.

Finally, a few words must be said about France, portrayed by many, including Sealy and Modood in this collection, as an "exception" in Western Europe because of its constitutional principle of *laicité*, which for Modood (2013, 2019a) means *"radical* secularism." The frequently made point that France is explicitly defined as secular in its constitution is insignificant, because even the Italian constitution stipulates, without ever using the term "secular," freedom of religion, separation of church and state, and protection of citizens from religious discrimination (see Magazzini *et.al.* in this volume), all of which signifies "secularism" for the European Court of Human Rights, as may be seen in its section judgment on *"Lautsi v. Italy"* (ECtHR, 30814/06, 3 November 2009).

Much is also made of the French ban on headscarves as a narrative of Islamophobia and Muslim victimization, although again France is hardly alone in this regard. This is not the place to examine the intricacies of French policies on its Muslim population, including the well-known role of the colonial background, entangled with issues of racism, poverty, and unemployment in the *banlieues*, or its less-studied aspects, such as the recent move away from classical secularism into a variant of multiculturalism and the right-wing appropriation of *"laicité"* in a move that is more anti-Muslim than pro-secular and brings French national identity into closer association with Catholicism (Akan, 2009; Ahearne, 2014; Almeida, 2017). But we may note more generally that dress codes are typically a premodern practice implemented to distinguish between different social and political strata in society. Thus, a veiling ban does not follow from, and is indeed opposed to, the logic of secularism as I have defined it, or it is a controversial matter to say the least (for my take on it, see Gülalp, 2010, 2013, 2019). By contrast, veiling seems to be mandatory in Muslim-majority nations where state and religion have merged, as in Iran, Afghanistan, and others. Beyond dress codes, moreover, an emphasis on such conservative themes as "family values" and gender inequality gains prominence in cases of strong SRCs, whichever religion the state may be embroiled with. We see, again, that "moderate secularism" is quite different from secularism proper.

Conclusion

Secularism, then, is a formula for social peace in a society composed of a variety of believers and non-believers, whereby individuals have the freedom of thought and conscience as specified for protection by international covenants. This freedom does not protect religion itself, but the right to believe in one. It follows that the tenets of a religion may be sacred for the believer, but they are not for anyone else. Belief, then, is a private matter, which may be practiced communally by those who choose to form or join such a community and thereby enjoy any dignity that may be derived from it, provided they do not interfere with the rights of others. Under these circumstances there will be freedom of conscience individually *and* collectively, but state affairs will be based on a common language of reason and negotiation. Therefore, an individual in a position of political power may not and should not bring into the public arena any rules that originate from their belief, for while they may be obligated to follow those rules, nobody else is. They may certainly have ideas that originate from their belief, which they may offer for discussion and debate, but the negotiation with others ought to be based on *reason* and not on any absolute truths, which may be valid for the believer but is not necessarily so for anybody else. Historically speaking, religion has always been at the center of politics; but if the aim is to create a democracy based on human rights, secularism as defined above is the necessary foundation for it. It is true that religion is about identity and community, defining the individual and his/her place within society, which in turn is the substance of politics. But it is also about *faith*, which renders it among all conceivable ideological vehicles the most convenient for authoritarian politics.

References

Ahearne, Jeremy (2014), "*Laïcité*: A Parallel French Cultural Policy (2002–2007)," *French Cultural Studies*, 25(3/4), pp.320–329.

Akan, Murat (2009), "*Laïcité* and Multiculturalism: The Stasi Report in Context," *The British Journal of Sociology*, 60(2), pp.237–256.

Almeida, Dimitri (2017), "Exclusionary Secularism: The Front National and the Reinvention of *Laïcité*," *Modern & Contemporary France*, 25(3), pp.249–263.

Balibar, Etienne (2004), "Dissonances within *Laïcité*," *Constellations*, 11(3), pp.353–367.

Bielefeldt, Heiner (2013), "Misperceptions of Freedom of Religion or Belief," *Human Rights Quarterly*, 35(1), pp.33–68.

Calhoun, Craig (2002), "Imagining Solidarity: Cosmopolitanism, Constitutional Patriotism, and the Public Sphere," *Public Culture*, 14(1), pp.147–171.

Gülalp, Haldun (2006), "Introduction: Citizenship vs. Nationality?" in Haldun Gülalp (ed.), *Citizenship and Ethnic Conflict: Challenging the Nation-State*, London: Routledge.

Gülalp, Haldun (2010), "Secularism and the European Court of Human Rights," *European Public Law*, 16(3), pp.455–471.

Gülalp, Haldun (2013), "Religion on my Mind: Secularism, Christianity and European Identity," in Haldun Gülalp and Günter Seufert (eds), *Religion, Identity and Politics: Germany and Turkey in Interaction*, London: Routledge.

Gülalp, Haldun (2017), "Secularism as a Double-Edged Sword? State Regulation of Religion in Turkey," in Anna Triandafyllidou and Tariq Modood (eds), *The Problem of Religious Diversity: European Challenges, Asian Approaches*, University of Edinburgh Press. Edinburgh.

Gülalp, Haldun (2019), "Religion, Law and Politics: The 'Trickle Down' Effects of ECtHR Judgments on Turkey's Headscarf Battles," *Religion and Human Rights*, 14(3), pp.135–168.

Habermas, Jürgen (1994), "Citizenship and National Identity," in Bert van Steenbergen (ed.), *The Condition of Citizenship*, London: Sage.

Habermas, Jürgen (2001), "Constitutional Democracy: A Paradoxical Union of Contradictory Principles?" *Political Theory*, 29(6), pp.766–781.

Klausen, Jytte (2005), *The Islamic Challenge: Politics and Religion in Western Europe*, Oxford: Oxford University Press.

Marx, Anthony (2003), *Faith in Nation: Exclusionary Origins of Nationalism*, New York: Oxford University Press.

Modood, Tariq (2013), *Multiculturalism: A Civic Idea*, (Second Edition), Cambridge: Polity Press.

Modood, Tariq (2017), "Multiculturalism and Moderate Secularism," in Anna Triandafyllidou and Tariq Modood (eds), *The Problem of Religious Diversity: European Challenges, Asian Approaches*, Edinburgh: Edinburgh University Press.

Modood, Tariq (2019a), *Essays on Secularism and Multiculturalism*, London: ECPR Press.

Modood, Tariq (2019b), "A Multicultural Nationalism?" *The Brown Journal of World Affairs*, 25(2), pp.233–246.

Taşkın, Yüksel (2021), "Lebanon: Confessionalism and the Problem of Divided Loyalties," in Anna Triandafyllidou and Tina Magazzini (eds), *Routledge Handbook on the Governance of Religious Diversity*, London: Routledge.

Yavuz, Hakan (2003), *Islamic Political Identity in Turkey*, London: Oxford University Press.

Some reflections on state-religion relationships and political secularism in the contemporary world

Gurpreet Mahajan

Concepts are context specific. They get redefined and layered with new meanings as they travel across space and time. Yet, even as they acquire different forms, a core idea, or set of ideas, persists and surfaces over and over again in various ways. This makes it possible for us to invoke the same concept in fairly diverse situations and histories. In the case of secularism, that core idea is – non-discrimination on religious grounds (Mahajan 2003). What constitutes religion-based discrimination; what is identified as a site of religious discrimination, policies formulated to remedy this, invariably vary. When state recognized (official or established) religion was identified as the source of discrimination, some responded by creating a "wall of separation" between state and religion; others focused on removing legal barriers that prevented non-recognized minority communities from enjoying equal citizenship rights; several extended recognition to other religions in the state. Thus, policies to deal with a perceived site of discrimination have differed enormously, and so have state-religion relationships. Nevertheless, as each tries to minimize religion-based discrimination, albeit in a specific form, they can be placed side-by-side and examined together as different modes of secularism.

What we have, as a consequence, are multiple secularisms, incorporating a range of diverse paths. Even within western Europe, and this point surfaces throughout the volume, secularism takes diverse forms. Not all countries disestablished religion or formally separated religion and state. In fact, most continue to have an established religion, albeit a "weak" form of it, while exploring ways of minimizing the disadvantages faced by minorities. Given the diverse forms of state-religion relationships that exist, one needs to abandon the dichotomies within which the discourse on secularism has been conducted for some time – namely, positioning "western" conception of secularism against the "Indian model or Asian models of secularism".

When we approach the issue of secularism from this perspective, we can appreciate the significance of the five-fold typology offered by Tariq Modood and Thomas Sealey (Modood and Sealey 2022). Not only do they draw our attention to the diverse forms of secularism, but also they construct each mode of religious governance as a complex whole, consisting of a set of allied norms. This means that even countries which follow a similar policy or endorse the same "dominant operative norm" – say, moderate secularism – may still differ significantly. These differences could be captured by analyzing the "qualifying operative norms" that accompany the operative norm (Modood and Sealey 2022:11).

The importance of this framework lies in its ability to capture the uniqueness and the dynamism inherent in a specific mode of religious governance. A state may, over a passage of time, incorporate other associated norms or abandon/reinterpret some existing qualifying norms. France is a case in point. As the chapter by Sealey and Modood shows, Laicite remains the dominant operative norm, but along with the insistence on privatizing religion, there is public recognition of religious bodies of Catholics, Protestants, Jews and now Muslims (Sealey and Modood 2022:8–9). In 2003, an elected body, Conseil français du culte musulman (CFCM), was established to give "official" representation to Muslims. The relationship between state and religion in each country is thus open to some modification, without being completely open-ended.

The five modes of governance that Modood and Sealey outline operate with categories that are both analytical and political in nature. Through them we can understand the differences between states while simultaneously underling the possibility of change. Politics entails negotiations and re-formulation in the light of new claims, changing circumstances and new ways of making sense of our social world. This dimension is frequently lost when we focus on analytical distinctions. The framework that Modood and Sealey outline, and the thinking that informs it, is remarkable and quite unique in this respect. Even though they see their models as a heuristic device, constructing ideal types, their methodological orientation and their classification of different kinds of secularisms are bound to shape the discussions around state-religion relationships for some time to come.

In this paper, however, I want to take a step back and turn to two questions that invariably arise when we endorse the idea of multiple secularisms; more so, when we maintain, as Modood and Sealey do, that having an established religion (Church) does not in itself alienate minorities (Modood and Sealey 2022:4). First, can we make a distinction between secular and non-secular states? Is this distinction at all tenable? Second, are we now living in a world where there are mainly secular states of various types: some with strong state-religion linkage, a few with a weak state-religion linkage, and others with no linkage, or separation of state and religion?

Modood and Sealey address this question briefly when they offer a "minimum" definition of secularism, by looking at "what all secularisms have in common" (2022:7). They refer to this minimum as "political secularism": that is, "…the state has a raison d'etre of its own and should not be *subordinated* to religious authority, religious purposes or religious reasons" (2022: 8. Emphasis added). This conception of secularism, unlike one anchored in strict separation, allows us to include a range of European democracies, where there is an established religion, as secular (also see, Modood 2017:52–74). One cannot but agree with them on this. Today, most analysts would describe England, Germany, Italy and Spain as secular democracies. In fact, one could justify this representation on the ground that each of them has extended religious liberty to people of all faiths and has minimized, to a considerable extent, religion-related discrimination. The task is far from complete but they have made significant changes in pursuit of that end.

Modood and Sealey, however, make a different argument. They give a more concrete and specific criterion for identifying these European democracies as secular – namely, *the state is not subordinated to religious authority, religious purposes and religious reasons*. While each of these elements may appear to be self-evidently clear, they require further elaboration and consideration, particularly against the backdrop of the changes that secular states are making to accommodate religious minorities. For instance, one could take non-subordination to religious authority to imply that state authority resides outside religious institutions; it does not derive legitimacy from the latter; the leadership/membership of the two is separate and religious institutions do not determine who should occupy state positions. However, if the state was to involve religious leaders in some of its activities or frame some of its policies – on health care, abortion, marriage, and education – in line with the sentiments of the religious leadership, would this make the state subordinate to religious authority, reasons or purposes? If some laws are aligned with religious norms, would that entail subordination to religious reasons and purposes? If the state was to allow religious dietary norms to be accommodated in public institutions or observe public holidays to mark religious festivals, would that entail subordination? One could add so many other cases: collection of taxes for religious institutions, recognition of religious bodies, giving the latter the authority to adjudicate on certain issues and impose penalties on the congregation, etc. What if, state officials and leaders themselves hold strong religious views (something that is becoming a familiar phenomenon in "secular" states). They may not derive their authority from religious institutions/authority but may acknowledge, and make space for, religious reasons in the laws and policies they frame. If religion is identified as a "public good" (as is the case in moderate secularism), then we are likely to see more of these connections between state and religion.

Modood and Sealey, and most contributors to this volume, would not see accommodation of religious practices as undermining secularism. In fact, Modood has for long been a strong advocate for the accommodation of minorities; under the circumstances, one needs further elucidation of what subordination of state, to religious reasons, purposes and authority, implies. When does partnership with religious institutions not undermine state autonomy? Modood and Sealey address this question, at least indirectly, by invoking the twin principles of "positive cooperation" and "principled distance". We could infer from the brief exposition of these principles that not all forms of cooperation between state and religious groups undermine state autonomy. More importantly, so long as the state can, and does, prioritize citizenship rights and constitutional values, cooperation with religious bodies does not subordinate the state to religious authority, reasons or purposes.

We could go a step further and conclude that when the state partners with religious groups for delivery of valued goods – education, care, health, and basic amenities – it acts to further citizenship rights. Hence, in this relationship it retains its autonomy and raison d'etre. The difficulty however is that in moderate secularism (a framework they regard to be accommodative of differences and conducive equal treatment), when religion is valued as a public good, the presence of, and cooperation with, religious groups is unlikely to be limited to delivery of services. Religious groups (one or many) are likely to be included in such things as, framing the national curriculum or other critical aspects of health policy. When one values the perspectives that these groups bring to the table, we can hardly set them aside or make a clear distinction between state's raison d'etre and religious reasons. The latter might well inform the former and the former might well employ the reasoning of the latter to affirm certain humanitarian ends and values.

These questions gain traction as many secular states resist accommodation of religious beliefs and practices in the name of state autonomy, principled distance and unacceptability of religious reasons – something that would subordinate sovereign authority to religion. Some take the idea of the state having a raison d'etre of its own to imply that rational arguments, anchored in personal autonomy and choice, alone should prevail in the affairs of the state. We hear arguments of this kind all around us everyday. We see them invoking (implicitly) the notion of principled distance to say that religious reasons for certain practices – such as partial and full covering of the face – are a sign of the subordination of women. It undermines the principle of gender equality, which is a basic constitutional norm, and the state should act and intervene to check these practices.

The point is, most practices are contested even within a community; and they are open to multiple interpretations. It is virtually impossible to imagine a neutral point of view or a rational perspective from which we can determine when an essential norm is being violated; when the state's raison d'etre is being subordinated even for it needs to intervene, setting aside all other considerations. If discrimination on religious grounds is to be minimized, and eventually eradicated, then we may need a new language for representing secularism and state-religion relationships: one that moves away from both the idea of separation of state from religion and non-subordination of state to religion.

When we step outside Europe and turn to Asia one cannot but notice the unease, and skepticism, that surrounds the concept of secularism. Indonesia, to take one example, identified itself "…neither as a state of religion nor a secular state" (Sealey, Ibrahim, Zulian et al. 2022: 3–4). To a considerable extent this is because secularism brings with it notions of separation of state and religion or subordination of religion to state, and neither of these seem to be appropriate for capturing the complex relationship between, and status of, the two entities – state and religion.

The journey outside Europe is important for another reason. In Asia (particularly the countries included in this volume) – a region where religion is a primary and important source of personal identity – there is greater willingness to accept and respect differences of practices. However, there is also a greater possibility of religious mobilizations and inter-community conflict. The latter poses the most serious challenge and is the main source of marginalization and disadvantage. By comparison, in much of Western Europe, the challenge is to accommodate diversity of religious and cultural practices, and inability to make space for minorities in this regard is a source of discrimination and disadvantage. There are, in other words, different sites of minority vulnerability, and they call for different strategies: dealing with inter-community violent conflict requires a strident defense of basic rights – right to life, liberty and property. Accommodating minorities in the public domain requires policies of recognition and often special consideration for a minority's way of life (see, Mahajan 2007). On reading the experiences and historical trajectories of different societies side-by-side, we realize that both a defense of basic rights and a positive recognition of difference are needed to address minority concerns. A democratic state fails the test of being plural and secular when it neglects either of these concerns.

The strength of this volume is that it draws our attention not just to the differences that exist across regions and states but also to the presence of similar trends and affinities. Most states today (including Russia, parts of the erstwhile Soviet Union and the MENA region) guarantee freedom of conscience, and, in varying degrees, they accord recognition to several minority (or previously non-dominant) religious groups. The case studies also show that after 9/11, there is a perceptible shift in state-religion relationships: from greater state regulation of religion (particularly, Muslim religious institutions and practices) to rise of the "far-right" spectrum. Should this trend not be identified as a shift to some form of "majoritarian nationalism"? Is the far right still a "fringe" group? Electoral results in many

GOVERNING RELIGIOUS DIVERSITY IN GLOBAL COMPARATIVE PERSPECTIVE

parts of Europe would compel us to question that conclusion, and even a passing glance at their political rhetoric will prompt one to reconsider the belief that these views are not significantly altering the conception of nationalism in that region.

Modood and Sealey make an important distinction between "liberal neutralism" and "moderate secularism", and it illuminates the differences that can be seen within Europe itself. These two modes of governance are starkly separated from what they term as "incorporated within majoritarian nationalism". However, one cannot but bring in here the insights that have come from multiculturalism: namely, that liberal neutralism has an in-built majoritarian bias. The language of moral individualism and state neutrality camouflages the multiple ways in which the majority culture (one that emerged around a dominant religion and way of life) prevails in the public domain. If we now examine what is identified in the case studies as majoritarian nationalism, it is evident that religious freedoms extended to diverse groups are not being withdrawn. Multiple forms of recognition continue to stay in these countries. What is being questioned, within majoritarian nationalism, is the idea of "differentiated citizenship" and the accompanying distinction between majority and minorities. It is the language of liberal neutralism that is being invoked to question special consideration given to minorities to accommodate aspects of their way of life and practices. Or, to put in another way, these societies (and regimes) are pushing for identical and the same treatment for all, and through that prioritizing the dominant cultural values. There is thus an easy transition between these two modes, and the distance between them, more blurred than what is suggested by their names.

We are living in a new and significantly altered world today. At a time when the Rawlsian individual – morally autonomous, rational and reasonable – was the dominant mode of personal identity, it was relatively easier to think of learning from each other and rethinking one's prejudices. Even if a "rationally motivated consensus" could not be achieved, one could pin one's hope on dialogue. One could argue, as Modood, Parekh and many other multiculturalists do, that understanding the other would allow us to overcome fears that may be triggered by the presence of the "other"; it would enable us to rethink our prejudices and compel a degree of critical self -reflection. Dialogue between self and other, between state and religious groups/leaders, between state and civil society, between religious and non-religious voluntary groups and between different religious and faith groups would pave the way for peaceful co-existence with diversity, and that too in a way that is mutually enriching. Today, that seems to be a distant reality. Individuals, who see themselves as deeply embedded, engage in solidarity formation and in that process draw boundaries that separate them from the "other". We appear trapped in an endless cycle of conflict and violence. Can self-affirming identities exist in ways that are simultaneously non-othering? That is the question before secular states today, and their survival as secular democracies depends critically upon the way they address this issue.

References

Mahajan, Gurpreet. 2003. "Secularism", In *The Oxford India Companion to Sociology and Social Anthropology,* edited by Veena Das, 908–934. New Delhi: Oxford University Press.
Mahajan, Gurpreet. 2007. "Multiculturalism in the age of terror: confronting the challenges", *Political Studies Review,* 5:3, 317–336.

Modood, Tariq. 2017. "Multiculturalism and moderate secularism." In *The Problem of Religious Diversity European Challenges, Asian Approaches*, edited by A. Triandafyllidou and T. Modood, 52–74. Edinburgh: Edinburgh University Press.

Modood, Tariq and Thomas Sealy. 2022. "Developing a framework for a global comparative analysis of the governance of religious diversity", *Religion, State & Society*, 50:4, 362–377, DOI: 10.1080/09637494.2022.2117526

Sealey, Thomas, Zawawi Ibrahim, Pradana B. Zulian *et.al.* 2022. "South and Southeast Asia: deep diversity under strain", *Religion, State and Society*, 50:4, 452–468, DOI: 10.1080/09637494.2022.2126258

Sealey, Thomas and Tariq Modood. 2022. "Western Europe and Australia: negotiating freedoms of religion", *Religion, State & Society*, DOI: 10.1080/09637494.2022.2119825

Index

Note: Page numbers followed by "n" denote endnotes.

accommodation 17, 19, 20, 23, 26, 29, 94, 95, 110, 113, 115, 121, 122, 135
actual secularisms 125–126
Albania 36–39, 41, 42, 45, 47, 48, 111, 117
Alevi community 83
Anderson, J. 66
Arab nationalism 85
Arab Spring 4, 76, 79, 80, 85, 87, 112
atheism 40, 97, 98
Australia 12, 17–20, 23, 27, 30, 108, 110, 116, 117
Australian multiculturalism 23
autonomy 19, 25, 28, 96, 97, 115–117, 120, 130, 135

Bahout, Joseph 81
Belgium 4, 18, 19, 21–24, 27, 28, 110, 116
Berger, P. L. 56
Bey, Ahmad 77
Bhargava, R. 5
Bourguiba, Habib 83
Bracewell, W. 35
Buddhism 93, 98
Bulgaria 36–39, 42, 43, 45, 47, 48, 111, 117

Catholic Church 19, 39, 40, 43, 46, 59
Central Eastern Europe 54, 55, 57, 58, 60, 68, 70, 112
Chin, J. 101
Christianity 55, 61–64, 68, 83, 91, 98, 100, 109
Church of England 3, 4, 19, 21
citizenship 12, 82, 121, 122, 128
civil war 39, 41, 80, 81, 86, 87, 130
constitutional settlements 95, 98
contemporary challenges 13, 109, 110
convergence 114, 116
covenantal pluralism 6, 7, 94, 95
cultural differences 6, 82, 94

de facto state church 66
de-secularisation 57, 62, 63, 65, 66, 69
deep diversity 4, 6, 91, 92, 95, 103, 113, 120, 130
deep religious diversity 86, 91, 93, 95
discrimination 8, 28, 45, 102, 119, 125, 133, 136
divergences 114, 116, 128
diversities 10–12, 26, 29, 93, 94, 108–122, 136, 137
dominant operative norms (DONs) 11, 44, 45, 61, 63, 65, 68, 87, 95, 98, 103, 117, 121
Drace-Francis, A. 35

Eastern Europe 2, 9, 12, 55, 110
education 19, 22, 57, 62, 63, 77, 78, 86, 96, 129, 135
Egypt 76–80, 82–88, 112
Eisenstadt, S. N. 56
Elbasani, A. 47
ethnic communities 88, 98, 102

faith communities 55, 60, 63, 64, 70, 112
Fisher, M. 103n3
Fox, J. 8
France 4, 5, 18–20, 24, 25, 27–29, 110, 111, 117, 130, 131
freedom: of belief 5, 80, 126, 127; of conscience 11, 12, 20, 21, 29, 45, 46, 65, 67–69, 83, 117, 118, 127; of religion 12, 18, 23, 25, 29, 45, 46, 48, 70, 93, 102, 110, 115–121, 130; of worship 115, 120
French law 78, 127, 128

Germany 18–25, 27, 28, 110, 116
Greece 36–40, 43, 45–49, 111, 117

Habermas, J. 56, 57
Habib, C. 86
Hefner, R. W. 93, 100, 101
Hindu culture 101

Hinduism 93, 98, 102
Hungary 54, 55, 59–65, 68–70, 112, 118, 129

India 5–7, 91–94, 96, 97, 101, 102, 113, 120, 121
Indonesia 6, 91–95, 97, 98, 100, 101, 103, 113,
 120, 121, 130
inductive generalisation 9
institutional accommodation 13, 23, 29, 67, 69,
 86, 95, 96, 111
institutional religious freedom 95, 98, 101,
 102, 120
institutionalisation 26, 88, 99
inter-regional comparative themes 108–122
Islam 26, 36, 40, 42, 58, 77–80, 82, 83, 87, 93,
 98–100, 110, 112, 119
Islamic law 77, 93, 95
Islamic Sharia 77, 79, 80
Italy 36, 37, 39, 40, 42, 43, 45–49, 111, 117,
 131, 134

Jehovah's Witnesses 19, 118
Jews 19, 24, 39, 58, 59, 67, 78, 83, 84, 134

Khrushchev, Nikita 59

Laborde, C. 3, 20
Lebanese exception 80
Lebanon 12, 76, 80, 81, 86–88, 113, 120, 130
liberal neutralism 30, 45, 60, 63, 65, 68, 111,
 112, 118, 137
Lithuania 12, 54, 55, 67–70, 112, 113, 118, 129

Maclure, J. 115
Mahajan, G. 5
majoritarian challenges 98
majoritarian nationalism 12, 45, 46, 48, 49, 63,
 65, 70, 82, 103, 117–119, 130, 137
Malaysia 91–101, 113, 120, 121, 130
MENA 2, 4, 12, 75, 87, 108, 109, 112, 115, 119,
 121, 136
moderate secularism 20, 21, 23–30, 45, 46, 48,
 61, 63, 65, 117, 118, 129, 135
modern nation-state formation 77
Modood, Tariq 4, 9, 110, 125, 126, 131, 134
moral individualism 12, 20, 23, 25, 29, 45–48,
 65, 67–69, 117, 118
Morocco 75, 76, 78–80, 82–84, 86–88
multiculturalism 17, 19, 99, 125–127, 130,
 131, 137
Muslim 2, 3, 26, 27, 38, 41, 42, 58, 64, 66, 69, 79,
 82, 83, 91, 93, 99, 101, 102, 131
mutual autonomy 6, 8, 22, 46–48, 65, 115, 117,
 127, 129

new accommodationist responses 2–4
New Religious Movements (NRMs) 20, 118
no-establishment principle 94

non-European responses 4
normative secularism 126–128

Orthodox Christianity 36, 38, 46, 48, 58, 65, 66, 70

Parmaksız, U. 57
pluralism 91, 92, 98–101, 120
pluralistic nationalism 23, 86, 95, 97, 98, 102,
 103, 114, 115, 120–122
pluralistic principles 100
political autonomy 8, 46, 115
political power 66, 88, 131
political regimes 75, 76, 81, 85
political secularism 5–9, 19–23, 109, 115–118
politics 41, 93, 97, 99–101, 109, 112, 113, 115,
 126, 130–132, 134
positive cooperation 6, 86, 94, 135
public goods 57, 62, 63, 68, 129, 135
public neutrality 9
public policy 97
public religion 2, 11, 20, 24, 25, 29, 110,
 117, 121
public spaces 24
public visibility 26, 27, 29
Putin, Vladimir 66
Puto, A. 47

qualifying operative norms (QONs) 11, 44, 45,
 61, 63, 65, 68, 82, 88, 95, 98, 117, 121

registered religious organisations 12, 60, 64,
 65, 69
religion-state relations 55, 76, 77, 80, 87
religious actors 75–78, 87, 97, 112
religious affairs 43, 79, 80, 86, 96, 97, 125,
 127, 128
religious beliefs 2, 23, 45, 46, 59, 83, 135
religious communities 41, 42, 45, 47, 57, 59, 62,
 64, 67, 68, 83, 86, 97, 120, 127
Religious Discrimination Act 24
religious education 22, 64, 66, 96
religious freedom 21, 23, 41, 46–48, 64, 65, 67,
 78, 98, 99, 101
religious identities 3, 4, 40, 41, 48, 82, 86, 97,
 111, 112, 119, 126
religious institutions 39–43, 48, 83–86,
 135, 136
religious minorities 2, 4, 17, 20, 22, 26, 42, 43,
 58, 59, 94, 109, 111
religious organisations 60–67, 85, 112, 115, 129
religious pluralism 47, 96, 103
religious revival 76, 78, 87, 112
religious rights 23, 45, 59, 60
religious signs 17, 26–28
religious symbols 17, 26–28
Russia 54, 55, 57, 58, 60, 61, 65, 66, 68–70, 112,
 118, 129

INDEX

Saat, N. 100
Sealy, Thomas 134
secularism 3–5, 7, 8, 17, 56, 93, 109, 110, 115,
    117–119, 126, 127, 131, 133, 134, 136
secularist statism 20, 24, 25, 27, 29, 30, 47, 48,
    70, 117–119, 121
Slovakia 54, 55, 60, 61, 63–65, 68–70, 112,
    118, 119
social classes 81
South Asia 2, 4, 6, 12, 91, 95, 102, 108, 109, 113,
    115, 120
Southeast Asia 2, 4, 6, 12, 91, 95, 102, 108, 109,
    113, 115, 118, 120
Southeastern Europe 2, 35–37, 39, 41, 44, 48,
    108, 111, 117
Southern Europe 2, 35, 37, 40, 43, 48, 109, 111
Spain 36, 37, 39, 40, 42, 43, 45–49, 111, 117
state-religion connections (SRCs) 2–4, 7, 9,
    19–25, 27, 29, 115–119, 125–127, 129

state-religion relations/relationships 35, 37–39,
    44, 45, 47, 49, 54, 55, 67–70, 109, 133,
    134, 136
Stepan, A. 6, 9, 94
Sunni Islam 78, 82, 83, 86–88

Tanasaldy, T. 101
Taylor, C. 115
Thompson, S. 110
traditional religious communities
    60, 67–69
Tunisia 75–80, 82–88
Turkey 75–79, 82–88, 112
Turkish-Islamic synthesis 79

Western Europe 2, 4–6, 17, 18, 20, 27, 29, 30,
    110, 118, 130, 133, 136

Zogy, Ahmet 39

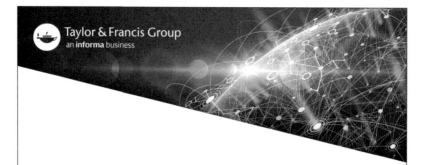